MANAGEMENT OF CONSUMER COOPERATIVES

MANAGEMENT OF CONSUMER COOPERATIVES

B. Tamilmani

Reader, Department of Cooperation
Gandhigram Rural University,
Gandhigram - 624 302
Dindigul Dist. (TN)

&

Frank Ratna Kumar

Reader, Department of Cooperation
T.B.M.L. College, Porayar – 609 307
Nagai Dist. (TN)

SERIALS PUBLICATIONS

NEW DELHI

First Published - 2008

ISBN : 978-81-8387-146-4

Published with the financial assistance of unassigned grants of U.G.C., New Delhi through Gandhigram Rural University, Gandhigram.

Published by

SERIALS PUBLICATIONS
4830/24, Prahlad Street, Ansari Road
Darya Ganj, New Delhi-110002 (India)
Phone : 23245225. Fax : 91-11-23272135
E-mail: serials@satyam.net.in

Contents

Foreword

"A Customer is the most important visitor in our premises. He is not dependent on us, we are dependent on him..... He is not an interruption in our work, he is the purpose of it. He is not an outsider to our business, he is part of it. We are not doing him a favour by serving him, he is doing us a favour by giving us an opportunity to do so".

—*Mahatma Gandhi*

The winds of change sweeping across the globe with the inking of the Dunkel proposals by the world community have touched the consumer sector also. Globalisation and technological development have brought in their wake a number of effects which have completely changed the face of market and the consumer environment. External attractions of package, label, sizes and shapes have overtaken quality and the value they provide for money. In fact, the changed scenario has helped create three distinct categories of consumers: (i) Consumer, who makes enough money to buy anything he wishes to buy at any price; (ii) Consumer, who mainly represents salaried classes with limited resources and also ignorant of the products he is surrounded with; (iii) The rural consumer who is completely unaware of the happenings around him and often unable to even afford the bare necessities of life for his family.

Therefore, in the complex market situation, the last two categories need protection. There are three agencies for ensuring consumer protection:

(i) Self-Help i.e. Consumer organization itself

(ii) Business, by self-regulation and by giving a fair deal to the retailers.

(iii) Government, by having special Acts and implementing those laws strictly.

In this context, the role of consumer co-operatives assumes importance for protecting the consumers while at the same time acting as a market regulating mechanism. There are over 30,000 primary stores and central/wholesale stores spread across the length and breadth of the country. They have more than 12,000 department stores with a membership of about 9.5 million. But they suffer from many deficiencies: the stock range is less, prices are comparatively higher, infrastructure, ambience and comfort level services are low, customer services are poor, cost structure is higher and modern style of marketing is absent.

But, the size of the organized retail segment to-day is estimated to be Rs. 2000 Billion. The co-operatives which serve primarily the salaried class and rural poor must gear themselves to meet the challenges posed by private retail giants like Pantaloon, RPG, Shoppers Stop, Life Style, West-Side, Pyramid, Globus and a host of other international retail giants who are also eyeing India with great interest.

Obviously this calls for a critical review and appraisal of institutional structure, business strategy, operations and management of consumer co-operatives for their effective repositioning and sustainability in the changed context. The Department of Co-operation, and in particularly Dr. B. Tamilmani who is the prime editor of this workshop proceedings, deserve our heartiest appreciation for their hard work to bring out this valuable study materials on Management of Consumers Co-operatives.

I hope this publication will be a useful reference material and will help visualize and formulate suitable strategies for strengthening consumer co-operatives in the globalised world.

T. Karunakaran
Vice-Chancellor
Gandhigram Rural University

Preface

The role of consumer cooperatives in the competitive world assumes great importance, as they strive for protecting the consumers, by means of serving them with quality consumer goods at a price comparatively lower to the private shops, with exact correct measurement. Consumer cooperatives here at commanding heights with all resources and in some places they served as market leaders by performing effective service to the public. For instance, the Chinthamani Cooperative Supermarket *(Tamilnadu)* the best in India two decades ago, has gone down. Apna Bazaar and Janatha bazars respectively of Delhi and Bangalore metros have also been indicating declining trend and unhealthy status.

In general, performance reports of consumer cooperatives show a dismal picture. Some consumer cooperatives survive mainly because of the margin gained through undertaking of public distribution system and with governments' patronage. Moreover, the liberalized era has opened up the gate for the multinational corporations in the retailing business. This will certainly be a great threat to the consumer cooperatives. At this Juncture, CWSs need to be adaptive in every respect and they must be capable of harnessing the opportunities and resources. They need to redefine their policies, management methods, procedural aspects and legal matters. Decisive strategies are to be evolved to strengthen CWSs to make them structurally strong and financially viable. Equipping the officials with necessary skills for enhancing the performance of CWSs is one way of getting close to make them functionally effective.

Keeping in mind the above issues and matters, a two day state level workshop was organized by the Department of Cooperation, Gandhigram Rural University, Gandhigram on 19th and 20th

January 2006, by involving the academics, managerial caders of CWSs, Research Scholars and students.

Financial assistance for the conduct of the two day workshop under unassigned grant of the University Grants Commission was made available. It is my bounden duty to thank the UGC. New Delhi.

Grateful acknowledgements due to our Vice-chancellor, Dr. T. Karnakaran, who always encourages the faculty members to organize programmes like this for the benefit of both sides. He has determined to introduce innovative spirits among the faculty and in the academic programmes and has motivated us in maintaining upward quality in academic and research activities.

I would like to place on record the support extended by Dr. R. Sundaravadivelu, the Registrar and Dr. Susila Kirubavathi, Academic Registrar and other officials of our University.

Thanks are due to Dr. P. Sivaprakasam Prof. & Head; Dr. B. Subburaj, Prof; Dr. K. Ravichandran, Dr. S. Manivel, Dr. D. Joseph Nelson and Mr. B. Basker the faculty members of cooperation, GRU for their help and encouragement.

My humble gratitude to my guide Dr. N. Narayanasamy, Prof. & Head, Department of Extension Education for his constant guidance and cheerful support.

I am very grateful to the Chairman and the members of Publication committee of GRU for having extended financial assistance for publishing this material.

Thankful acknowledgements are due to Mr. R. Jeyachandramani, General Manager, Erode District CWSs, Mr. S. Jeyakuamr, Head, Department of Commerce, Gangatharan Arts and Science College, Pondichery for their guidance and suggestions extended especially during the pre workshop period.

I am privileged to have Dr. Frank Ratna Kumar as the Co. editor of this useful material.

Dr. S. K. Gopal, Chief Training Officer, KVK,GRU, Dr. Rajamohan Rao, and Sri S. Nehru faculty members of Economics, GRU, are very much remembered here for their help during the workshop.

I am thankful to the Research Scholars of GRU namely Raja Rajeswari, S. Dhanasekarn, K. Gunaseelapraphu, V. Murugan, S.Velanganni, P. Kamaraj, S. Mohan and the Students of Cooperation for their assistance during the workshop.

B. Tamilmani

List of Contributors

A. Abdul Rahman, Research Scholar, Department of Gandhian Thought, Gadhigram Rural University, Gandhigram.

S. Adaikala Charles, Lecturer in Cooperation, T.B.M.L. College, Porayar, Nagai District, Tamilnadu.

N. Baluswami, Reader and Head, PG Department of Cooperation, Sri Ramakrishan Mission Vidyalaya College of Arts and Science, Coimbatore, Tamilnadu.

F.Basker Chandrasekar, Lecturer, Department of Cooperation, T.B.M.L. College, Porayar, Nagai District, Tamilnadu.

B. Basker, Lecturer, Department of Cooperation, Gandhigram Rural University, Gandhigram , Dindigul, Tamilnadu.

S. David Amirtha Rajan, Reader and Head, Post Graduate and Research, Department of Commerce, The American College, Madurai, Tamilnadu.

S. Dhanasekaran, Lecturer (SG), Department of Mechanical Engineering, Thigaraja Engineering College, Madurai, Tamilnadu.

Frank Ratna Kumar, Reader, Department of Cooperation, T.B.M.L. College, Porayar, Nagai District, Tamilnadu.

J. Gayathri, Lecturer, Department of Cooperation, Tiruppur Kumaran College for Women, Tiruppur, Tamilnadu.

P. Gnana Sundari, Reader in Economics, Lady Doak College, Madurai, Tamilnadu.

K. Guna Seela Prabhu, Department of Cooperation, Gandhigram Rural University, Gandhigram-624302, Tamilnadu.

R. Jayachandramani, General Manager, Erode District Consumer Cooperative Wholesale Store, Erode, Tamilnadu.

S. Jayakumar, Head, Department of Commerce, Gangatharan Arts and Science College, Pondicherry.

C.P. Jayaseelan, Research Scholar, T.B.M.L. College, Porayar, Nagai District, Tamilnadu.

P. Jeyachitra, P.G. Student, Department of Cooperation, Gandhigram Rural University, Gandhigram-624302, Tamilnadu.

D. Joel Edwinraj, Lecturer in Cooperation, T.B.M.L. College, Porayar, Nagai District, Tamilnadu.

P. Kalaiselvi, Lecturer, Department of Cooperation, Tiruppur Kumaran College for Women, Tiruppur, Tamilnadu.

X. Lorudes Xavier Wilson, Lecturer, PG Department of Cooperation, Sri Ramakrishan Mission Vidyalaya College of Arts and Science, Coimbatore, Tamilnadu.

G. Madhruai, Vice Principal, Institute of Cooperative Management, Pondicherry.

S. Manivel, Reader, Department of Cooperation, Gandhigram Rural University, Gadhigram, Dindigul, Tamilnadu.

V. Manohar, Lecturer in Commerce, V.H.N.S.N. College, Virudhunagar, Tamilnadu.

M. Maruthamuthu, Senior Cooperative Auditor, Dindigul District, Tamilnadu.

V. Murugan, Research Scholar, Department of Cooperation, Gandhigram Rural University, Gandhigram-624302, Tamilnadu.

M. Nagavel, Senior Cooperative Auditor, Dindigul District, Tamilnadu.

P. Pirakatheeswari, M.Phil. Research Scholar, V.V. Vanniaperumal College for Women, Virudhunagar.

R. Pothi Reddi, Convenor, Campaign Committee for Liberal Cooperative Law in Tamilnadu.

W. Raja Solomon, Lecturer in Cooperation, T.B.M.L. College, Porayar, Tamilnadu.

Samuel Kakuko Lopoteum, Post Doctoral Research Fellow, Department of Cooperation, Gandhigram Rural University, Gandhigram-624302, Tamilnadu.

B. Santhi, Lecturer, Vellalar College of Arts and Science, Erode District, Tamilnadu.

R. Seerangarajan, Reader, Department of Rural Industries Management, Gandhigram Rural University, Gandhigram. Tamilnadu.

K. Selvarani, Reader in Commerce, V.V. Vanniaperumal College for Women, Virudhunagar, Tamilnadu.

P. Sivaprakasam, Professor & Head, Department of Cooperation, Gandhigram Rural University, Gandhigram-624302, Tamilnadu.

S. Sugumar, Reader, Department of Cooperation, T.B.M.L. College, Porayar, Tamilnadu.

P. Sundara Pandian, Reader in Commerce, V.H.N.S.N. College, Virudhunagar, Tamilnadu.

B. Tamilmani, Reader, Department of Cooperation, Gandhigram Rural University, Gandhigram-624302, Tamilnadu.

S. Velanganni, Research Scholar, Department of Cooperation, Gandhigram Rural University, Gandhigram-624302, Tamilnadu.

R. Velu Raj, Lecturer, Department of Cooperative, Management, Tagore Government Arts College, Pondicherry-605008.

A. Xavior Selvakumar, Lecturer, Department of Cooperation, T.B.M.L. College, Porayar, Nagai District, Tamilnadu.

1

Consumer Cooperatives: Status, Problems and Prospects

B. Tamilmani

INTRODUCTION

A consumer cooperative is an autonomous association of consumers united voluntarily to obtain their requirements of consumer goods and services on terms of greatest advantage, through a jointly owned and democratically controlled enterprise. Consumer cooperatives play a vital role in distributing consumer goods and necessary provisions to the public at large through wholesaling as well as retailing. The modern cooperative movement originated from consumer cooperatives called 'Rochdale Society of Equitable Pioneers' which was started way back in 1844. The principles evolved by them are still very relevant to cooperatives. The first consumer cooperative in India was started in 1904, known as Triplicane Urban Cooperative Society, in the then Madras province. *(presently Tamilnadu)*

The consumer cooperatives in India have been working for achieving the following objectives: (i) to ensure the availability of quality consumer goods to the common man and more so to the vulnerable sections of the community, at affordable prices, (ii) to develop fair trade practices, (iii) to create employment opportunities to the local people, (iv) to develop consumer awareness and take effective measures in the areas of consumer protection, and (v) to keep the prices of essential items under check as the presence of consumer cooperatives would provide the consumers an idea of comparative rates in the market.

INSTITUTIONAL NET WORK

Consumer Cooperatives in India have been following 'Federal Structure'. It means that a consumer cooperative at lower level could have business relationship with similar cooperatives, in order to get financial, technical, and other supports from them. This system does not affect the democratic functioning of lower level organizations. This structural system leads to creating a stronger and mighty consumer cooperative network in order to serve the consumers in a better way. What follows is the structure of consumer cooperatives along with a short profile on each level of organizations.

National Consumer Cooperative Federation-1

↓

State Consumer Cooperative Federations-30

↓

District Consumer Cooperative Wholesale Stores - 794

↓

Primary Consumer Cooperative Stores- 24078

National Cooperative Consumer Federation(NCCF) acts as a spokesman of consumer cooperative movement. By assisting and guiding member-organizations, it improves their operational and managerial efficiency. It also involves in procuring and marketing consumer goods and undertakes liasion with governments, National and International level bodies on matters of consumer cooperatives and consumer protection.

State Consumer Cooperative Federations (SCCFs) promote consumer cooperative movement in their respective states. They procure goods in bulk and supply them to member-organizations for distribution to the public. They also assist member organizations to enhance their efficiency. They also act as an agent of the respective state governments in distributing essential consumer goods and in ensuring food security.

District Consumer Cooperative Wholesale Stores (DCCWS) purchase goods in bulk and supply them in wholesale as well as retail to the members and non-members. They practice fair trade, stabilize the prices of consumer goods and take all possible measures to protect interests of consumers.

Primary Consumer Cooperative Stores (PCCS) involve in distributing consumer articles in retail to the members and the general public. As they are closely associated with consumers, they can easily understand their taste and behaviour. Therefore, they give information to the higher level organizations on consumer taste and behaviours and other relevant market information.

In addition, there are more than 58000 Primary Agricultural Credit Societies (PACS) and Large Sized Adivasi Multi-Purpose Societies (LAMPS) in the rural areas, which are also distributing essential consumer goods of daily use to the people living in rural as well as hilly and inaccessible areas. Around 4180 Students Cooperatives are making available books and stationery items to the college/university students, in addition to running canteens. Over 125000 Fair Prices shops in cooperative sector are handling and distributing of selected essential commodities of daily use under the public distribution system of the Government of India.

THE STATUS OF CONSUMER COOPERATIVES

At attempt is made here to describe the status of the consumer cooperatives in India. This has been done with the help of relevant data gathered from articles appeared in NCDC Bulletin and the profile of Indian Cooperative Movement. The data were pertaining to 2005 and in some cases the data of earlier years are also used for description and analysis.

NCCF has been functioning since 1965 with the membership of 136 cooperative organizations and government institutions including government of India. The paid up share capital found with NCCF on 31.03.2003 was Rs. 185.62 millions, of which government's share alone was Rs. 156 millions(84 per cent). The total turnover of the NCCF was Rs. 6740.60 millions and it was able to get a profit of Rs. 41.93 Millions.

There were 30 SCCFs as on 31.03.2005. These SCCFs and working with the branches of 737 (inclusive of departmental stores). The membership of the federations was 21000 of which almost 50 per cent was constituted by institutional membership. The share capital was collected to the tune of Rs. 1174.4 millions, of which the respective state government's participation was 85 per cent. The working capital of the SCCFs was Rs. 4306.1 millions *(2003)* and the sales was effected to the tune of Rs. 14371.2 millions *(2005)*, which indicates that a two and half times higher than the working capital. Of the sales effected, the portion of wholesale trade constituted 77 per cent and the rest was by retail trade. Almost 50 per cent of the federations were on profit *(2002)*.

There were 794 DCCWSs in India, functioning through 5001 branches and departmental stores. The membership of these stores was 2229 millions. These stores were able to mobilise share capital to the level of Rs. 867.43 millions, of which governments' participation was 68.06 per cent *(2002)*. The working capital of the stores was maintained at Rs. 5393.9 millions and the sales of the stores was Rs. 20656 millions*(2005)*, which indicates a sale of three and a half times higher than the working capital. Of the sales components, it was found that 52 per cent was constituted for retail trades and the rest was by wholesale trade. A 44.5 per cent of the stores was running on profit.

The PCCSs are organized at grassroot level catering to the requirements of consumer provisions of rural and semi urban consumers. There were 24078 PCCSs with 7484 branches and departmental stores as on March 2005. The Share capital of these stores was Rs. 1098.1 millions, in which government's participation was 29.18 per cent. At lower level, the government's participation was found at reduced level. The working capital maintained was Rs. 3357.6 millions. The sale of controlled commodities constituted 60.7 per cent and the rest was the sale of non-controlled commodities.

The consumer cooperatives altogether achieved sales of about Rs. 95 billion during the year 1999-2000. This was around 2.5 per cent of the total retail sales of the consumer goods in the country. Although, the sales coverage was not very significant, but the very presence of the consumer cooperatives creates an impact in the market to stabilize the prices and availability of consumer goods. The consumer cooperatives like Apna Bazar, Sahakari Bhandar in Mumbai, Kendriya Bhandar and Apna Bazar in Delhi, Triveni and Neethi Stores in Kerala are some of the notable consumer cooperatives in India.

PROBLEMS

The performance of consumer cooperatives was declining year by year excepting a few cases. That too, a sharp decline was noticed from 1990.91 onwards. The Liberalised environment has opened up a bundle of pressures and threats to consumer cooperatives. A large number of private players have already started entering in the retail sector, which poses a tough climate to the consumer cooperatives. Very recently, the Reliance group and Mittal group have entered the retail market with a big bang. The ambience and outlook, branded items, attractive packages have overtaken the inner aspects of goods. Therefore, consumer cooperatives must work better than ever before in order to compete with private players.

To study the poor performance of consumer cooperatives, an Expert Committee was appointed by the Government of India in 1993-94, headed by Shri G.K. Sharma, the then Regional Director, International Cooperative Alliance with the members from different Central Government Departments, State Governments, Cooperative Institutions and the NCCF: The terms of reference of the Committee were: (i) to study the functioning of the consumer cooperatives of all tiers to find out the extent of sickness, (ii) to find out the bottlenecks and the hurdles, which have contributed to the sickness, (iii) to study the effect of the policy of the liberalized economy of the government and, (iv) to suggest the strategies and remedial measures for improving the working of the consumer cooperatives.

The expert committee in its report mentioned that 57 per cent of primary stores were either in loss or defunct. The remaining 43 per cent was in profit that too, in most cases marginally. At the District/Central level, 61 per cent of the stores were in loss and 39 per cent were somewhat running viably. Out of 29 State Federations, only 16 were in profit and remaining were in loss. The committee identified the following structural and organizational problems which affected the growth of consumer cooperatives: (i) registration of societies without proper scrutiny, (ii) lack of member participation, (iii) lack of democratic functioning, (iv) absence of professionalism, (v) discontinuation of centrally sponsored scheme for providing financial assistance for development of consumer cooperatives through State Governments and Government approach.

The managerial problems associated with consumer cooperatives and the reasons responsible for the downward performance were: (i) unplanned business operations,

(ii) higher establishment cost and low margin available from their commercial operations, (iii) inability to devise strategy to face stiff competition from multi-national companies, which are entering retail trade in a big way, (iv) non-availability of working capital from banks/financial institutions on preferential terms, (v) business indiscipline among the consumer cooperatives resulting in competition among themselves, (vi) improper business attitude of the manufacturers for allowing preferential treatment to the private trade.

PROSPECTS

It is the right time to make an indepth internal as well external analysis which would help to proceed further. With the experience of a century of existence, consumer cooperatives must evolve practicable and operable strategies for their prospects.

They must develop a tendency of standing on their own without looking forward for financial assistance from the government. These require drastic changes in their structure, system of purchases, sales, inventory/assortments and building of regular clientele. The below mentioned suggestive measures could help sortout present problems and take them to a right future.

The responsibilities and activities of the consumer cooperatives will have to be increased to the changing behaviour of consumers and the environment. The consumer cooperatives must have strategies to meet the increased demands of the people. However, this could be possible only by professionalising themselves with modern techniques of retail as well as wholesale management.

Consumer cooperatives have to develop professional management by training their staff to improve their operational efficiency and professional competency. Special training modules must be prepared by taking into consideration of the changes that take place in the globalised environment. Modern marketing concepts must be adopted. Also new blood must be injected in consumer cooperatives.

In the context of globalized trade and economy, consumers get a lot of avenues and choices. Therefore, the consumer cooperatives should improve the quality of goods and their services, so that they could retain their clientele of consumers for ever. They must take effective customer care so that consumers do not switch over to private traders.

In the days of stiff competition, the operations of the consumer cooperatives must be made qualitative and cost effective. This could be done by increasing labour productivity, which could be achieved by linking it with productivity incentive scheme.

Maintaining inventory control at an optimum level without adversely affecting the sales would be appreciated. As also having maximum rotation of the capital by way of stock-turn over in order to minimize the capital cost are some of the essential requisites of profit earning capacity of the consumer cooperatives.

In the modern world consumers cannot be taken for granted. Hence, consumer cooperatives stores have to adopt a package of sales promotional techniques so that consumers could be retained. There should also be regular performance review to maintain their profitability and take corrective actions wherever necessary.

The unviable small consumer cooperatives, which have no infrastructure, should either be liquidated or merged with the nearest successful cooperative stores. They should adopt modern techniques and systems of retail management and gear up their activities to satisfy the changing needs of the consumers.

The consumer cooperatives would need government and institutional support for some more time, to build up a strong consumer movement in the country and for protecting the interests of consumers and common masses.

CONCLUSION

The greatest plus point of consumer cooperatives is that it has an effective organizational network with an experience of existence over a century. Lot of wonders could be done with this much net work, resources and experience. But, the present status of consumer cooperatives is not encouraging. On an average around 40 per cent of them run on profit that too on a very marginal amount of profit. The liberalized environment has unleashed innumerable problems from various corners. They must be adaptive to changing environment and active in devising strategies to the sustainability of their operations. The suggestive measures described above could help them for better functioning.

2

Consumer Cooperatives: Problems and Prospects

P. Sivaprakasam

INTRODUCTION

There are 26500 primary consumer cooperatives, 700 wholesale/central stores and 28 state federations, besides the NCCF, which is the apex body of the consumer cooperatives in the country. About 2.35 crore individuals are the members of primary and wholesale/central cooperative stores spread all over the country. The current level of estimated sales turnover of the consumer cooperatives is in the range of Rs. 6500 crores. Because of various factors, about 50 per cent of the consumer cooperative societies have been incurring losses.

CAUSES FOR THE SICKNESS

The following are the main factors for the sickness in the growth of consumer cooperatives in India:

- The various tiers of consumer cooperatives have a little or no linkages.
- Weak capital base of the consumer cooperatives.

- The average sales turnover of the individual units remains low and stagnant.
- Inadequate margin available to the consumer cooperatives for distributions of controlled commodities.
- Political and official domination in the functioning of the societies.
- Managed by non-professionals which leads to inefficient management.
- Lack of autonomy in the decision making process.
- Ineffective functioning of the sub-committees constituted for purchases and price fixation
- Underutilization of the processing/manufacturing units of the consumer cooperatives.
- Absence of the need-based training programmes.
- High labour turnover due to the ineffective personnel policies.

MEASURES FOR IMPROVING THE BUSINESS EFFICIENCY OF THE COOPERATIVE WHOLESALE STORES

Assortment

With a view to winning the confidence of the customers the management of store should aim at formulating an assortment policy which ensures supplying all the requirements of the consumers. In this respect, need based purchasing policy can be followed.

Pricing

The management of the store should follow 'active price policy' which means pricing the goods just below the market price but above the cost price.

System of selling

Some of the common systems of selling are home delivery, cash sales and credit sales. Under the home delivery system, salesman visits customers' homes, collects orders against cash and delivers the goods ordered at the doors of the customers. Under the system of cash sales the customer buys goods from the salesman across the counter and pays the cash for the goods purchased. Credit sales can also be made available for those, particularly employees who are not able to make the payment at the time of purchasing goods. The value of the goods purchased by them is deducted from their salary on the basis of an agreement between the employer and the cooperative store.

Responsibility of Salesmen

He is responsible for the entire section, he must be made responsible for pilferages, leakages and shortages of goods kept in his section. If there is a shortage or leakage or pilferage at the time of taking the stock, the value of the goods should be deducted from the salary of the concerned employee.

Formation of Local Committee

The selfless and service-minded persons representing all groups of customers without having political background should be encouraged to become members of the committee. To become a committee member, it should be made as a pre-condition that he should have the business participation of atleast Rs. 1000/- in the previous year with the store.

The Incentive System for the Employees of the Store

A salesman, if he is not motivated may even misguide the customers. As a result the sales turnover will come down. Therefore, sales incentive system can be introduced. This will aim at achieving the objective of motivating the employees and at the same time helping the society to increase its turnover also. The management of the store can follow the example given below for adapting the sales incentive system. Salary of each salesman - Rs. 1000/- per month or minimum wages as per the act. Average sales expected from each salesman–Rs. 2000/- per day Incentive for every additional sale of Rs. 100/- Rs. 1.00/-.

Thus, a salesman who sells the goods worth of Rs. 3000/- per day on an average will get a monthly salary of Rs. 1300/- (Rs.1000 as salary plus Rs. 300 as incentive). The incentive given to the salesman encourages him to increase his remuneration on one side and increase the turnover of the society on the other side.

Viability of the Store

- All the measures suggested under improvement of business and incentive schemes suggested for the employees of the store are to be implemented without fail.
- Reduce the establishment cost of the store.
- Increase in the business transactions.
- The government should meet the expenses incurred by the Special Officer until the election is held for the board of management of stores.
- Accountability to the special officer should be fixed by financial analysis like cash flow, fund flow, and ratio analysis should be done by the special officer and steps must be taken to correct the deviations, if any.
- Continuous assessment on the business performance of employees by the Special Officer.
- Computerized MIS should be followed.

Other Measures

- Common cadre system can be followed.
- Management should be in the hands of elected members. If at all Special Officers are appointed, they should work atleast for three years in a particular society. Transfer in between the period should be strictly avoided.

- General body meeting should be convened atleast once a year even under the regime of Special Officers.
- Dividend to the members must be distributed every year.
- Surplus staff of the cooperatives can be absorbed by the needy cooperatives.
- Training to the salesman, office bearers should be arranged periodically so as to improve their efficiency.
- Computerization of the billing and accounting system in the stores is the need of the hour.

3

Cooperative Wholesale Stores in the Globalized Era: A SWOT Analysis

Frank Ratnakumar

"All were glad; the plants, the birds, insects and children. But men, grown up men and women did not leave off cheating and tormenting themselves and each other. It was not this spring morning they thought sacred and important, not the beauty of God's world given to benefit all creatures- a beauty which inclines the heart to peace, harmony and love–but only their own devices for getting the upperhand of each other"—*by TOLSTOI.*

The current pace of economic development not only widens the gap between the rich and the poor but also damages ecological foundations essential for sustainable productivity namely land, water, flora, fauna, forests, oceans and the atmosphere. (M.S. Swaminathan, 1998). The Global environmental changes such as 'Green House Effect', 'Global Warming' and 'Depletion of Ozone Layer' have all been contributed by market economy. So we need a broader concept of sustainable development which encompasses environmental, economic, ethical and social parameters.

SUSTAINABLE DEVELOPMENT AND CONSUMER COOPERATIVES

Sustainable development, as a model and an important environmental theme is evolving. In essence the sustainable development promotes development which:

1. Reduces the disparities in life styles and global consumption.
2. Improves and maintains a healthy local environment and
3. Then and only then Contributes towards solving critical global environmental management of the global commons-such as global climate change, oceans, fisheries and forests.

Therefore, it is vital to ask;

1. What kind of growth is desirable?
2. What kind is not ? and
3. How to develop economic policy and environmental policy accordingly while maintaining consumer choices and a sense of equity within a market economy?

So we need a broader concept of sustainable development which encompasses environmental, economic, ethical and social parameters. This is possible only in a high synergy society. As Ruth Benedict, an anthropologist pointed out "in cultures with high social synergy, institutions ensure mutual advantage in low synergy society, the disadvantages individual becomes victory for another and the majority who are not victorious must shift for themselves" Most evil in this world is due to excessive preoccupation with material wealth and power. Mahatama Gandhi, through his life and work emphasized the need for ethical underpinning of civilization and for a systems view in matters relating to life on earth. There is a distinct possibility that global civilization might collapse within our life time or that of our children. Increasing number of intelligent people including Lord May, David King,

Jared Diamond, Harold Pinter, Noam Chomsky have been warning that global collapse is a genuine possibility. Many cilvilisations from Maya in Mexico to Polynesians of Eastern Islands have collapsed in the past due to the very same dangers that threaten us to day i.e deforestration, depletion of resources, ecological problems and war (Dylan Evans, 2005).

It is in this background P.Kotler and Levy originated the concept and coined the term " Creative demarketing" as that aspect of marketing that deals with discouraging customer in general or a certain class of customers in particular on either a temporary or permanent basis. So the public has to be enlightened about these problems such as wastages, environmental degradation and depletion of natural resources. So consumer cooperatives have to play an increasingly important role not only in consumer satisfaction but in 'Creative demarketing. They have to, not only protect the interest of the consumers but also, educate the members about wastages, environmental degradation and depletion of natural resources.

GLOBALIZATION

Thomas Friedman in his book, The World is Flat–A brief History of Globalised world in the 21st Century, Classified Globalization into 3 eras.

1. Globalisation 1.0: The first lasted from 1492–when Columbus set sail, opening trade between the old world and the new world until around 1800-the dynamic force driving the globalization was power of the countries.
2. Globalisation 2.0, lasted from 1800–2000 the dynamic force driving global integration was multi national companies global integration was powered by falling transportation costs and in the second half by the falling telecommunication costs–thanks to the diffusion of the telegraph, telephones, P.Cs, satellites, and WWW.etc.
3. Globalisaton 3.0 began around 2000–shrinking and flattening the world and empowering individuals.

Individuals from every part of the world are being empowered.

Even though windows, internet, work flow and open sources software, outsourcing, off-shoring etc may appear to make the world more equal and flat, the fact remains the real value addition is still creamed off by the big multi national corporations. (Siddharth Vardarajan, 2005). Further, the model followed by India relies heavily on imported technology, designs and equipment through foreign collaboration and FDI with far too little attention and effort at building indigenous capability which will seriously erode the extent of autonomy the country can have in shaping its development inconsistent with equity and sustainability.

PRECONDITIONS FOR SUCCESS OF COOPERATIVE ORGANIZATION IN THE GLOBALIZED ERA

"The continuance of the cooperative idea does not rely on cooperatives living forever but on being reborn time and again" said Charles Gide.

SOCIETAL PRECONDITIONS

1. An act of grass roots collective mobilisation.
2. Grass roots mobilisatoin can take place under a minimum of guaranteed civil liberties.
3. Process of societal change in which large segments of society experience drastic reduction of their relative economic and social position and wish to reaffirm it.

ECONOMIC PRECONDITIONS

Success in established cooperatives will depend on serving member's interest efficiently. The globalization process is expected to;

1. Improve allocative efficiency of resources.
2. Reduce the capital output ratio.
3. Increase labour productivity.

4. Increase capital.
5. Increase technology.

To face the challenges cooperatives have to;

1. Ensure patronage and participation of members
2. Effective structure to ensure effective management and control
3. Efficient capitalization
4. Modern technology

CONSUMER COOPERATIVES

Consumer cooperatives in India were established to safeguard the consumer from the ruthless exploitation of middlemen in unethical malpractices, adulteration, under weighment, poor quality of goods, duplicate goods, high prices, creation of artificial scarcity of goods etc. The consumer cooperatives which were approximately 23 towards the end of 1911 rose to 78 towards the end of First World War. The consumer cooperatives suffered huge losses during the great depression.

The Consumer Cooperative movement received, support of the government since the 1st Five Year Plan. The Consumer Cooperatives suffered a set back because of the abandment of controls and rationing in 1952. The establishement of fair price shops in the cooperative sector in II Five Year Plan proved a fillip to the movement. During the III Five Year Plan centrally sponsored 200 cooperative wholesale stores and 400 primary branch stores were started with an outlay of Rs. 10 crores. The IV Five Year Plan saw the establishment of National Consumers' Cooperative Federation.

During the Vth plan with increased government support and encouragement the retail trade handled by them increased from Rs. 400 crores to Rs. 550 crores registering an increase of 37 per cent. The VI plan marketed, increased governmental assistance to set up departmental stores, Large Sized Retail Outlets, Janatha Shops, Regional Distribution

Centre by the State Federations and wholesale stores. The VII five year plan witnessed assistance to the tune of Rs. 997.4 millions by NCDC to promote consumer stores and the annual business operations of the stores registered an increase of 11.09. per cent.

According to Images–KSA technoprak study (2005) in 2004 the size of the organized retailing market stood at Rs. 28000 crore, making up a mere 3 per cent of total retailing market. Organized retail maketing is projected to grow at the rate of 25-30 per cent per annum and expected to reach Rs. 100000 crores by 2010. In this backdrop, the performance of consumer cooperatives, particularly cooperatives wholesale stores present a sorry picture, on an average more than 60 per cent of the CWSs had been working on loss and according to the expert committee on consumer cooperatives the remaining 40 per cent were in profit, that too in most cases marginally. They dependent heavily on government for their share capital and government schemes for their resources. Even though sales registered growth this was mainly due to 3 states i.e Tamilnadu, Maharashtra and Delhi, they together accounted for 35 per cent. Of the total sales, retail sales, accounted for more than 50 per cent during 1991-2001 and of the total sale of controlled goods accounted for more than 55 per cent. The cost of management showed an increasing trend.

SWOT ANALYSIS

India is on the radar of global market and retailers and suppliers world wide are willing to partner with retailers here. Further, large Indian corporate groups like the Tatas, Reliance, the Rahejas, ITC, Bombay Dyeing, Murugappa and Priramal and also foreign investors are planning to enter India's retail market in a big way. So consumer cooperative movement, particularly CWS with their already established infrastructure and branches have to prepare on a war footing to meet the challenges from private retailers and also to develop the concept of creative demarketing.

STRENGTHS

Safeguard the Interest of Men of Smaller Means

The world commission on social dimension of globalization (2004) observed that the current process of globalization is generating unbalanced outcomes, both between and within countries, wealth is being created, but too many countries and people are not sharing in its benefits. They also have little or no voice in shaping the process. Seen through the eyes of vast majority of women and men, globalization has not met their simple and legitimate aspirations for decent jobs and better future for their children. Cooperation alone safeguards the interest of men of smaller means.

Cooperative Values and Principles

Very few Indians have a broader sense of community than that circumscribed by that of blood, caste affiliation or village. We take care of those we consider dear and near and remain largely indifferent to the rest. This was demonstrated during and after Tsunami struck the coast of Tamilnadu. Other ills affecting the society are violence and corruption. Corruption violates human rights, undermines rule of law, distorts development process and disembowels the Indian state. Cooperatives alone instill values and sense of community among the people and bring about social integration.

Structure

The four tier structure of consumer cooperatives, with 28290 primary societies, 696 Wholesale stores and 29 Apex Federations and one National Federation with a total membership of 16.5 million is formidable. With proper networking and coordination they can take up the best of Retail chain stores and beat them also.

Community Concern and Environment

As locally based institutions, cooperatives are naturally concerned about their communities in which their members live. The consumer cooperatives in Japan have adopted a uniform slogan, "Let us watch our life and the earth" and consumer cooperatives have been consistently concerned with changing life styles and the need to promote more sustainable consumption patterns.

WEAKNESSES

Lack of Members' Support

Lack of active participation of the members in the affairs of the stores. In U.K. the market share of consumers' shop has been dwindling. In France the National Cooperatives de consummator has collapsed. The Dutch consumer movement has ceased to exist. Widespread passive member control has been considered an important factor for the debacle.

Lack of Democratic Management

The involvement of government in managing the affairs of the societies affects the democratic character. In Tamilnadu the cooperatives have been virtually under govt. control and some world renowned cooperatives like Chinthamani cooperative super market in Coimbatore have been destroyed because of lack of democratic management.

Unplanned Business Operation

The CWS were burdened with PDS with accounts more than 50 per cent of their sales. Further their organic link with the primaries as well as Apex Federation was almost absent as they don't supply the requirements of primaries and inturn CWS dont get any support from the Apex organization. They also suffer chronic stock deficit, lack of choice of goods etc.

Failure to Adopt Modern Technology

Even though consumer cooperatives have been responsible for opening super markets and self services, they are now lagging behind in the age of theme malls and computerization.

Non-availability of Funds

Increasing capital intensity of retail trade has led to the downfall of many European consumer movements. Non-availability of funds from banks and financial institutions and dependence on government for funds restrict the operations and efficiency of CWS.

Lack of Professional Management

Shortage of professional managerial staff due to poor resources available with consumer cooperatives affected their functioning while countries like Sweden, Japan, Germany have adopted the principles of corporate governance.

High Establishment Cost and Low Margin

Higher establishment costs have been the bane of cooperative and CWS are no exception. Because of their heavy dependence on local purchase, they necessarily get low margin from their commercial operations.

OPPORTUNITIES

There is a consumer boom in India. The organized retailing is projected to grow at the rate of 25-30 per cent per annum and is estimated to reach Rs. 100000 crore by 2010. Global retailers and suppliers are wiling to partner with retailers here in India.

Expanding Organized Retail Market

The expanding retail market and consumer awareness provide opportunities for CWS. With their already available infrastructure and member base, if they go in for modernization and technology upgradation, they can make a real impact in Tamilnadu.

Consumerism

Consumerism is the name given to the consumer protection movement. P. Kotler defines consumerism as the social movement seeking to augment the rights and powers of the buyers in relation to sellers. Besides that, Consumers skepticism, Anti- hypocrisy and concern about the environment are the factors responsible for the rise of consumerism. In such an environment cooperatives have a better chance of surviving because of their insistence on fair practices.

Consultancy Services of NCCF

The consultancy and promotional cell of NCCF is providing technical guidance and assistance in different fields of management like management accounting system, wholesale and retail management, setting up of self service department stores, education and training , preparation of project reports for rehabilitation of sick consumer cooperatives. Consumer cooperatives can make use of their services

NCDC–Financial Assistance

The NCDC provides financial assistance to consumer cooperatives for; (i) expansion/renovation of existing infrastructure or construction of new shopping centres/ godowns (ii) margin money for raising working capital and (iii) rehabilitation of weak societies.

THREATS

India Retail Forum (IRF), a platform for private retail industry, was launched recently. With the industry growing at 7 per cent CAGR and organized retailed growing at 30 per cent CAGR, the organized industry is expected to grow to 110000 crore by 2010 with a potential to employ 2 million people, it is attracting huge foreign and domestic interest.

Foreign Direct Investment in Retail Sector

Foreign players are displaying a keen interest in India. Kearney rated India as the most attractive market in preference to countries like China, Russia etc., India has jumped from the 30th to 16th position in the foreign direct investment index.

More specific to retail, India has moved-up from the 6th to the 1st position in the Global retail index.

Indian Retail Industry in Urban Areas

Large Indian groups like the Tatas, Reliance, Rahejas, ITC, Bombay Dyeing, Murugappa, Priramal etc. are planning to enter retail market in a big way. Reliance has set up 725 gas stations across the country as well as 55 'A1 plazas' which include hospitality services for the trucking community and trans connect, a complete fleet solution. Reliance is adding 3-4 new Reliance Petroleum Outlets every day. Reliance is planning a tie-up with Walmart.

Emergence of other forms of Marketing

E-commerce companies are making it possible to small town people to log on to the Net and order branded products. Further appearance of Margin Free Supermarkets, Tele-shopping, direct marketing, Cheap foreign goods etc pose a direct threat to consumer cooperatives.

Indian Retail Industry in Rural Areas

Some corporates such as ITC, Godrej and Reliance have successfully tapped the rural retail markets. ITC has set up 'Choupal Sagar' which sells fertilizers, hair oil, cloths etc and also double–up as facilitation centres fo the farming community through their agricultural advice, training and other assistance services, Godrej has launched 'Adhaar' Agri. Stores to sell agricultural products.

CONCLUSION

With the concept of 'creative demarketing' gaining ground and the rise of consumerism the scope for consumer cooperatives has increased. Consumer cooperatives can rise to the challenge, provided they improve their purchase practices, supply chain networking, information system and technology and last but not the least adopting the low cost culture. I believe like Martin Luther King "I say to you to-day, my friends, so even though we face the difficulties of to-day and to-morrow, I still have a dream. I have a dream that some day this nation will rise up and live out the true meaning of its creed......." I have a dream that one day the cooperative movement in this country will live to the true meaning of its culture.

4

Essential Mantras for the Success and Sustenance of Consumer Cooperatives in the Globalised Era

B. Tamilmani and S. Velanganni

INTRODUCTION

Consumer Cooperatives came into existence mainly to safeguard the interests of consumers from the onslaughts of profiteering middlemen. Supplying the member-consumers with pure, unadulterated goods at reasonable price is the maxim of the consumer stores. They have taken the role of price stabilizer, quality controller and leader of the market over the years. The Consumer cooperatives had a proven record of success in many parts of the country. But in recent past, the performance was highly descending. Many thrive mainly because of the patronage extended by the government in the form of distribution of controlled commodities. Many are at the subsistence level. The pathetic situation could be attributed, interalia, ineffective customer service, poor ambience, absence of competitive spirit, financial instability, lack of forsightedness, and lack of professionalism. Hence, it would be appropriate and pertinent to provide a few mantras for the success and sustenance of cooperative especially in the globalised era.

REASONABLE PRICE

Consumer satisfaction on price is of paramount importance for it would definitely reward the organization with good turnover. "Pricing policy of cooperatives should be framed keeping in view the following three essential points: the selling rates should be acceptable to the consumers, all costs should be adequately covered; and store should earn surplus at the end of the year, partly for distribution as dividend among members and partly for ploughing back in the business to ensure proper growth". Active Price Policy, which is in vogue, can be adopted without affecting the profitability of the cooperatives. It is a price slightly higher than the cost price and lower than the market price, fixed mainly on the basis of open market price. Price monitoring system could be effected for controlling the price based on the price that prevails in the market. Walmarts, the retailing giant in the globe is positioning on "Always low prices. Always Walmart".

SUPERIOR QUALITY GOODS

Quality speaks louder than any other mantras. Selling of pure, unadulterated and superior quality articles to the clientele is the key activity of consumer cooperatives. Consumers trust in superior quality and they prefer to buy such goods. They could be retained for ever by supplying superior quality goods. An efficient organization will not let their consumers compromised. Therefore, satisfying the consumers with quality goods is of prime importance. A quality control system is a prerequisite in order to monitor the quality aspects in consumer cooperatives.

Establishing well equipped quality testing laboratory, appointing quality controllers, purchasing of standard goods, grading of goods based on quality are the prime activities to be performed carefully. An analysis on the periodical feedback from the consumers would keep always alert on quality.

Goods supplied must be correct at weighment and at measurement. This in turn will enhance for greater business participation of the consumer cooperatives. Underweigh-ment will dissatisfy the consumers and would create a negative impression about the cooperatives among the consumers. Pre-packed goods would solve this problem: (i) pilferage of goods is prevented; (ii) it saves the time of both salesman and consumer; and (iii) it avoids both the under and over measurement of goods. (iv) and it would also make the sales personnel free from getting into liability.

CUSTOMER RELATIONS

It is true, business could be enlarged through large number of customers. It is they who determine the destiny of the business concerns. That is why, modern marketing emphasizes on customer relationship management (CRM). Gandhiji has described the position of the customers in unequivocal terms as "a customer is the most important visitor on our premises. He is not dependent on us. We are dependent on him. He is not an interruption on our work. he is the purpose of it. He is not an outsider on our business. We are not doing favour by serving him. He is doing us a favour by giving us an opportunity to do so".

Peter Drucker, a great authority on management, has rightly said that the ultimate object of any business is "to create a customer". Creation of customers alone is not just enough. His interests in the products should be sustained and he should be retained at any cost. This, of course, depends on exemplary customer-service at reasonable cost and maintaining cordial relationship with the customers.

Sales personnel who frequently meet customers, must be very polite, cordial, and patient towards them. They must be very prompt in attending to the customers. There should not be any delay in delivering the goods. In the process of persuading customers, the salesman must ensure that there shall be not any argument or disagreement with them.

OPTIMUM INVENTORY LEVEL

Timely availability of variety of required articles will definitely create a sense of dependability and confidence in the minds of consumers which will ultimately give a fillip to business operations. Unlike some of the private sellers who work for high profit through hoarding and artificial scarcity, consumers cooperatives absolutely aim at satisfying the genuine consumers' needs through fair means. Making the articles available at all time would be the solution to solve the above problem and maintaining inventory at an optimum level would be the best way in fulfilling the customers' requirements. This could be done by forecasting the requirements of consumers with their preference at periodic intervals. On the basis of immediate previous years' purchases and sales, consumers demands can effectively be forecast.

AMBIENCE AND OUTLOOK

Location and layout of the stores play a greater role in satisfying consumers. Stores should be located in the heart of cities/towns or in the thickly populated places. The area surrounded by the stores should be pollution free.

Evolving standard shop layout with separate godowns, parking section, display of articles, cash counter, accounts and records section, children's park and canteen will improve the image of the consumer stores. Size of the store is the one which must accommodate the current requirements with the future expansion. Stores constructed lavishly without there being any practical need or keeping its size small though there is need for expansion, will adversely affect the profitability of the organization.

Neatness with proper interior and outer decoration, and proper ventilation, are some of the crucial features in attracting the consumers. Since stores are dealing with food items, cosmetics, luxuries, toiletry, medicine etc., the quality, colour and features of the goods are to be preserved. Systematic arrangement of goods in different shelves at consumer eye-sight level is a trait of good sales personnel. In short, an attractive store could easily convert an unwilling consumer into a willing customer.

EFFECTIVE PLANNING AND CONTROL

Consumer Cooperatives must go for systematic planning and realistic control. While planning, the performance made in the past, and the prospects of the future must blend together to arrive at the systematic planning. Planning on the key functional aspects namely purchases, sales, inventory and working capital, cost cutting and profitability are very crucial in consumer cooperatives. Planning directs where to go and how to go. Consumer cooperatives must institute for a realistic control at the end of the each financial year. Such control must be realistic not ritualistic. A realistic control would review the performance periodically, unearth the potentials, inabilities and suggestive measures for the future. In the process of continuous planning and control, the consumer cooperatives would understand their strengths, weakness, opportunities and threats.

PROFESSIONAL MANAGEMENT

Modern business world opts professional touch in every aspects of managerial functions. Consumers also are in favour of goods and services rendered with professional flavour. Therefore, keeping in mind the changes taking place, consumer cooperatives must go for professionalizing its managerial activities. One of the mantras of modern business world is "professionalize or perish". Initially, professionalism could start with appointing skilled and technically competent personnel to the suitable job at higher positions. Then gradually the whole spectrum of consumer cooperatives have to be professionalised.

The reason being, most of the officials and employees in consumer cooperatives remain unskilled. They need to be given rigourous professional training on managerial functions. Consumer cooperatives must think of injecting new blood especially in the field of marketing. When the private players come with high professional means, the consumer cooperatives must also go along. In the absence of professionalism they cannot win the race.

TECHNOLOGY IN BUSINESS AND ADMINISTRATION

Now- a-days technology plays a major role in bringing about efficiency in business and administration. They help take decisions on time, as well as communicate the decisions down the line quickly. With the help of technology, the business proceedings can be known within fraction of seconds. If computerized accounting is practiced, it would facilitate for quickening the accounting as well as audit process. In a way, it helps assessing the strengths and weaknesses of the organization. The updated market information could be easily accessed by the consumer cooperatives through technology, in order to set price for the goods. Consumer cooperatives must move along with the time. Therefore, usage of information and communication technologies, and other electronic devices must be encouraged for better performance and to get quick results. No doubt, it involves heavy cost, but consumer cooperatives must find resources to get involved in the technology-adoption process.

ORGANIC INTEGRATION

By having business relationship with different types of cooperatives, consumer cooperatives can develop an organic integration at horizontal level as well as at vertical level. The horizontal integration could be of two types-having integration with other consumer cooperatives within the state or within the country and having business relationship with other types of cooperatives. This would facilitate for enormous growth options to the cooperatives which take part in the integration process. The integration would help reducing overhead costs, unnecessary competition and finally reduction in price of the goods. The vertical integration by a lower level consumer cooperative with higher level consumer federations, would get financial, technical, and leadership guidance and continuous support. These forms of assistance would refine their functional means and enhance their business performance.

ADD-ON SERVICES

Flexible working hours must be had in such a manner as it would be convenient for the clientele to have more dealings. On important occasions namely market days, local festival days, and other notable days, the stores must work. The very rigid banking sector too has changed their working hours "seven days in a week".

In the modern world, life has become more mechanical. Most of the urban dwellers are either office-goers or engaged in businesses, who hardly find time for shopping. Door delivery system could be the answer to such consumers. This can be well practiced in the towns and cities and a nominal amount can also be collected as service charges. This system is well practiced by Japaneese Cooperatives and has got overwhelming support among the Japanese.

Consumer cooperatives must have arrangements among themselves whereby the goods purchased by a consumer from a store can be serviced or exchanged in any other consumer cooperatives stores in Tamilnadu. Gradually this arrangement can be widened to consumer cooperatives in south India and India.

CONCLUSION

Change is the order of the day. Change is everywhere and in every aspect of life. Consumers are no exception to this. There is change in their taste, preference, buying behaviour and consuming pattern. The consumer cooperatives, if at all to thrive in the open market economy, must take cognizance of the changing taste, preference and behaviour of not only the current customers but also potential and prospective customers. They need to carefully study their customer options and behaviour and change their style of functioning. Dynamism should be the watchword of consumer cooperatives. For the success and sustainability of consumer cooperatives essential mantras discussed would be pertinent.

5

Cooperative Retailing in the Liberalized Era: Challenges and Opportunities

S. Dhanasekaran and B.Tamilmani

INTRODUCTION

Cooperatives have emerged as a form of business organizations to give solutions to economic problems through collective means and ends. It enabled the people of small means of the society to actively participate in them, and help to reap the benefits of collective advantages and bargaining. Over the years of existence and development, cooperatives have branched out and taken different forms like producers' cooperatives, Employees' cooperatives, Workers' cooperatives, consumers'cooperatives and what not. Cooperatives with different forms have touched all walks of human life across the world. Consumer cooperatives have become more popular because of their reach, and their commitment to protect consumers from the on slaughtering unfair trade practices in the form of underweighment, adulteration, unreasonable prices, inferior quality of products and services.

The prime objective of consumer cooperatives are (i) selling of consumer articles and necessary provisions at a price advantage, (ii) supply of pure, unadulterated and superior quality goods, and (iii) protection of consumers in all possible respects. Consumer cooperatives are the one which not only cater to the requirements of the members but also serve the entire community which approaches them.

INDIAN CONSUMER COOPERATIVES: A GLANCE

Consumer cooperatives have crossed a century by their existence. The first consumer coooperative was registered in 1904 in Triplicane as urban consumers' society. Thereafter a large number of consume cooperatives came into being towards serving the community. Comsumer cooperatives with its large network, functioning through federal structure, has covered almost all parts of the country. The structure of cooperatives is as follows:

National Consumer Cooperative Federation
State Level Federations 30
Wholesale and Central Cooperative Stores 794
Primary Cooperative Stores 24078

Indian consumer cooperatives had a lot of success in the past. The performance and progress of consumer cooperatives have been indicating a declining trend over the years. For instance, the number of primary stores had declined from

26,426 stores in March 2002, to 24,078 in March 2005. Likewise the departmental stores have also declined from 10,760 in March 2002 to 7484 in March 2005. Consumer cooperatives have a massive individual membership of 10.574 millions in March 2005, which shows an increasing trend from 9.52 millions in March 2002. However a decreasing trend is being noticed when it comes to the number of primary consumer stores, and branches of primary consumer stores including departmental stores and their sales. The total sales effected by primary cooperatives and their branches including departmental stores have also registered a decline. Their sales in 2002 put together accounted for 18160 million whereas they achieved a sales turnover of 16024 million in 2005.

The status of Indian Consumers' Cooperatives During the Last 3 years is described below:

Key variables	*Primary consumer stores*		*Wholesale/ central stores*		*State coop federations*		*Pacs/ lamps*
	2002	2005	2002	2005	2002	2005	2005
Number of stores	26426	24078	712	794	29	30	58000
Branches including departmental stores	10760	7484	5793	5001	731	737	12320
Total sales (Rs. in million)	18160	16024	22007	20656	14822	14371	563828
Membership (000)	9520	10574	2637	2229	18	21	62118

Source: Indian Cooperative Movement–A Profile, 2004: and NCDC Bulletin, August 2006.

Consumer cooperatives are enjoying an enviable position when it comes to the availability of working capital. The working capital available in all consumer cooperatives put together comes to 13057.6 million.

LIBERALIZATION AND CONSUMER COOPERATIVES

At present, consumer cooperatives are passing through a difficult time in their business history because of a wide variety of reasons. Till nineties, consumer cooperatives had to compete with Indian Retail players. Due to the liberalization and its aftermath, consumer cooperatives were put in heavy pressures. Financial assistance and other forms of assistance extended by the state were reconsidered and likely to be rolled back. State itself changed its role from "supplier" to facilitator. Survival of the fittest, self-development, organic collaboration and self-sufficiency are the watch words of business world. At this juncture, the consumer cooperatives which are already showing a passive performance status, by their inherent hurdles, the liberalization process definitely would pose a rough climate. Consumer cooperatives have, of late, been exposed to another major threat unleashed by the globalization and liberalization process called "the emergence of organized retailing by major players like Kishore Biyanis Pantaloon retail, K. Raheja group's Shoppers Stop, Tata group's Trent, RPG's Spencers, Landmark Group's Lifestyle Stores and the likely entrants Reliance group and Bharti, Subhikshas, Big Bazaars, Value Cities. All these groups are gearing themselves up, in order to make a dent when it comes to organized retailing. Their eyes are set on Metropolitan cities in India, and other Tier I, Tier II, and Tier III cities. They are drawing up grand plans to establish their own outlets in all the cities and capture a sizeable per centage of the retail market. When they actually set their foot on organized retailing, the condition of the existing players like Indian consumer cooperatives would become more difficult with reduction in sales turnover and profits.

However, with its large institutional network, with more than 10 millions of membership they had done a lot and capable of doing a lot in the future. It depends on the style, approaches, preferences, and behaviour of the leaders, officials, members, and consumers. How the consumer cooperatives view the liberalization process-will it be a threat to consumer cooperatives or will they reap the benefits of liberalization–is the theme of the article. It attempts to explore and analyze the challenging factors that stand in the way of cooperatives attaining their noble objectives. Besides this, an attempt has also been made to visualize the emergence of organized retailing fuelled by the Globalization and Liberalization and their impact on consumer cooperatives. This paper also looks at the opportunities that were thrown open to the consumer cooperatives also.

INHERENT WEAKNESSES OF CONSUMER COOPERATIVES

1. **Inactive Membership**: Members are the owners and users of consumer cooperatives. However members' participation in business operations was found unencouraging. Only a few members make purchase in the stores contributing to the poor performance of the stores.
2. **Absence of Democratic Management**: As the involvement of the government in the affairs of the consumer cooperatives is high, cooperatives are losing their democratic character. In most cases, state dictates things, determines the targets to be achieved by the cooperatives. Cooperatives are put in the hands of non-serious players.
3. **Unplanned Business Operations:** Cooperative wholesale stores are burdened with public distribution system which account for more than 50 percent of their sales. The business operations must be planned well in advance by considering their past performance and future visions. If at all plans are made, it would be ritualistic one.
4. **Poor Ambience and lack of Modern Technology**: Even though consumer cooperatives have been the pioneers on supermarkets, and self service stores, they lagged behind theme malls and in computerization of accounts. Attractive business centers are much sought after by the consumers. Poor ambience will not attract the consumers.

5. **Inadequacy of Funds**: Retailing requires huge funds Non-availability of funds from banks and financial Institutions is a great hurdle. Dependence on funds from government has developed only spoon-fed tendancy which restricts the business operations.
6. **Lack of Professional Management**: Shortage of professional managerial staff due to poor resources affects their functioning. Consumer cooperatives are neither affordable to meet the cost of professional management nor should be able to mobilize funds.
7. **High Establishment Cost:** Low margin has been the social objective of consumer cooperatives which can not be given up for profitability. It does not cover up the establishment cost. Increased establishment cost is one of the impediments for the growth of cooperatives.

CHALLENGES OF CONSUMER COOPERATIVES

Liberalization has opened up the gates of retailing sector to private and foreign players. As of now foreign players could invest 51 per cent of the capital in retailing when it comes to dealing with single brand. Days are not far off, when retailing sector would be opened up fully.

- According to various estimates the overall retail industry in India is worth between Rs. 9,30,000 crore to 15,75,000 crore. In dollar terms, it ranges between $206 to 350 billion.
- According to Technopak, a Delhi based Consulting Firm, $12 billion (Rs. 54,000 crore) will get invested in retail over the next five years.
- Out of Rs. 54,000 crore, half that is Rs. 27,000 crore, will get invested in food related retail and another Rs. 27,000 crore will get invested in non-food related retail.
- The spread of the retail pie is tabled below:

Item	*% of pie*	*Item*	*% of pie*
Clothing	39	Watches	4
Food and Groceries	11	Books and music	3
Consumer durables	9	Health and beauty	3
Footwears	8	Jewellery	3
Entertainment	2	Mobile accessories	3
Catering services	7	Furniture and furnishings	8

Note: Clothing and food and groceries account for half of the retail pie.

- India is at the peak of attractiveness for retailers right now. Burgeoning middle class and upper middle classes with growing spending powers, coupled with proliferation of domestic and international brands have propelled the retail growth. The spectacular growth in top cities has infused confidence in local and international players to expand into newer markets. The continued stellar performance of the economy with increasing urbanization is pushing organized retailing deeper into the country.
- As growth slows down in their home markets, more and more foreign retailers will want to tap the Indian market.
- It is propelled by a 300 million strong consumer class spread across more than 35 state capitals, economic centers and educational hubs, from Cochin to Chandigarh to Lucknow and Surat.
- Of the 700 upcoming malls in India almost 40 per cent will come up in tier II and tierIII cities. The strong demand for retail space has in fact pushed up rental values by more than 100 per cent in cities like Jaipur, Chandigarh, Surat and Lucknow.

OPPORTUNITIES FOR CONSUMER COOPERATIVES

1. **Expanding Retail Market**: Expanding retail market and consumer awareness, is an opportunity for cooperative wholesale stores. If cooperative wholesale stores go for

modernization and technology upgradation they can make a real impact.

2. **Strong Working base and Membership Base**: The working capital base of all types of consumer cooperatives put together works out to Rs. 13,057.6 millions. Apart from this cooperative membership runs into 95921 thousands.
3. **Planning for Joint Ventures between Leading Cooperative Stores:** Cooperatives can think in terms of joint ventures between leading consumer cooperative stores and foreign consumer cooperative movement for strengthening the cooperative structure in India. The amendments made in the Multi State Cooperative Societies Act, 2002 provide for setting up of subsidiary institutions under other acts prevailing in the country so that growth of business is not held up as in the past.
4. **Change in Taxation Policy and Interest Rates:** The taxation policy as well as the tax structure is undergoing a lot of changes in our country. The domestic rate of interest on bank borrowing has also shown a downward trend signifying the availability of bank finances for the setting up of viable projects in the country. This will encourage the setting up of joint ventures in this country and abroad.
5. **Consultancy Services of NCCF**: The Consultancy & Promotional Cell (CPC) provides technical guidance and promotional assistance to the consumer cooperatives in India for improving their managerial & operational efficiency. It also helps in setting up of Self service department stores. Consumer cooperatives can make use of their services.
6. **Direct Financial Assistance from NCDC**: The National Cooperative Development Corporation provides financial assistance to consumer cooperatives for (i) expansion/ renovation of existing infrastructure or construction of new shopping centres/godown; (ii) margin money for raising working capital (iii) rehabilitation of weak societies.

CONCLUSION

Even though there are formidable threats for the consumers cooperatives, it has so many opportunities also. Using its rich experience in the field of Departmental stores, and Self service store, it can revive its activities. In order to achieve its past glory, the consumer cooperatives have to introspect its past path, and get rid of the shortcomings, and move ahead towards their goals and objectives. Consumer cooperatives need to take decisive managerial strategies, redefine their policies and concepts for the survival and sustenance of the movement.

6

Business Parameters for District Consumer Cooperative Wholesale Stores

R. Jayachandramani

BUSINESS ANALYSIS

It is estimated that 50 per cent of our population is youth and further it is expected that in the year 2010 three out of four would be youth in our population. Hence the present retail business of around Rs. 3 Lakh crores estimated will further increase with the support of real estate boom making available another 25 million sq.ft. for retail in the new malls to come up in the Metros with employment opportunities to 1.25 Lakh persons @ 200 sq.ft./one person.

We live in the globalised world where the winds of free trade blow stronger than ever before. Hence the cooperatives cannot be isolated or insulated from these changes to face tough competition to stay ahead in the competition. In this transition period with bright opportunities for FDI (Foreign Direct Investment) to create level playing field the CWS must analyse their business to improve their efficiency.

BUDGET

As the saying goes if you wish to be happy set goals in your life. People who set goals will enjoy life as they know where they are going. But once you set the goals you should have the will to achieve the goals. Accordingly, CWS should prepare every year "Sales budget" to achieve its goals. So all CWS before the end of the current financial year, must prepare the budget for the next year. The budget that is prepared is to be realistic based on the past. Further, the budget should meet the ends and leave reasonable surplus. Normally the budget period starts from 1st April, however in the first 3 months one cannot anticipate maximum increase from the 1st April as we pull down the shutters at the end of the working hours on 31st March, again the shutters will be opened the next day (April) at office hours. In the gap of available several hours one cannot anticipate a sizable increase in the sales. Hence target should be fixed in such a manner taking other relevant factors into account with reasonable increase month after month for the year.

DIVERSIFICATION OF BUSINESS

Traditionally, the CWS is concentrating only on essential commodities where the percentage of margin in the business is very thin. Of-late the life-style of the people has changed drastically and people are spending sizable part of their income on industrial and service sector goods.

Hence, the CWS should diversify the business. There are around 20-30 thousand advertised brand commodities in the business. The Supply of should think of diversifying the business like building materials, hardware, paint, electrical, electronics, fast food, I.T. peripherals etc. But before they go for diversifying their business activities, they should ensure that adequate technical/professional persons are available in the stores, for running the show successfully.

PERCENTAGE OF MARGIN

While fixing retail price, the scientific method of price fixation is to be adopted in the CWS. It should consider the following factors: Nature Commodities, Movement of goods (Fast moving, slow moving), Size, Taxes, Incidentals, Packing, and Percentage of net margin for wholesale business and retail business.

STANDARDIZATION OF ASSORTMENTS

Normally most of the CWS do not adopt standardization in assortments. Purchase orders are to be placed for only select fast moving brands which are contributing sizable percentage in the sales. Effective standardization will lead to additional margin from the companies, besides accumulation of non-saleable goods.

PURCHASE POLICY

Every CWS should have rigid purchase policy. The CWS should purchase their requirements preferably on credit terms. While placing orders with FMCG (Fast Moving Consumers Goods) company, the orders should be placed only after negotiation with the concerned representative for rates, dealer offer, consumer offer etc., to derive more profit to the institution.

While placing orders the closing stocks, schemes, damages, season, exact requirements etc., are to be taken into account. If any CWS is financially sound such CWS may embark on cash purchase to avail cash discount if any.

AMBIENCE

Most of the supermarkets are situated in private buildings. Hence adequate ambience is not provided in the building, which resulted in less customer traffic in the coop. super markets. Whether the supermarket is located in the rented building or in the own building. required minimum ambience should be provided to attract the customers, thereby sales can be increased. Further, to increase the foot falls, frequently, the Customer Relationship Management (C.R.M) should be developed by regular meetings, home delivery, maintaining individual customer's particulars, festivals, discount sales etc.,

TECHNOLOGY

It is an era of I.T(Information Technology). Hence all CWS should introduce computers in the day to day administration. Introduction of computers will definitely improve the business in addition to providing various particulars for improvement of business. Further 'e' business 'e' commerce can also be introduced through computers.

LIABILITY SYSTEM

By using computers in the retail counters, Unit Control Liability system can be maintained against the present obsolete value control system. Unit control system is more vibrant system in the retail counters for sales analysis.

Unit control system is fool proof system to ensure that the sales are affected at the rates fixed by the CWS and to prevent the escalation of selling price for personal gains under value control system.

RECRUITMENT POLICY

The present recruitment policy is to be re-visited. The retail industry badly needs professionals. The educational qualifications are to be prescribed accordingly with reasonable emoluments. Further in the selected area the B.P.O(Business Process Outsourcing) and system should be practiced especially in case of Sales personnel (Contract basis), Pre packing, Load men, Security and Petrol Pump Boys etc.

TRANSFERS

The existing transfer policy which is adopted in the CWS requires a paradigm shift. It is an era of specialization.

Frequent transfers will certainly stall the specialization. Therefore, a new transfer policy is to be framed in consultation with employees.

REALISTIC SYSTEM

Periodical reviews and feed back on the following will certainly improve the business efficiency: Hence critical review should be conducted periodically and follow up action is to be taken. Budget, Financial statements, Funds management, Sales, Credit policy, Stock out, Stock turn, Sale of unsold stocks, Disposal of damaged goods, Stock deficit, Debtors Balance, Gross profit, Net profit, Productivity and Ratio analysis.

7

Business Analysis in Consumer Cooperative Wholesale Stores

S. Sugumar

INTRODUCTION

Modern marketing revolves round the consumer. A highly integrated cooperative consumer structure can help to develop much consumerism in India. There is need to activate member support that will improve cooperative performance. The consumer cooperatives therefore must strive to meet their expectations. Every sale is an opportunity for growth. The share of consumer cooperatives in the total retail market however is very meager today. The cooperatives have to adopt appropriate strategies to meet the needs of the competitive situations to secure maximum advantages.

PROTECTION AND PROMOTION OF INTEREST OF MEMBER-BUYERS

Price increase is inevitable in the present economy because of increased capital. Holding price line is one of the objectives of consumer cooperatives. Consumer cooperatives have special responsibilities under such conditions. Care should be taken to control prices through efficient productivity. Schemes like public distribution of essential items, help to offer protection to the vulnerable section of the people.

By controlling cost and maintaining the supply line of essentials, consumer cooperatives endeavor to afford protection to their members. 'Active Price Policy" will help the cooperatives to increase and improve member support to their retail business. The cooperatives need not disturb the prevailing market price level but confer benefits on members by giving them bonus on their purchases by the end of the business year.

BUSINESS ANALYSIS: A TOOL TO IMPROVE THE EFFICIENCIES OF CONSUMER COOPERATIVES

Viability

Economic benefits can accrue only if the operation of the cooperative is viable. Sales, margin and cost structure of the consumer cooperatives should be estimated and monitored regularly. The common mistake in this regard relates to over estimating sales and margin and under estimating cost. Unless the stock rotates at least 15 times in a year, a store cannot be viable. A special care should be taken in this regard.

The problems for not achieving viability are often created from the following activities: Bad purchase (Purchase of stocks not required by the members), Over stocking, Excess borrowing, High staffing and Faulty merchandising.

Self-reliance

The cooperative stores should be self-reliant to meet monthly committed expenditures, like salary, rent, telephone, electricity bills etc. Capital requirements can be correctly estimated and raised from the members. One third (1/3) of capital can be borrowed from cooperative banks and if more money is borrowed, cost of interest will go up, which may affect the viability.

There is no harm in getting government assistance in the form of loans, equity or subsidy and it should be however be treated as loans to be paid back. If the store requires to invest on fixed assets it must do after stabilizing the business.

Working capital is important for holding sufficient stocks. To reduce the quantum of working capital requirement, the stores must get 50% of goods by way of credit purchase from suppliers.

Stock Productivity

The entire gross profit earned by the stores is by the gross force of margin and stock turn. If the average margin of the stores is 7% and stock turn is 15 times, the stock productivity is 105% (7 X 15). Successful consumer co-operatives should invariably achieve a stock productivity of 125% and above. The consumer co-operatives should appreciate this concept and plan accordingly. The margin and gross surplus is usually equal to the private retáil shops. However if the co-operative store sells its goods at a cheaper rate, the margin will be slightly less. This can be compensated at a higher rate of stock turn.

Financial Analysis

A financial performance appraisal should be made at the end of every month from the profit and loss account and balance sheet. The appraisal should be on the following lines:

(a) Sale: Monthly sales at the end of every month should be compared with the sales of the corresponding period of the previous year and the inflation rate. Increase in sales should be at least 5% higher than the inflation rate. If not, sales policy has to be checked, analyzed and suitable remedial action, including sales promotion measures should be taken.

The composition of sales for each commodity group can be in the following pattern food and grocery 70%, textiles 10%, general merchandise 10%, cosmetics and drugs 10% and total 100%.

(b) Purchase: Monthly purchase should never be more than the monthly sales for the running business. Reasons for major variations, if any, are to be analyzed and rectified. Seasonal purchases are separate from normal purchases and it should be assessed based on past experiences and future requirements.

(c) Stock Holding: There should be an overall stock holding policy. It is also advisable to formulate the stock days for each commodity group. Reasons for variations in actual performance and norms should be analyzed and necessary remedial action should be taken.

The norms for stock holding days of different commodities are as follows:

(i) food and groceries	12–15 days (25 times stock turn)
(ii) textiles	60–75 days (5 times stock turn)
(iii) general merchandise	35–45 days (8 times stock turn)
(iv) Cosmetics and drugs	25–30 days (12 times stock turn)
(v) Overall stocks	20–25 days (15 times stock turn)

(d) Area (floor space): Sale per square foot in respect of each session/department should be analyzed and compared with norms as well as past performances. Such an analysis may be helpful to increase or decrease the store space of different sections to increase the productivity.

The percentage of floor area or space of a co-operative store can be on the following levels are: (i) Food and grocery 50%, (ii) Textiles 20%, (iii) General merchandise 20%, (iv) Cosmetics and drugs 10% and (v) Total space 100%.

(e) Sale per man day (SPMD): Sale per man day will reveal over staffing and understaffing. Rapid increase in sale in a particular session may require recruitment of a few employees. Conversely, if sale of particular section is poor the staff should be reduced.

(f) Customer: Customer is a big asset of a co-operative store. Any symptom fall in the customer traffic requires detailed analysis and rectification measures. In the sales day book, it is advisable to have an exclusive column to record the daily flow of customers, in order to monitor the trend in the customers flow.

The reasons for fall or decline in customer's flow may be due to the following reasons; missing inventory, stock out, wrong pricing and wrong layout or service.

(g) Trade creditors: With the gradual stability in a retail business, the trade creditors payable should go on increasing each month till it is equal to stock holding and trade debtors (if credit sale is admissible). By increasing trade creditors payable, bank borrowing requirements are reduced and interest cost is saved.

(h) Total expenses: If the expenditures are more then income, there will be a loss. Most of the expenditures are fixed, like salary, rent, interest, electricity, telephone charges etc., So they can be estimated well ahead. Monthly expenditure should be compared with monthly budget and norms. Reasons of variations should be analyzed and necessary steps taken. The following norms can be followed for the expenditures of the stores are staff cost 3.5% to sales, interest, insurance, bank charges 1% to sales, rent and depreciation1.5% to sales, other expenditures 1% to sales and overall expenditure cost 7% to sales.

(i) Gross profit (margin): Every month the gross profit margin should be ascertained and percentage to sales of gross profit should be worked out and compared with the budget, norms and past performances. The suggested norms for gross profit margin can be determined as follows: (a) Food and grocery 6.5% to sales, (b) Textiles 12% to sales, (c) general merchandise 10% to sales (d) Cosmetics and drugs 8% to sales and (e) Average margin 8% to sales.

CONCLUSION

By not following these guidelines a number of consumer co-operatives face serious problems ending up with liquidation. Today Indian consumer co-operatives are passing through a a revolution of rising expectation and therefore they must equip themselves to face the emerging challenges in the competitive consumer markets. Therefore, the management of co-operative consumer stores should analyze the business every month by interpreting the Trading Account, Profit and Loss Account and Balance Sheet, so that performances can be judged and problems can be identified and sorted out immediately.

This business analysis should, therefore, be a standing agenda in the monthly meeting of the Board of Directors, and all the directors may be trained for this purpose to have a detailed knowledge in this record.

8

Business Diversification of the Pondicherry Cooperative Wholesale Store: A Paradigm Shift

R. Velu Raj and Samuel Kakuko Lopoteum

INTRODUCTION

Business diversification in cooperative wholesale store is a sin-qua-non for ensuring reduction of mounting losses, gaining higher profitability and better economic viability in the changed new economic environment. In this paper, it refers to carrying out business operations to meet the demands and wants of customers in a diversified manner and this can be done by adopting concentric diversification and horizontal diversification. The Pondicherry Cooperative Wholesale Store is practicing simplified diversification methods. But it could not earn sufficient profit due to heavy cutthroat competition from private businessmen and traders. Even though, they have adopted cost price shopping services, they have not shown cut-edge competition to face the stiff challenges posed by the changed economic situation which includes liberalization and open market economy.

Diversification strategies adopted by them includes getting license from the government for running one wholesale and eight retail Indian Made Foreign Liquor (IMFL) units, entering into Liquid Petroleum Gas (LPG) business, operating several sections such as self service section, general merchandise, HMT Time Art, Textile and Readymade under one roof situated in the heart of the city, running petrol bunk, dealing with cosmetics and beauty parlor goods. In business diversification growth strategies, it makes sense to adopt the best strategies and methods if the core marketing system does not yield additional opportunities for growth, financial stability, and profitability. Also, the opportunity outside the present core marketing system is superior and competitive, therefore the researchers are advocating for the adoption of concentric and horizontal diversification techniques and methods by the stores. They can engage themselves in profitable investments and dealership of products existing in the open market. However, it is earnestly hoped that business diversification will enable the store to recoup the net loss within shortest period.

ORIGIN AND GROWTH OF THE COOPERATIVE WHOLESALE STORES IN INDIA AND IN PONDICHERRY

The then Madras province was birth place to the consumer cooperation leading to the famous Triplicane Urban Cooperative Stores being started. Infact, this happened prior to the passing of the first cooperative societies Act of 1904. In the advent of the world war situation, people were mainly confronted with innumerable problems which necessitated starting of consumers' cooperative stores movement in India. At the end of 1950-51, the number of stores was 9751 which consisted of 18450 members. After Independence, cooperation was chosen as an important socio-economic agency and the building up of the cooperative stores sector became one of the central aims of the National Policy. At this stage, Dr. P. Natesan Committee on consumer cooperatives made far-reaching recommendation on the organization of strong wholesale stores.

The devaluation of the Indian Rupee by 36.5 per cent in June 1966 resulted in and has necessitated the introduction of an accelerated programme for strengthening consumers' cooperative movement in the country by organizing central stores in all the districts. Moreover, at the end of 1999, there were 647 wholesale stores in the country and presently the number has enlarged.

In the case of Union Territory of Pondicherry, separate consumer cooperatives stores were organized for sale of consumer goods in urban and rural areas only after the enactment of the Pondicherry Cooperative Societies Act 1965 (Act No. 11 of 1965). At present, there are 17 consumer cooperative stores in Pondicherry (includes one state level Federation and one wholesale store), 2 at Karaikal (includes one wholesale store) and 3 at Mahe are functioning to cater to the needs of members and public at competitive rates. Besides, the consumer stores, there are 417 fair price shops which have evolved under the Public Distribution System (PDS). However, the PDS are now-a-days separated from the stores and controlled by separate (isolated) cooperatives society.

CURRENT TREND OF COOPERATIVE WHOLESALE STORES IN THE UNION TERRITORY OF PONDICHERRY

The cooperative wholesale stores in the Union Territory of Pondicherry namely the Pondicherry Cooperative Wholesale Stores in Pondicherry popularly named as *'Amudhasurabhi'* and the Karaikal Cooperative Wholesale Stores in Karaikal popularly named as *'Mangani'* supply essential commodities to its member cooperatives at wholesale prices. These two stores control the prices of products whenever there is a hike of prices in the open market. It is interesting to note that the prices of the products of the private stores in both the regions are fixed only after the prices are fixed by these stores. The *'Price Control Mechanism'* is operating through the stores in the

Union Territory as well. The Concept of Cost Price Shop is the key aspect of price control mechanism adopted by the consumer wholesale stores which refers that, the fixation of the margin price of the products is slightly higher than the actual price and not up to the maximum retail prices. This can give advantages and benefits to the consumers and stabilize the open market environment.

The competition posed from the private stores is controlled through the cost control mechanism adopted by these stores. Strictly speaking, though, the stores are controlling the prices of the products, it could not compete with the sales turnover of other private stores prevailing in the market. The main reasons behind this are; (i) the approach of sales personnel are not admirable or unsuitable, (ii) the system of service delivery is not effective and mostly inefficient, (iii) time taken for delivery of service and goods are extremely lengthy, (iv) the unavailability of products at all times, and (v) availability of different brands and varieties of products which may not be required and demanded by the customers. However, those stores and many other primary stores have carved an important place and gained momentum in extending services to the middle income group. They have also played a significant role in meeting the consumers' need of the lower income group people living in the region.

CRITICAL ANALYSIS OF THE PONDICHERRY COOPERATIVE WHOLESALE STORES

The Pondicherry Cooperative Wholesale Stores was started as a primary cooperative store in April 1956 with 56 members. Later, it was converted into a wholesale store in the year 1966 and the super market popularly known as 'Amudhasurabhi' was started during September 1969, with 9 sales sections including groceries, cosmetic, household, electrical, textiles, readymade garments, utensils, medicine, etc. It was the first time that Amudhasurabhi started the selling of grocery items in pre-packed form with correct weight.

Considering the rapid growth and development in the consumer sector, the stores constructed a multistoried shopping complex to run its super market in the heart of the Pondicherry city, with the government loan assistance of Rs. 60.00 lakhs. The following sections are functioning in the shopping complex at present: 1. Self Service Section, 2. General Merchandise, 3. HMT Time Art, and 4. Textile and Readymade.

Even though, the stores took much pain and strain, it could not run on profit lines due to heavy competition from the private traders. Besides, the stores faced much hardship to run 46 fair price shops functioning under its control up to September 2001. Infact, fair price shops played a vital role in making the consumer wholesale stores incurring heavy losses.

At one point of time, the functioning of the stores was at stake and its survival was not even assured. As a result, various remedial measures were taken-up by the management of the stores leading to the mounting of net loss starting to decline. Subsequently, the stores was able to save a sum of Rs. 2 lakhs per month being which was incurred for running fair price shops as from October 2001 onwards. When we looked into the percentage of gross profit to sales, it is surprising that the stores have earned a substantial portion of profit from the sales to an extent of Rs. 6.00 lakhs to Rs. 15.00 lakhs per month.

The Stores have started the conversion of self service sections into cost price shops (the nomenclature of the stores and the price fixation of the products were changed), since it has made remarkable impact on the minds of the consumers in recent times. This has resulted in a very good response among the public at large. In that way, the stores began to increase its sales turnover considerably. On the basis of this success, all the branches of the stores have been converted into cost price shops to improve services to the public in and around Pondicherry region.

Table 1
Details of Trading Operations (Rs. in lakhs)

Year/ Particulars	*Purchase*	*Salas*	*Gross Profit*	*% of GP to Sales*
2000-01	758.74	828.19	76.23	9.20
2001-02	705.72	761.10	68.72	9.03
2002-03	940.21	990.57	93.45	9.43
2003-04	1503.26	1619.34	138.40	8.55
2004-05 (Tentative)	1753.02	1942.97	188.18	9.69

Source: Data Collected from the Audited Reports of the Pondicherry Cooperative Whzolesale Stores.

Besides, the management of the stores has strongly felt that by merely running of the cost price shops, will not fetch much profit and, as such, the situation warrants diversification of business. After making exhorting steps, the stores is successful by getting licence from the Government for running one wholesale and eight retail Indian Made Foreign Liquors (IMFL) units, of running petrol and diesel bunk, of dealing with cosmetics and beauty parlor goods, of running medical shop at the JIPMER complex which is one of the major hospitals run by the central government in Pondicherry, etc. The stores had an idea of opening Jewellery Park in Pondicherry city and of entering into Liquid Petroleum Gas (LPG) business.

FACTORS CONTRIBUTING TO THE SUCCESS AND/OR FAILURE

Every business organization aims at maximizing the profit with efficient and effective utilization of available scarce resources. By undertaking utilization of such resources, it may sometimes bring profit or loss. The business community must keep this in mind. There are so many factors determining the success/ profit and/or failure/loss of the business. The study reveals that the Stores have both the success and failure stories in respect of utilization of its efforts on normal business operations.

The factors responsible for the success are:

- It has managed to create good image among the consumers, customers and public at large.
- The changeover process from self service sections into cost price shops.
- Separation and conversion of fair price shops into a cooperative society.
- Support and assistance are obtained from the government from time to time.
- Promotion of business diversification measures and strategies.
- Adoption of suitable price control mechanism.
- Adoption of prudent purchase policy practices and procedures.
- Taking advantage of seasonal operations such as selling crackers, silk saris, text books, etc.
- Direct purchase from the manufacturers and wholesalers,
- Involvement of repacking processing activities.
- Cash sales and computerized system of billing.
- Efficient supply management especially from the suppliers and often being specifically requested to reduce the prices, to offer schemes, to allow discount, etc.

The factors responsible for the losses are:

- Proclivity towards payment of higher salary to the staffs
- Retail agent of the CONFED
- Payment of interest cost on borrowings
- Payment of turnover tax at the rate of 0.5 %, if exceeding the sales of Rs. 5 crores

- Absence of democratic board of management.
- Frequent change of administrators.
- Reluctance of sales personnel to involve themselves fully in the affairs of the stores.

BUSINESS DIVERSIFICATION

The Stores is keen to call for sustained efforts to improve the working of the stores which includes raising the level of sales improvement, ensuring that the expenditure comes down and the stores are brought out of the *"Red Environment"*. These efforts shall bear fruit under the banner of *"Better Diversification Measures"* which shall be based on the selection of the right business options/alternatives. Infact, it is imperative for the stores to adopt the concept of Strategic Business Units (SBU) to evolve themselves and to compete effectively in the open market. Concentric diversification and horizontal diversification are highly essential methods to be adopted by stores in the new economic environment. Concentric diversification refers to adding new products that posses technological and marketing synergies with the existing product line namely it would appeal to new classes of customers. Horizontal diversification refers to adding new products that appeal to present customers even then not technologically related to the present product line. Therefore, the stores has adopted a few concentric and horizontal diversification measures. Some of the business diversification methods advocated by the stores are:

- Conversion of self service sections into cost price shops which has widely promoted customer attraction.
- Conversion and separation of fair price shops into a cooperative society which is fully assisted by the government.
- Running of diesel and petrol bunk.
- Opening of retail outlets as viable branches located in important places in the city.

- Sales outlet for beauty parlor goods.
- Running medical shop at JIPMER complex.
- Maintaining of wholesale and retail Indian Made Foreign Liquors (IMFL) units.
- Opening of repacking godown infrastructure.
- Maintaining of sales outlet for household vessels.
- Running business unit for stationery and note books.
- Maintaining show room for HMT watches.
- Maintaining sales outlet for textiles and readymade garments.
- Running STD booth and Xerox services centre.
- Doing seasonal business operations.
- Entering into "Jewellery Park" business as well as Liquid Petroleum Gas (LPG) business (These diversification strategies are under consideration).

Table 2
Details of Payment of Salaries to Sales

(Rs. in Lakhs)

Year/Particulars	*Salary Cost*	*Salas*	*% of Salary Cost to Sales*
2000-01	70.27	828.19	8.48
2001-02	87.55	761.10	11.50
2002-03	90.76	990.57	9.16
2003-04	109.88	1619.34	6.79
2004-05 (Tentative)	125.61	1942.97	6.46

Source: Data collected from the Audited Reports of the Pondicherry Cooperative Wholesale Stores.

Some of the strenuous efforts, which had been taken by the stores, have yielded a very good profit within a short span of time. However, it is suggested that the stores should keep on watching over the establishment and management expenses, which should not escape from the desired level of cost. [As per the norm of the National Cooperative Consumers Federation, the desired level of salary cost of sales should not exceed 3.00% to 4.5% at the places like Pondicherry].

THE IMPACT AND EFFECT OF BUSINESS DIVERSIFICATION

The diversification of business brings forth the impact and effect to the stores on the followings dimensions:

- It creates good image among the public at large.
- It creates employment opportunities to the youth and the community at large.
- It helps to improve productivity and profitability in the new economic environment in the long-run.
- It helps to recoup the losses as well as to overcome the hurdles arising out of the competition.
- It attracts new customers and initiates new marketing methods of doing business in the new economic environment.
- It fulfils the customers' satisfaction and wants in the long-run.
- It brings quality goods at a reasonable price.
- It controls the price escalation by adopting best methods and strategies of diversification.

LESSONS FOR OTHER COOPERATIVE WHOLESALE STORES

The demonstrations, lessons and experiences from other organizations may count for improving the success of business profile in the long run. The Pondicherry Cooperative Wholesale Stores has come out with certain superior calibers and secrets of professional management skills, methods and techniques which can be borrowed by Tamil Nadu State and other States. The lessons learnt from the stores, may be taken into consideration for the growth and development of wholesale stores in the Tamil Nadu State. Some of the lessons are:

- There is an imperative need for cooperative wholesale stores for undertaking best diversification strategies by adopting the right selection of viable business units.
- There is a need to get required level of financial assistance from the government.
- There is a need to separate Public Distribution System from the stores and convert it into a cooperative society.
- Change of nomenclature of the self service sections of the stores into cost price shops.
- Opening viable branches of the stores in important places of the town and in the district.
- Undertaking seasonal business operations such as sales of crackers, text books, silk saris counter, etc.
- Need to get licence from the government for liquor shop, LPG business, petrol and diesel bunk, etc.

POLICY IMPLICATIONS AND DEVELOPMENT OF CONSUMERS WHOLESALE STORES

- The Department of Cooperation in the State to start one or more cooperative society exclusively for the fair price shops in each district. The society would also get financial assistance fully from the state government.
- All the cooperative wholesale stores in the state should convert its self service sections into cost price shops (the nomenclature is very important) and to install branches in important places.
- There is a constant call for removing the turnover tax from the stores, and to bring the net results on possible way, if applicable.
- Selection of viable business units (like opening of petrol and diesel bunk, maintaining medical shop at leading hospitals, opening of show rooms for selected goods (for example beauty parlor and cosmetics, readymade and textiles, etc), involving themselves in the business like STD

booth, Xerox centre, sale of computer peripherals, etc) which will lead to the success of the stores.

- The stores would need to take steps to get licence from the state government for running liquor shops in the important towns (at least one each at block level) in the district.
- A golden handshake scheme namely voluntary retirement scheme may be introduced to dispense with the surplus staff of the establishment wing of the stores.
- The financial support from the state government may enable the stores to undertake business diversification strategies.

SUGGESTIONS AND CONCLUSIONS

- The need of the hour is to constitute a democratic board of management in the Pondicherry Cooperative Wholesale Stores in particular and even in the entire cooperatives movement in general.
- It is suggested that a the Pondicherry State Consumers Cooperative Federation should not be a wholesaler of the wholesale stores. Rather, it could be a regulatory body/ organization.
- Purchase security scheme may be introduced in the stores so as to enhence the sales turnover.
- There is need for calling for immediate stop/withdrawal of turnover linked taxation of stores system in Pondicherry.

CONCLUSION

Business diversification is the need of hour. The consumer wholesale stores can adopt the best Business Diversification Strategies as stated in this paper. Subsequently, there is an imperative need for adopting the concentric and horizontal diversification strategies in the long run. These two strategies are highly necessary in the New Economic Environment. This may include adding new products that poss technological and marketing synergies in order to attract to the new emerging classes of consumers and customers. Also, the consumer wholesale stores can add products to appeal to the present customers, even though the products are not technologically related to the products handled by the stores in the current scenario. Thus, the Cooperative Wholesale Stores will succeed in competing and coping with the changing environment.

REFERENCES

Lopoyetum, S.K. (2001), "Operational Improvement of Consumer Cooperative Store:Gandhigram Rural Scenario", Tamil Nadu Journal of Cooperation, Vol. 49 (10), July 2001, pp. 54-60.

Lopoyetum, S.K. and Velu Raj R. (2003), "Fundamental Management Dimensions of Cooperative : An Analysis of Major Imperative Issues", Indian Cooperative Review, Vol. 40(4), April 2003, pp. 239-24.

Davidsson R. and Taimni, K.K. (1971), "A Study of Personnel Management in Selected Cooperative Super Markets in India" ICA, New Delhi.

Consumer Cooperative in Asia, Africa and USA (ACOCD): Financing Cooperatives in Developing Countries: Report of a Seminar held on October 24th 1969, Washington: Overseas Cooperative Development, 1969.

Rao, S.B. (1969), "A Study of Finances of some Best Wholesale Central Consumerist Cooperative societies in 1963-64", VAMNICOM, Pune.

Davidson and Shiro Futagami (1970), "Distribution of Consumer Goods through Cooperatives in Japan", ICA, New Delhi.

Kamat G.S. (2001), "New Dimensions of Cooperative Management", Himalaya Publishing House, Mumbai.

9

An Analysis on the Status and Trend of Business Performance of a Consumer Cooperative Wholesale Store in Tamilnadu

B. Tamilmani and P. Jeya Chitra

The Consumer cooperative wholesale stores are in a competitive setting. They are district level organizations catering to the requirements of necessary provisions through wholesaling and retailing. The liberalized economic environment has unleashed a lot of challenges to the cooperative wholesale store rather than opportunities. Competitive trading, reduction in financial assistance by government, introduction of cost cutting measures at various levels, goal oriented performance are some of the serious issues pertaining to the consumer cooperatives. Moreover big industrial concerns and multi national companies are targeting on the retail market. At this juncture, consumer cooperatives should make an introspective analysis over its functioning. They must redefine their policies and methods of functioning. They must be adaptive and effective in their operational means. In the absence of the above, their survival becomes tougher. It is therefore decided to take up a unit and make an analytical study on the status and trend of the business performance of the unit. What is the status of key business areas of cooperative wholesale store? Will they sustain with the present status? What would be the trend projection of the store in future? These are the few issues which need to be addressed. Hence this study.

OBJECTIVES OF THE STUDY

(i) To analyze the present status of business performance of the cooperative wholesale store, with reference to the key areas.

(ii) To project the future trend of the key business areas of the study unit.

METHODOLOGY

The present study is a 'case study'. The Dindigul District Consumer Cooperative Wholesale Store was selected purposively. It aims at analyzing its business performance especially with reference to the present status and the future trend. One of the reasons for selecting the above case is that it has started earning profit for the last three years, after a continuous loss.

SOURCES OF DATA

The study is based on secondary data. The data and information required for the present study have been gathered from the records, annual reports and audit reports of the sample store. The researchers have also held discussions with the personnel of the store to elicit further information and supportive clarification.

TOOLS FOR ANALYSIS OF DATA

The data collected were tabulated and analyzed using simple statistical tools such as average, percentage, compound growth rate and trend chart for a meaningful presentation.

The following formula was used to find out the growth rate of the performance of the store.

$$\text{Growth Rate} = \frac{\text{Current year} - \text{Base year}}{\text{Base year}} \times 100$$

In order to find out the compound growth rate of the performance of the store, the formula mentioned below was used.

$$\text{CGR} = \frac{\text{Log Current year} - \text{Log past year}}{\text{No. of years}} \times 100$$

The formula which described below indicates the trend projections of the business performance of the store for the future.

$$Y_c = a + bx$$

ANALYSIS AND DISCUSSION

For analysis, the key variables considered here are membership, major sources of funds, purchases, sales and profit. Before getting into the analysis of the key variables, a brief note on the constitution of the store is given.The present status of each variable was analysed using simple statistical tools. Based on the analysis, future trend was also projected by using trend line projections.

Constitution of the Store

The Dindigul District Consumer Cooperative Wholesale Stores was registered on 19.03.1964 under the Madras Cooperative Societies Act, 1961 and commenced its functioning on 03.04.1964. The area of operation of the store is confined to the entire district of Dindigul.

The objectives of the store are: (i) to purchase in bulk articles of domestic consumption and sell them wholesale and retail; (ii) to purchase or hire processing plants, transport vehicles, godowns, for processing and manufacturing goods into a state fit for consumption or use; (iii) to act as the agent of the government and cooperative societies to procure, stock and supply food-grains and other commodities; (iv) to sell the goods purchased, processed or manufactured by it to its affiliated primary stores at wholesale rates; (v) to undertake retail distribution of goods purchased, processed or manufactured by it; and (vi) to open retail units or super markets for retail distribution at suitable places within its area of operation.

The store has two self service sections. The wholesale store is running fair price shops through its member organizations within the area of the operation. In total, there are 71 shops run by the wholesale store. A well equipped quality testing laboratory is owned by the store. All commodities including edible oils are put under rigourous quality test before sent to pre-packing section.

Membership

Members are the owners and users of cooperatives. The level of membership is considered essential, as there is greater possibility for the expansion of the business. That too in consumer stores, the frequency of member's participation is more, comparing to other types of cooperatives. Every primary cooperative store, marketing society, employee credit society, multi-purpose credit society, anybody of persons or institutions approved by the government and are working within the jurisdiction of the store are eligible to be admitted as a 'A' class members. Individual persons over 18 years of age competent to contract and residing within the area of operations of the stores are admitted as 'B' class members. The growth of membership is shown in the following table.

Table 1
Membership Position

Year	*Membership*			*Total*	*Growth Rate (%)*
	Govt.	*Individuals*	*Cooperative Institutions*		
1994-95	1	23490	250	23696	-
1995-96	1	23751	250	23957	1.102
1996-97	1	23991	206	24198	1.015
1997-98	1	24094	206	24301	0.425
1998-99	1	24495	206	24702	1.650
1999-2k	1	24495	206	24702	-
2000-01	1	24495	206	24702	-
2001-02	1	24496	206	24703	0.004
2002-03	1	24496	206	24703	-
2003-04	1	24496	206	24703	-
Average	1	24220	205	24437	-
CGR				0.42	

Source: Compiled from Audit Reports.

The above table shows the growth of membership of the selected store for a period of ten years, from 1994-95 to 2003-04. Though there was an increasing trend in the growth of the membership, it was not very significant. The number of members had increased from 23,696 to 24,703, indicating an increase of 1007 members. It could be inferred that on an average the store admitted 100 members in a year. The members were admitted especially during the first half of the study period.

Share Capital

Share capital is one of the sources of funds. As share capital forms part of owned funds, it is associated with the borrowings of the store. An increase in share capital would increase the borrowings of the store, as the level of borrowings depends on the level of owned funds which includes share capital and reserve fund.

The share capital position with the contributions made by different types of members is presented in the table 2.

Table 2
Share Capital

(Rs. in lakhs)

Year	*Share Capital*			*Total*	*Growth rate (%)*
	Govt.	*Individuals*	*Cooperative Institutions*		
1994-95	9.28 (70.0)	3.10 (23.5)	0.79 (6.0)	13.17	-
1995-96	9.28 (70.0)	3.12 (23.0)	0.79 (7.0)	13.19	0.15
1996-97	9.28 (70.0)	3.16 (24.0)	0.79 (6.0)	13.23	0.30
1997-98	9.28 (70.0)	3.26 (24.0)	0.79 (6.0)	13.33	0.75
1998-99	9.28 (67.7)	3.64 (26.5)	0.79 (5.8)	13.71	2.85
1999-2k	9.28 (67.7)	3.64 (26.5)	0.79 (5.8)	13.71	-
2000-01	9.28 (67.7)	3.64 (26.5)	0.79 (5.8)	13.71	-
2001-02	9.28 (67.7)	3.64 (26.5)	0.79 (5.8)	13.71	-
2002-03	9.28 (67.7)	3.64 (26.5)	0.79 (5.8)	13.71	-
2003-04	9.28 (67.7)	3.64 (26.5)	0.79 (5.8)	13.71	-
Average	9.28	3.45	0.79	13.52	
CGR				0.40	

Source: Compiled from Audit Reports.
Note: Figures in parentheses are percentage to total.

The share capital of the stores had slightly increased from Rs. 13.17 lakhs in 1994-95 to Rs.13.71 lakhs in 2000-01. In the second half of the period, the share capital position remained constant as no member was admitted during the study period. However, the overall CGR was 0.40. Government contribution in the share capital position constituted 69 per cent.

Deposits

Deposits are another important source of funds which are mobilized both from the members non-members, and staff of the store. The store also collects staff security deposits from the sales personnel of the store, fixed deposits from public, traders and trade deposits from customers.

Fixed Deposits: It was collected by the store in the earlier years, but not now. The purpose of collecting fixed deposit was to use the same in business and to minimize working capital borrowings from District Central Cooperative Banks.

Trade Deposits: Trade deposit is collected from the members (Customers). It is an advance paid by the members to the store, in order to avoid paying cash every time while buying goods. It is not allowed to be withdrawn in cash unless membership is withdrawn. Every member making a trade deposit is supplied with a pass book and a counterfoil indent book at free of cost. Interest is paid on the trade deposit. At present, the trade deposit is not collected.

Staff Security Deposits: Salesmen working in each section of wholesale store or retailing unit are made liable for the goods under his/her control. In order to have a control over the salesmen, a fixed amount is collected at the time of appointment of salespersons. It is therefore mandatory on the part of the staff to give security to the society to certain amount. The staff security deposit also bears interest, on par with the interest on fixed deposit.

Table 3
Deposits

(Rs. in lakhs)

Year	*Deposits*			*Total*	*Growth rate (%)*
	Fixed Deposits	*Trade Deposits*	*Staff Security Deposits*		
1994-95	0.38	1.42	0.92	2.72	-
1995-96	0.38	1.42	1.80	3.6	32.35
1996-97	0.38	1.42	2.86	4.65	29.17
1997-98	0.38	1.42	2.86	4.66	0.22
1998-99	0.12	1.42	2.86	4.40	-5.58
1999-2k	0.11	1.42	3.65	5.18	17.73
2000-01	0.11	1.42	3.43	4.96	-4.25
2001-02	0.11	1.42	3.43	4.56	-8.06
2002-03	0.03	1.42	5.20	6.65	45.83
2003-04	0.03	1.42	5.30	6.75	1.50
Average	0.20	1.42	3.23	4.85	
CGR				9.51	

Source: Compiled from Audit Reports.

The total deposits position shows a fluctuating trend over the years. Staff security deposit constitutes a major portion in the deposits position because all other deposits are not collected. That is why, fixed deposits and trade deposits constituted a meagre position.

Borrowings

Borrowings constitute the major source of funds, which helps to meet the requirements of working capital of the stores. The total borrowings of the store not allowed to exceed ten times of the paid up share capital plus the reserve fund. The wholesale store borrows working capital from the Central Cooperative Bank of the district concerned in the form of cash credit (CC), over drafts and other means. The amount of loans borrowed by the store is described in the following table.

Table 4
Borrowings

(Rs. in lakhs)

Year	*Govt. loan*	*CC-I*	*CC-II*	*CC-I*	*NAMT*	*Total*	*Growth rate (%)*
1994-95	3.67	74.67	16.04	1.85	2.76	98.99	-
1995-96	3.67	88.72	18.96	1.77	1.31	114.42	15.59
1996-97	5.67	102.94	14.73	2.59	-	125.93	10.06
1997-98	5.67	114.22	17.98	7.26	-	145.13	15.25
1998-99	5.67	114.22	17.98	7.26	-	145.13	-
1999-2k	5.67	133.02	12.50	4.87	6.26	162.32	11.84
2000-01	5.67	123.35	52.58	9.69	9.53	201.01	23.84
2001-02	5.67	123.55	52.58	9.69	9.53	201.01	-
2002-03	5.67	128.57	43.80	9.72	6.50	194.27	-3.35
2003-04	5.82	84.63	34.59	10.78	3.44	128.47	-33.87
Average	5.30	108.81	33.92	6.55	3.93	151.67	
CGR						2.64	

Source: Compiled from Audit Reports.

The loan amount borrowed by the store had increased from Rs. 98.99 lakhs in 1994-95 to 128.46 lakhs in the year 2003-04 with a CGR of 2.64 per cent during the study period. The borrowings stood at high in the years 2000-01 and 2001-02, as there was an increase on CC-II and NAMT (Non-Agricultural Medium Term) loan. The trend projection of the borrowings of the store in 2008–09 would be Rs. 231.66 lakhs.

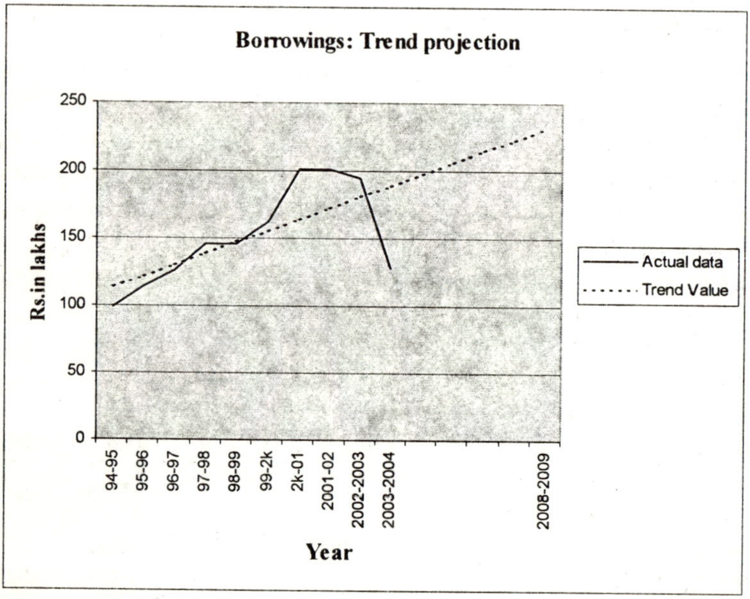

Purchase

Purchases are made to meet the requirements of the member-societies, individual members and the general public. The wholesale store deals with the two kinds of goods viz., controlled (items under public distribution system) and non-controlled (groceries, cosmetics, general merchandise, oil, text book, crackers and so on). In Tamilnadu, the responsibility of running ration stops (Public Distribution System) is with the cooperatives. They distribute the controlled items supplied by civil supplies corporation, to the ration-card holders in the respective regions.

The commodities required by the store are being purchased through a joint purchase committee (JPC), from the approved dealers and the production centers. In Tamil Nadu, the purchase function is executed through the system of a centralized purchasing body called JPC. The 29 wholesale stores operating in TamilNadu are divided into four regions, for each region there was a JPC.

Table 5
Purchase Details

(Rs. in lakhs)

Year	*Controlled*	*Non-controlled*	*Total*	*Growth Rate %)*
1994-95	1522.47 (86.10)	245.78 (13.9)	1768.25 (100)	-
1995-96	1687.35 (89.45)	199.09 (10.55)	1886.44 (100)	6.68
1996-97	2331.84 (92.91)	177.82 (7.09)	2509.66 (100)	33.04
1997-98	2414.75 (93.3)	173.46 (6.7)	2588.21 (100)	1.93
1998-99	2110.67 (92.4)	174.11 (7.6)	2284.78 (100)	-10.68
1999-2k	2465.01 (89.52)	288.69 (10.48)	2753.70 (100)	20.52
2000-01	2351.67 (91.3)	224.81 (8.7)	2576.48 (100)	-6.44
2001-02	2424.63 (87.66)	341.43 (12.34)	2766.06 (100)	7.36
2002-03	2198.92 (84.52)	402.84 (15.48)	2601.76 (100)	-5.94
2003-04	1595.90 (63.73)	908.38 (36.27)	2504.28 (100)	-3.75
Average	2110.32 (87.1)	313.64 (12.9)	2424.06 (100)	
CGR		3.54		

Source: Compiled from Audit Reports.
Note: Figures in parentheses are percentage to total.

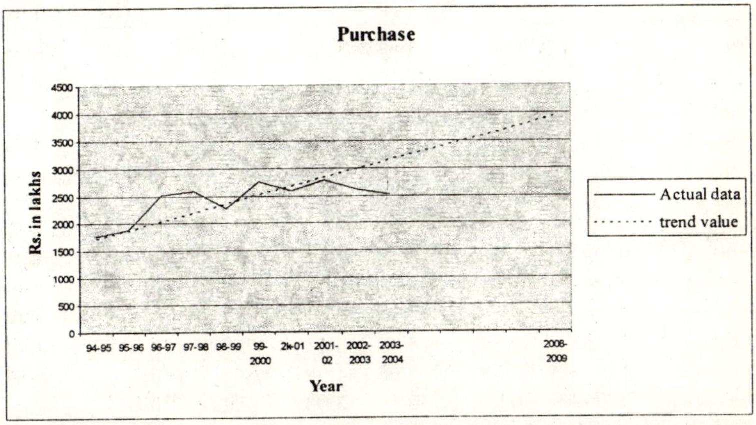

It could be seen from the table the purchase details of controlled and non-controlled items. On an average, the controlled items constituted 87 per cent of the total purchase and the rest was constituted by the non-controlled items. It must be noted that the percentage of non-controlled items must be higher so that it will strengthen the business operations and efficiency by competing with private trading. The percentage of controlled items in the recent three years indicates a down ward trend while at the same time, the percentage of non-controlled items shot up, which is a positive signal. The trend projection of purchase in 2008–09 would be Rs. 3915.03 lakhs.

Sales

The store undertakes the trade activities of both wholesaling and retailing. The wholesale trade is done with affiliated societies and institutions and such trade is done on credit basis. Similarly, credit sales are allowed to the employees who are working in the store. Cash sales are also made simultaneously. The following table shows the sales particulars in respect of controlled and non-controlled goods (table 6).

Table 6
Sales

(Rs. in lakhs)

Year	*Controlled*	*Non-controlled*	*Total*	*Growth Rate %)*
1994-95	1553.15 (86.17)	249.26 (13.83)	1802.41 (100)	-
1995-96	1744.55 (89.57)	203.16 (10.43)	1947.71 (100)	8.06
1996-97	2393.43 (91.99)	208.40 (8.01)	2601.83 (100)	33.58
1997-98	2464.35 (91.89)	217.36 (8.11)	2681.71 (100)	3.07
1998-99	2168.04 (88.78)	208.20 (8.76)	2376.24 (100)	-11.39
1999-2k	2528.97 (88.49)	319.66 (11.22)	2848.63 (100)	19.88
2000-01	2456.95 (91.21)	236.68 (8.79)	2693.63 (100)	5.44
2001-02	2596.92 (88.49)	337.74 (11.51)	2934.66 (100)	8.95
2002-03	2340.92 (84.88)	418.43 (15.11)	2759.35 (100)	-5.97
2003-04	1796.63 (65.08)	902.68 (34.92)	2699.31 (100)	-2.18
Average	2204.39 (56.97)	330.16 (33.03)	2534.55 (100)	
CGR			4.12	

Source: Compiled from Audit Reports.
Note: Figures in parentheses are percentage to total.

Of the total, controlled sales constituted 57 per cent and the rest was the sale of non-controlled items. The sale of controlled items was high in 2001-02 whereas that of non-controlled items was high in 2003-04. But the total sales was high in 2001-02 which was influenced by non-controlled items. The projected sales would be Rs. 3451.49 lakhs in 2008–09.

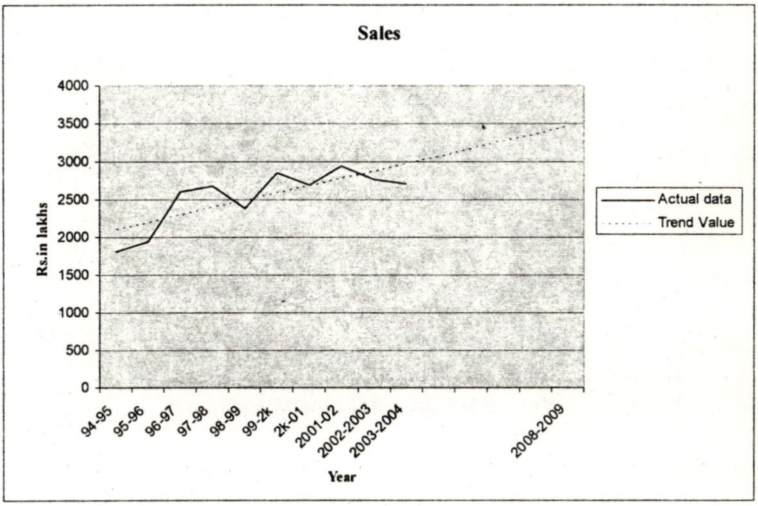

Cash Sales and Credit Sales

In the wholesale store, sales are made both on cash as well as credit basis. Most of the sales are made on credit basis to the member cooperatives. The sales performance in respect of cash and credit is shown in the following table.

The credit sales constituted three-fourth of the total sales. The reason being most of the sales was done to the member-organizations. The duration of credit sales normally runs upto 3 months. The reason for being low cash sales is that the sales are effected for public through retailing. Credit sales have the advantages of increasing the sales volume, while at the same time the risk of realisability is there.

Table 7
Cash and Credit Sales

(Rs. in lakhs)

Year	*Cash sales*	*Credit sales*	*Total*
1994-1995	490.2 (27.20)	1312.21 (72.80)	1802.41 (100)
1995-1996	482.97 (24.80)	1464.74 (72.80)	1947.71 (100)
1996-1997	558.89 (21.08)	2042.94 (78.52)	2601.83 (100)
1997-1998	536.38 (20.00)	2145.32 (80.00)	2681.71 (100)
1998-1999	529.67 (22.29)	1846.67 (77.71)	2376.24 (100)
1999-2000	563.10 (19.77)	2285.53 (80.23)	2848.63 (100)
2000-2001	777.91 (26.88)	1915.72 (71.12)	2693.63 (100)
2001-2002	896.43 (30.55)	2038.23 (69.45)	2934.66 (100)
2002-2003	747.59 (26.10)	1857.53 (68.81)	2759.35 (100)
2003-2004	841.78 (31.19)	1892.06 (74.65)	2699.31 (100)
Average	642.49 (25.35)	1880.10 (74.65)	2534.55 (100)
CGR	5.56	3.54	4.12

Source: Compiled from Audit Reports.
Note: Figures in parentheses are percentage to total.

Profit

Gross profit is the result of the relationship between prices, sales volume and costs. The difference between net sales and cost of goods sold is known as Gross Profit. The earning capacity of the business can be ascertained by taking the margin between cost of goods sold and sales. It is useful as a test of profitability and efficiency of the organisation. It is generally contented that the margin of gross profit should be sufficient to cover all operating expenses and other expenses and also leave adequate amount for net profit. The gross profit indicates a fluctuating trend during the study period. In the years 1996-97 to 1999-2k, there was high gross profit with an amount respectively of Rs. 54.95 lakhs and Rs.64.19 lakhs. The year 2000-01 witnessed a lower gross profit as the sales was lower but cost of goods was higher.

Table 8
Gross Profit

(Rs. in lakhs)

Year	*Gross Profit*	*Growth rate*	*Net Result*
1994-1995	39.1	-	-40.23
1995-1996	50.1	28.13	-59.90
1996-1997	54.95	9.7	-77.36
1997-1998	53.95	-1.82	-124.11
1998-1999	53.30	-1.2	-159.24
1999-2000	64.19	20.43	-193.46
2000-2001	17.77	-72.32	-217.88
2001-2002	22.39	26.0	+2.07
2002-2003	22.44	0.22	+2.16
2003-2004	55.22	146.1	+1.51
Average	43.34		
CGR	3.51		

Source: Complied from Audit Reports.

The surplus (net profit) earned by the cooperatives is one of the yardsticks to measure the efficiency of the organisation. Eventhough cooperatives are not working for profit, practically they need to add margin to cover the expenses and losses. In the modern competitive world, profit earning capacity is considered imperative for withstanding as well as sustaining in the future.

The business results of the store shows a sorrowful state to the stakeholders. The quantum of loss was also high. However, the recent three years of the study period shows profit, but the quantum of profit was very low. It must be appreciated that the store started earning profit continuously for three years. In a way it has started recouping its business status. The trend projection shows that the store would earn net profit of Rs. 336.78 lakhs in 2008–09.

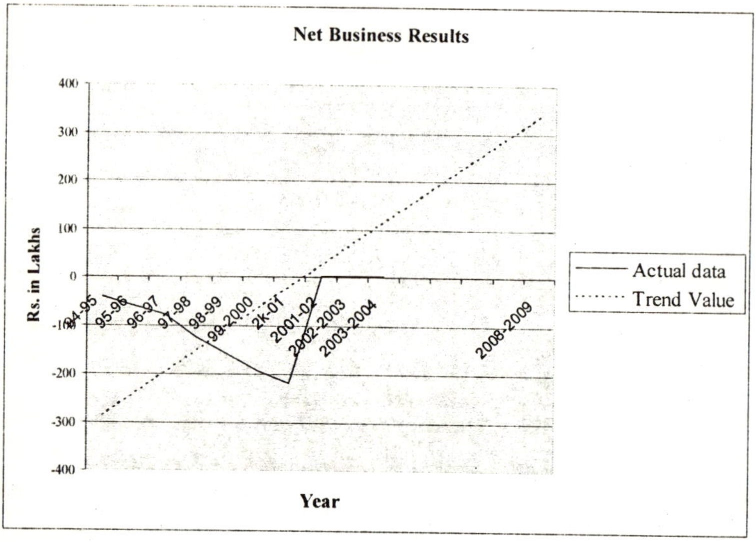

FINDINGS

The important findings of the study are:

(i) The membership position of the store found to be slightly increased that too in the first half of the study period.

(ii) A lower growth rate of the share capital was witnessed.

(iii) 'Borrowings' of the store shown a fluctuating trend throughout the strudy period. The future trend projection will be of Rs. 231.66 lakhs in the year 2008-09.

(iv) The purchase position also indicated a fluctuating trend. The trend projection value will be of Rs. 3915.03 lakhs.

(v) The sales position was found increasing from Rs. 1802.41 lakhs to Rs.2699.31 lakhs in the beginning and end of the study period. The trend value will be Rs. 3451.49 lakhs.

(vi) Credit sales constituted a three-fourth of the total sales.

(vii) The Gross profit shows a fluctuating trend during the study period.

(viii) The store started recovering with profit especially in the recent three years of the study period. However, the quantum of net profit was very low. The trend value will be Rs. 336.78 lakhs.

CONCLUSION

It is concluded that the status on the performance of key areas of the stores namely membership, sharecapital, borrowings was less than 3 per cent of compound growth rate. The compound growth rate of sales was higher than the purchases by 0.58 percent. This has to be increased. The volume of credit sales was three-fourth, when compared to the credit sales. The compound growth of the same found to be 3.54 which was lower by 2.02, the deposits position was found to be increased by 9.51 per cent, this is mainly because of staff security deposit. The trend projections of key variables for 2008–09 will be as follows, on borrowings Rs. 231.66 lakhs; on purchase Rs. 3451.99 lakhs; on profit Rs. 336.78 lakhs. The trend projections on the key variables was done with the assumption that all other things are being equal.

10

Purchase Management of the Consumer Co-operative Wholesale Stores in Tamil Nadu

B. Santhi

INTRODUCTION

In India, Madras was the pioneer province in the field of consumer co-operation, where the first such society formed in Triplicane, in the name of "Triplicane Urban Co-operative Society" in 1905. The Tamil Nadu has the largest number of Consumer stores organised to cater to the needs of the ultimate consumers by purchasing goods in bulk from production centres and supplying them at reasonable price to the members.

PURCHASE MANAGEMENT

The success of the consumer co-operatives depends on the purchase committee constituted in terms of their bye-laws. The purchase committee lays down is the policies which should be followed while purchasing goods. Now-a-days, the de-facto power is exercised by the special officer, chairman/ Secretary/the executive officer in consultation with one another in the committee.

JPC IN TAMIL NADU

In Tamilnadu the Consumer Co-operative Wholesale Stones are located at District level to cater to the needs of the ultimate consumers through its branches and primary stores. There is a JPC (Joint Purchase Committee) consisting of 3 to 5 districts. The special officer of CWSs in the particular district is the convener of the JPC. From the other districts an employee participates in the JPC as a member. In earlier stage, JPC convened once in 15 days, by the convenience of the members. Now, it meets once every month i.e on second Thursday.

MEMBERS

The Co-operative Marketing Societies, the leading merchants of State of Tamil Nadu and other States, local stockist, and rice mill owners are the members of the JPC. To act as a member of the JPC, they should pay a membership fee of Rs. 5000/- This member ship fee is refundable.

PURCHASE MADE BY JPC

The Joint Purchase Committee makes 15 days prior advertisement in leading news papers about the meeting. (It is not necessary because now-a days it meets one particular day i.e., second Thursday of every month). The member societies, merchants submitt samples of rice and groceries, like dhal, cashew nut, pepper, etc., as early as possible before the convening of the meeting. On the basis of quality and price the rice and groceries are purchased by JPC. If the JPC decided to buy the goods, then it gives purchase order to the merchant/marketing society. The requirements of each district are sent directly to the concerned wholesale stores.

The sample is given to all the member wholesale stores for checking the quality. The Co-operative Wholesales Stores make payment within 30 days from the date of purchase of goods.

COSMETICS, OIL AND OTHER ITEMS

The cosmetics are purchased directly from the companies and manufactures by CWS. The Co-operative Wholesale Stores makes advance payments for the purchase of cosmetics.

The stores buys oil and household articles from local merchants through tenders and also from other states. (Eg. Iron buckets from Kolkatta, pepper from Kodaikanal cashew nut from Panrutty).

The life saving medicines are purchased from the distributors of neighboring districts and also from local stockists as per the terms and conditions i.e., one week later payment with 3% discount.

The store purchase spirit from Sugar Mills for the use of Government Doctors in the Hospital and Health Centres.

The CWS supplies goods to Primary Stores/Super Markets/Department Stores, Student Co-operative Stores, Government Institutions on credit. The Co-operative Wholesale Stores makes payment with in 30 days (30 days is the maximum limit) form the date of purchase made by them.

PROBLEMS OF CWS

1. Limited merchant-members participating in JPC.
2. Lack of proper and effective purchase and pricing policy.
3. Some time the rate is higher than the market price.
4. The Govt. compels the stores to run Fair price shops.
5. Brokerage (1.5%) received by TNCC for the sale of crackers.
6. The stores buys adulterated goods from well known merchants. (Lab - cut)
7. The prices of goods increased to some extent by imposing sales tax to consumer stores.

8. Another important problem faced by the Co-operative Wholesale Stores is political interference.
9. Lack of co-operation among the employees.

SUGGESTIONS

1. To induce merchants to be present/participate in JPC.
2. It should have a genuine management.
3. The CWS should be exempted from sales tax to reduce the prices of goods.
4. The stores should emphasis suitable purchase and price policies.
5. It should sell quality goods for retaining the good will of the stores.
6. The staff should be properly trained.
7. There must be co-operation among the employees and the management.
8. The stores should be free from political interference.

CONCLUSION

The Government should take necessary steps to overcome all the problems faced by that consumer wholesale stores. The management must be genuine and employees should co-operate with one another to develop themselves and the public as a whole.

11

Purchase and Inventory Management in Consumer Cooperatives

F. Basker Chandrasekar

Consumer Cooperative Wholesale Store is an association of Primary Consumer Cooperatives aimed at pooling the purchasing power in order to enable the consumers to reap the benefits of collective buying.

Purchasing is the first and foremost function of the business. The efficiency of purchasing is a stepping stone to the successful performance of Consumer Cooperative Wholesale Stores. The efficient conduct of purchasing implies the existence of well defined set of intelligent and scientific purchase principles and policies. The proverb "Well bought goods are half sold" signifies the importance of right purchasing. Wrong purchases lead to overstocks and stockouts which in turn affect the success of Consumer Cooperatives.

The purchasing function in a Consumer Cooperative Store is performed within the limitation of the following considerations:

(a) It should be totally oriented towards the customers in the area of operation of the store.

(b) It should directly contribute to the effectiveness and efficiency of the Consumer Cooperatives.

A check on purchases, investments and sales is exercised by working out certain minimum norms of stock-turnover for a given margin of profit. This stock turnover ratio is worked out to ensure that so long as this is achieved, the profitability of the operations and the ability to survive and grow are not undermined. Thus the question like what to buy, how much to buy, how much to keep in stock and what should be the investment in stock-in-trade are answered in relation to what rate of stock turnover has to be achieved. The objectives of purchasing function in Consumer Cooperatives in the opinion of Taimini are:

(1) to satisfy the demand of the consumer at the least cost;

(2) to maintain the continuity of supply and to avoid stock-outs;

(3) to keep investments in stock-in-trade to minimum and ensure maximum rate of stock turnover;

(4) to maintain minimum standards of quality based on consumer preference; and

(5) to avoid waste and obsolescence of goods.[1]

PURCHASE POLICY

Rules, regulations and clear guidelines are to be framed while formulating purchase policy. Purchase policy is mainly concerned with 'what' and 'who' is to be purchased and who will take the purchasing action[2]. It describes the powers and authorities of purchasing officer and the limitations with regard to the type of the product and quantity of the product to be purchased. It gives a clear picture about the prospective suppliers, their ability to supply the required commodities in required quantity in conformity with the needs of the consumers.

While formulating a purchase policy one should bear in mind two important considerations.

(1) Their policies should be intune with the general objects of the organisation.

(2) To recognise the importance of consumer[3].

In addition, it will be influenced by various factors viz., availability of funds, assortment of stock, extent of competition, general conditions of business such as seasonal and cyclical variations and requirements of consumers as a whole.

In most of the consumer's stores the purchase committee has been constituted. Normally this committee should lay down policies which may be executed by the General Manager. The success of purchase management very much depends upon the efficiency with which the purchase department acts. The timely action of the purchase department not only meets the needs of the consumer's stores but consuming public at large. In Tamil Nadu election is not conduced to constitute a board and Special Officer is vested with the powers of the Board. The Special Officer is not fully aware of the business practices which results in violation of purchase policy and ultimately in the failure of Consumer Wholesale Stores.

ELEMENTS OF PURCHASING

Purchasing is the process of buying. According to George Ajian the basic elements in performing the purchasing function are "obtaining the proper equipment, material, supplies and services in the right quality, in the right quantity, at the right price and from the right source at the right time".

Buying Right Quality

In purchasing, this term refers to "the suitability of a product for its intended use". The Grocery manufactured and General Merchandise are procured from the business organisations or from the reputed production centres in order to maintain the quality. The Textiles are purchased from reputed mills.

Buying the Right Quantity

Determination of right quantity is a difficult task. Right quantity is one which is enough for uninterrupted selling. If too small quantity is purchased the unit cost will be higher; the stockouts will be more, more expediting work is necessary, the relationship between vendor and purchaser may suffer. In case too large quantity is purchased, excess of funds will be locked up, obsolescence will be more, additional storage require additional investment. Right quantity of purchase is judged with the two indicators viz (1) Proportion of annual purchase value to average stock value; and (2) Ratio of non-movable items to total inventory.

Buying from Right Source

While selecting the source of purchase proper consideration must be given with regard to the total (true) cost of commodity i.e., product cost, transportation cost and tax, if any, to be paid and then decision will be arrived at whether to purchase from manufactures/producers or in open market or producers directly.

Buying at Right Time

Right time means making availability of goods for sale at the required time. It also means, purchase of these goods which are in demand and make them available in right quantity so that it ensures continuous supply and not to face stock-outs and avoids over-stocking.

Buying at Right Price

Price is an important factor in purchasing. Reasonable price coupled with quality leads to more volume of sales which in-turn results in more profits. Price includes manufacturing cost plus all other costs incurred in getting the goods (services) namely (a) transportation (b) deterioration in storing (c) handling (d) cost of capital (e) leakages (f) evaporation etc. The price of the unit must accompany the quality, assured delivery and continuous supply of goods.

INVENTORY MANAGEMENT IN CONSUMERS' COOPERATIVES

Consumer business is one of the fields in which there is intense competition from private trade which has several advantages such as small establishment cost, personal care and efficient customer service. If cooperatives are to achieve the twin objectives of profit and better customer service they have to improve their system of inventory control. They should aim at most efficient and optimum use of capital and avoid the capital being locked up unnecessarily in heavy stock of inventories. At the same time they should keep desired level of inventories to offer satisfactory customer service. Therefore, there is a great need to improve the inventory management techniques in Consumer's Cooperatives.

Systematic Purchase

The Consumer's Stores should pursue a judicious and intelligent purchase policy. A list of inventories to be purchased should be prepared well in advance. A purchase budget should also be prepared on the basis of the sales targets and it should be approved by the board. They should plan the purchases in such a way to replenish the inventory before the stock is depleted. The percentage of 'stockouts' should be kept at minimum since frequent 'stockouts' will adversely affect the efficiency of cooperatives in meeting the demands of the customers.

Systematic reordering is necessary to maintain a desired level of inventory. Routine reordering is possible in the case of staple items, for which the demand is constant and continuous. The reordering of non-staple item is a genuine problem faced by the consumer's cooperatives, which can be overcome by proper understanding of demand pattern.

To calculate the 'reorder point', the level of stock that protects the store from 'stockouts' should be decided first.

This level is called 'safety level' or 'buffer stock'. To this 'safety level' the amount of stock that must be held to cover the 'lead time' from the movement an order is placed for a replenishment batch to the time it will probably be received should be added. These two calculations together give the reorder level. The reorder point can also be explained with the help of the following formula.

$P = B + Sd\ L$[4]

P = Reorder Point (in units)

B = Buffer Stock (in units)

Sd = Average Daily Sales (in units)

L = Average Lead time (in days)

Inventory reorder should be made regularly and fresh orders should be placed when an item of inventory falls below the reorder point. In order to maintain satisfactory inventory throughout the year, forecasting of future requirements is essential.

Proper Storage

A clean record of stock movement should be kept upto date. This is possible by the proper maintenance of purchase, issue and stock register. Use of computers has made this task simple. The main stock should be kept in the main godown and the periodic issue may be made to retail outlets. Allowances must be made for spoilage, pilferage, leakage and driage of goods. The unusable and damaged goods should be written off from time to time. Assortment and display of goods should be arranged in such a way that the items which sell rapidly are picked up by customers easily and the fast moving staple goods are used as a magnet to attract the customers to other articles. The display of goods should also ensure the possibility of visual control in order to avoid shop-lifting and pilferage.[5]

Regular Source of Supply

To ensure continuity of supply and quality of goods, the Consumer Cooperative Wholesale Store should select right sources from which they can arrange their supply. The wholesale stores should rely more and more on their federations and arrange the supply channels by integrating the consumer's movement with other cooperatives. Only then they can play a purposeful role in eliminating the middlemen operating in the private trade channel and in reducing the price-spread. It is not safe to depend heavily on private suppliers and such a practice should be discouraged, except in unavoidable circumstances. The Board of Directors should exercise control over the purchase policy and the purchase committee should have a constant watch over the supply sources. Large purchases should be made only with the approval of purchase committee and they should be made on the basis of tenders and quotations.

Periodic Checking of Inventories

A system of constant control over inventory is an essential element in inventory management. In order to locate any shortage and to determine the quickly moving items, atleast once in a month physical verification of stock should be undertaken. Arrangement should be made for the prompt recovery of stock deficits. Periodic stock verification will also help to determine the reorder points for each commodity. For effective inventory control, a separate inventory committee should be constituted which may be held responsible for proper control of inventories.

Rate of Stock-Turn over

Stock turnover is an indicator of the efficiency of the store in optimum utilsation of the capital invested. It is determined by calculating the number of times the stock has rotated itself in a year by way of sales. It is arrived at by the value of average stock $\frac{\text{(Average Stock = Opening Stock + clo sin g stock)}}{2}$ held by the store.

The stock turnover for the fast moving items will be more, whereas for the slow moving items it will be less. On the average for a city store handling groceries and other essential commodities, if the average merchandise inventory corresponds to less than three week's sales (that is the rate of stock-turn is more than 14 times a year) it generally indicates good and efficient management. In rural stores if the average inventory corresponds to less than two months sales (indicating a stock-turn of more than 5 times a year) the management efficiency may be termed as good.[6]

The Santhanam Committee on Cooperation, 1966, has recommended a stock-turn of at least 12 times for super markets. In many consumer stores the rate of stock-turn is far less than the desirable levels. Unless the stock-turn is improved the consumer's cooperatives can not hope to earn a decent profit.

Keep Down the Cost of Holding Inventories

The cost of holding inventories is directly related to the size of inventories and the period for which it is held. Therefore, the size of inventory should not at any time exceed the desirable level and should not be held for an unduly long period. If the cost of holding inventory is more than the expected, profit margin will be automatically reduced and finally the store has to incur loss. In order to keep down the cost of holding, the consumer's stores should periodically arrange for special sales promotion campaigns such as 'clearance sales, reduction sales' etc.

Thus the inventory control is concerned with purchase planning, reorder policy, proper storage, control over stock, regular supply channels, optimum stock turnover and low cost of holding inventories. Cooperative stores can evolve an efficient system of inventory management by adopting the above guidelines.

PROBLEMS

The major problems faced by the consumer cooperative wholesale stores are:

1. No trained sales personnel
2. Lack of scientific management practices
3. Wrong pricing policies
4. Poor display and salesmanship
5. No proper supply of commodities to primaries
6. Lack of publicity and propaganda.

SUGGESTIONS

1. Well trained and experienced staff even at higher cost would lead to better performance of the store. Strategy in this regard is to have less people with better pay than more inefficient people with poor pay, if economic performance of the store is to be improved.
2. Periodic review of purchase policy is necessary. Right source, right price, right quantity and right quality have to be the guidelines for purchasing decisions of Cooperative Wholesale Stores.
3. Stock replenishment must be made from time to time. For this purpose maximum level, minimum level, danger level, reorder level may be fixed for different commodities. The salesman concerned may be instructed to report the position to the management periodically.
4. The Cooperative Wholesale Stores should develop cooperative branded merchandise of selected mass consumption items for which an assured off take of minimum economic scale has already been developed in the cooperative sector.
5. Adopting "Active Price Policy" will help the wholesale stores to increase and improve member support to their retail business. Under this policy, Cooperative Wholesale

Store need not disturb the prevailing market price level but confer benefits on members by giving them bonus at the end of the year.

6. To improve the sales, goods may be displayed properly to catch the eyes of the customers. Importance to publicity and propaganda should be given. Slow moving goods should be sold by clearance sales every year.
7. Markets are in the grip of competition and suppliers are coming to the doors of the consumers through joint efforts of selling organisations. Telemarketing system is catching up fast in cities and other urban areas. Large sized stores are also now accepting credit cards. This may help to increase turnover of wholesale stores.

CONCLUSION

To day Indian Consumers Cooperatives are passing through a revolution of raising expectations. Therefore, their total structure must equip itself well to face the emerging challenges in the globalised competitive consumer markets.

NOTES AND REFERENCES

1. K.K. Taimini, Studies in Retailing Consumers Cooperation and Public Distribution System, Pune: Harshad Prakashan 1975.
2. John Stapleton, Marketing Hand book.
3. Duncan J. Delber & Charles F. Philips, Retailing Principles and methods, (London: Richard Irvin INC, 1976).
4. V. Kulandaisamy, Inventory Management in Consumers' Cooperatives.
5. John Argenti, Management Techniques, London : George Allen and Unwin Ltd, 1969.

12

Inventory Management in Consumer Cooperatives: An Overview

P. Kalaiselvi and J. Gayathri

INTRODUCTION

Consumer cooperatives are the earliest forms of the cooperative enterprises. They are the associations of consumers aimed at pooling the purchasing powers in order to enable the consumers to reap the benefits of collective buying. Besides fulfilling the economic aspirations of the group of consumers, the consumer cooperatives have a national role in the distribution front. Distribution of consumer goods is one of the basic functions of an economic system. In a mixed economy all the three sectors viz., private , public and cooperative sectors are engaged in the task of distribution. The objectives of public distribution is to eliminate profiteering middle-men, to do away with artificial scarcities by balancing the distribution between regions and seasons and to control the price-line. The consumer cooperatives are considered to be eminently suited to achieve the above tasks.

Organizational Structure

NCCF (National Consumer Coop. Federation)

↓

Sate Level Cooperative Consumers Federations

↓

District level Cooperative Wholesale Stores

↓

Branches | Primaries | Super Market

INVENTORY MANAGEMENT

Inventory management is one of the problem areas to the management of consumer cooperatives. It is complicated and cumbersome because even a small store has to handle hundreds of items and in bigger ones the number of items handle may even run to thousands. Inventory is the single largest item in the assets side of the balance sheet of consumers' business. It is one of the fields which needs to be considered. Low establishment cost, personal care and efficient customer service centre round to the effective inventory management. If cooperatives are to achieve the twin objectives of profit and better customer services they have to improve their system of inventory control. They should aim at most efficient and optimum use of capital and stock of inventories, and at the same time keep desired level of inventories to offer satisfactory customer services. In order to achieve the above objectives, a scientific system of inventory management should be adopted at least in large consumer cooperatives and super bazaars. Therefore, there is a great need to improve the inventory management techniques in consumer cooperatives.

CRITERIA FOR AN EFFICIENT SYSTEM OF INVENTORY MANAGEMENT

The important criteria for an efficient system of an inventory management are as follows: Systematic Purchase, Proper

Storage, Regular Supply Arrangement, Periodic Inventory Checking, Rate of Stock–Turn, Cost of Holding Inventories.

Systematic Purchase

The consumer stores should pursue a judicious and intelligent purchase policy. A list of inventories to be purchased should be prepared well in advance. A purchase budget should also be prepared on the basis of the sales target and it should be approved by the Board. They should plan the purchase in such a way to replenish the inventory before the stock is depleted. The percentage of 'Sock–outs' should be kept at minimum since frequent 'Stock–outs' will have adverse affect on the efficiency of cooperatives in meeting the demands of the customers.

Systematic recording is necessary to maintain a desired level of inventory. Routine reordering is possible in the case of stable items, for which the demand is constant and continuous. The reordering of non-staple items is a genuine problem faced by consumer cooperatives which can be overcome by proper understanding of demand pattern. The consumer cooperatives should work out 'reorder points' for each and every commodity, To calculate the reorder point, the level of stock that protects the society from 'stock–outs' should be decided first. This level is called 'safety level' or 'buffer stock'. To this 'safety level', the amount of stock that must be held to cover the 'lead time', from the moment an order is placed for a replenishment batch to the time it will probably be received should be added, These two calculations together give the reorder level. The reorder point can be explained with the help of the following formula:

$$P = B + Sd\ L$$

P = Reorder Point (in units)

B = Buffer Stock (in units)

Sd = average daily sales (in units)

L = average lead time (in days)

Inventory reorders should be made regularly and fresh orders should be placed when an item of inventory fails below the reorder point, in order to maintain satisfactory inventory throughout the year, Forecasting of future requirements is essential. Though it is difficult due to the unpredictability of buying public, forecasting with some degree of accuracy is possible in the case of stable items.

Proper Storage

A consumer stores should exercise strict and continuous control over the stock. A clear record of the movement of stock should be kept up to date. This is possible by the proper maintenance of 'Purchase, Issue and Stock Register'. The main stock should be kept in the main godown and the periodic issue may be made to retail outlets. Allowance must be made for spoilage, pilferage, lekage and driage of goods. The unsaleable and damage goods should be written off from time o time. Modern methods of cleaning and packaging of goods should be adopted. Assortment and display of goods should be arranged in such a way that the items which sell rapidly are picked up by customers easily and the fast moving stable goods are used as a magnat to attract the customers. The display of goods should also ensure the possibility of visual control in order to avoid shop-lifting and pilferage.

Regular Supply Arrangements

To ensure continuity of supply and quality of goods, the consumer cooperatives should select right source of supply. Generally here are three different sources from which the consume cooperatives can arrange their supply viz.;

(a) Producer cooperatives or the federations of producer or consumer cooperatives.

(b) Private manufactures and wholesalers.

(c) Government agencies like Civil Supplies Corporation, State Trading Corporation, Textile Corporation, Food Corporation of India etc.,

The consumer cooperatives should rely more and more on the wholesale consumer sores for arranging the supply of goods. Only then they can play a purposeful role in eliminating the host of middlemen operating in the private trade channel and in reducing the price–spread. It is not safe the consumer stores that depend heavily on private suppliers and normally such a practice should be discouraged, except in unavoidable circumstances. In case supply arrangement is made from private wholesalers, it is not wise to change he suppliers frequently. The Government policy is now favourable for the cooperativization of public distribution system and encouragement of consumers' cooperatives. The commodities like baby food, drugs, safety matches, razer blades, vanaspathi, cycle tyers etc, are being supplied by the consumer cooperatives. These concessions should be availed to the best advantage by the consumers' cooperatives. The purchase committee should have a constant watch over the supply sources, purchase should be made on the basis of tenders and quotations.

Periodic Inventory Checking

A System of constant control over inventory is an essential element in inventory management. In order to locate any shortages and to determine the quickly moving and nonmoving items, at least once in a month physical verification of stock should be undertaken. Cooperatives should also arrange for the prompt recovery of stock deficits. Periodic stock verification will also help to determine the reorder points for each commodity. Inspite of this, a systematic verification of stock is not undertaken in consumer cooperatives. Inventory in many small cooperatives is taken only once in a year, often by members of the committee who have little knowledge and are not good at judging the conditions of stock, and their future saleability. often they rely on the manager or shopman and he may well have made mistakes either in buying or in failing to buy. Therefore, for effective inventory control, a separate inventory committee should be constituted, which may be held responsible for proper control of inventories.

Rate of Stock–Turn

Stock turn is an indication of the efficiency of the consumer stores in optimum utilization of the capital invested in stock. Besides high cash flow, greater volume of business, smaller margin and improvement in the ability of the reailer to meet the current needs of the consumers are the obvious advantage of high stock turn. The stock turn is determined by calculating the number of times the stocks has rotated itself in a year by way of sales. This is arrived at by dividing the total value of sale by the value of average held by the society.

$$\frac{(\text{Average Stock} = \text{Opening Stock} + \text{clo sing stock})}{2}$$

The stock–turn varies from item to item and from locality to locality. The stock–turn for the fast moving items will be more, whereas for the slow moving items it will be less. However, on the average for a city stores handling groceries and other essential commodities, if the average merchandise inventory corresponds to less than three weeks' sales (that is the rate of stock–turn is more than 14 times a year). It generally indicates good and efficient management. In rural stores, 'if the average inventory corresponds to less than two months sales (indicating a stock–turn of more than 5 years) the management efficiency may be termed as good'.

The Santhanan Committee on Cooperation–1996 (Tamilnadu) has recommended a stock–turn of at least 12 times for super–markets. In many consumer sores the rate of stock-turn is far less than the desirable levels. Unless the stock–turn is improved the consumer cooperatives can not hope to earn a decent profit. By proper product mix, sales and price policies, the consumer cooperatives should strive achieve greater stock–turn.

Cost of Holding Inventories

A scientific inventory management should include an accurate judgement of the cost of holding inventories. It is directly related to the size of inventories and the period for which it is held. Therefore, the size of inventory should not at any time exceed the desirable level and should not be held for an unduly long period. If the cost of holding inventory is more than the expected profit margin, the society has to incur loss. In such a situation, it is always profitable to dispose the stock by reducing the cost of holding from the current price, than holding them. In order to keep down the cost of holding, the consumer cooperatives should periodically arrange for special sales promotion campaigns such as 'clearance sales', 'reduction sales' etc.

CONCLUSION

Thus, the inventory control is inextricably linked with purchase planning, reorder policy, proper storage, control over stock, regular supply channels, optimum stock–turn and low cost of holding inventories. Cooperatives can evolve an efficient system of inventory management by pursuing a judicious purchase policy, regularizing the supply arrangements, proper handling and storage of stock, periodic stock verification, achieving an optimum level of stock–turn and by keeping down the cost of holding inventories.

13

Inventory Management in Cooperative Wholesale Stores

S. Jayakumar

Inventory control has assumed a key position in consumer cooperatives. Efficient and effective management of inventories contributes to the profitability of the business by minimizing different types of costs, associated with the holding of inventories. Efficient inventory management reduces investment in current assets.

Inventory control is a planned method of determining what to intend, how to intend and how much to stock so that purchasing and storing costs are maintained at the lowest possible level.

Therefore, the inventory management includes the following aspects: (i) Size of inventory (ii) Lead Time and lot size of purchase orders and Minimum safety level stock (iii) Proper storage facilities (iv) Proper recording of inventory transactions (v) Inventory control functions.

OBJECTIVES OF INVENTORY CONTROL

Proper inventory control is necessary to reduce the cost of material purchased, stored and used. The main objectives of inventory control are: (i) Continuous availability of materials (ii) No excessive investment in the material (iii) Minimum level of wastages (iv) Reasonable price (v) Risk of spoilage and obsolescence.

FACTORS DETERMINING THE OPTIMUM LEVEL OF INVESTMENT IN THE INVENTORY

The decision of investment in the inventories can be classified into two parts.

(a) General Factors for Investment Decision

(i) Type and nature of business (ii) anticipated volume of sales (iii) operational level–price level variations and (iv) availability of funds.

(b) Special Factors for Investment Decisions

(i) Seasonal nature of goods (ii) Terms of purchase (iii) Time factor (purchasing time and selling time) (iv) Price level variations (v) Loan facilities and (vi) Management policies.

Techniques of Inventory Management

For management of inventory the following techniques are adopted: Stock level settings, Economic order quantity, Proper storage, Inventory system, Budgetary control system, ABC Analysis technique and Usage of control ratios.

Stock level settings

The purchase department should decide well in advance as to what quantity of materials should be maintained, when re-order should be placed and what should be purchased. The following points are to be considered with regard to the quantity of materials to be stocked: (i) Lead time (ii) Consumption rate (iii) investment in inventories (iv) store capacity (v) nature of materials (vi) cost of storage (vii) market conditions (viii) change in prices (ix) economic order quantity (x) loss due to deterioration, obsolescence, theft etc.

It is necessary to fix optimum limits of inventory so that there should not be any over stocking nor shortage of goods. The different stock levels are: (i) minimum level (ii) maximum level (iii) reorder level (iv) danger level.

The Formula for Determining Different Stock Levels are as follows

(i) minimum level = reorder level–(normal consumption X normal reorder period)

(ii) maximum level = (reorder level + reorder quantity) – (minimum consumption X minimum consumption period)

(iii) Reorder level = Maximum consumption X maximum reorder period

(iv) Danger level = Average consumption X lead time for emergency purchase

Calculations of Various Stock levels

Data for calculation:

Normal consumption	= 3600 units p.m
Maximum consumption	= 5400 units p.m
Minimum consumption	= 1800 units p.m
Re-order quantity	= 7200 units p.m
Re-order period (lead time)	= 1 to 3 months (Emergency purchase ½ months)

Calculation

Re-order level	= 5400 x 3 = 16,200
Minimum stock level	= 16,200–(3600 × 2)
	= 16,200–7200
	= 9000
Maximum stock level	= (16,200 + 7200)–(1800 × 1)
	= 21,600

Average stock level	= 21,600 + 9000/2
	= 15,300
Danger level	= 3600 × 0.5
	= 1800

Points to Ponder

- For the average or normal consumption of 3600 units, the average stock level is 15,300 units.
- For the average stock level of 15,300 units, the minimum stock level is 9000 units and maximum stock level is 21,600 units.
- At the time when reorder stock level of 16,200 units is reached, order should be made based on re-order quantity i.e. 7200 units.
- At any point of time, the stock level should not be allowed to go below the danger level of 1800 units.
- These levels are applicable only to the condition that the lead time is at the minimum of 1 month and the maximum of 3 months.

Economic Order Quantity (EOQ)

It is the quantity to be ordered when the stock reaches the re-ordering level.

For determining this level, ordering cost and carrying cost are taken into account. The formula used for determining EOQ is:

$$EOQ = \sqrt{\frac{2AB}{CS}}$$

Where,

A = Annual consumptions (in units)

B = Buying cost per order (fixed cost)

C = Cost per unit

S = Storage and carrying cost

Calculations for Economic Order Quantity (EOQ)

Data for calculation:

Annual consumption	= 10,000 units
Buying (Ordering) cost per order	= Rs. 50
Cost per unit	= Rs. 2
Storage cost	= 8% on inventory cost

$$EOQ = \sqrt{\frac{2AB}{CS}}$$

$$= \sqrt{\frac{2 \times 10,000 \times 50}{2 \times 8/100}}$$

$$= 2500 \text{ units}$$

Proper Storage

There should be an effective storage control to avoid losses from misappropriation, damage deterioration, evaporation and carelessness. The stores are of three types : (i) Centralised stores (ii) Decentralised stores (iii) Central stores with sub stores

Inventory System

There are two types of inventory system:

(a) **Permanent Inventory System:** Under this system, stock taking is undertaken at the end of accounting year and on the day of stock-taking, the business is suspended.

(b) **Perpetual Inventory System**: Under this method, stores balance is recorded after each transaction i.e., for each receipt and for each issue. This system involves maintenance of bin card and stores ledger simultaneously. Continuous stock taking is possible to compare the actual stock shown in the bin card and the stores ledger.

Discrepancies in Physical Stocks

There should not be any difference between book balances and physical balances. However discrepancies appear owing to many reasons and they must be rectified. The reasons of discrepancies may be classified into two categories:

1. **Avoidable causes are:** (i) clerical error in making records (ii) pilferage, theft etc (iii) placing stocks in wrong bins (iv) careless material handling (v) short or excess issue (vi) mistake in identifying items.
2. **Unavoidable causes include:** (i) evaporation, shrinkage etc. (ii) loss due to breaking in bulk or cutting to sizes (iii) loss on account of fire, riot etc. (iv) loss due to approximation (without count)

Budgetary Control System

The inventory budget is a plan for investing funds in stock at regular intervals. Through inventory budgets, inventory consumption levels are coordinated to expected usage. It serves the purpose of controlling cash and debtors' position.

ABC Analysis Technique

Where there are many items in the inventory, it becomes essential to have a value item analysis. The ABC Analysis is an outgrowth of "Pareto Analysis" (80:20 analysis).

A category stock–more costly	(10% items–70% value)
B category stock–medium costly	(10% items–10% value)
C category stock–less costly	(80% items–20% value)

Besides ABC technique, there are other techniques also. They are: (a) FSN Classification (b) VED Classification (c) SDE Classification (d) SOS Classification (e) GOLF Classification

(a) FSN (Fast, Slow, Non-Moving) Classification

Fast moving items are to be replenished very frequently than the slow moving items. If non-moving items are not required, they are to be declared as surplus items and action is to be taken to dispose them at discount rate.

(b) VED (Vital, Essential and Desirable) Classification

These classifications are applicable mainly in manufacturing industry, where Vital class spares are to be stocked adequately and desirable spares can even be done away with if the lead time for procurement is less.

(c) SDE (Scarce, Difficult, Easy) Classification

To avoid stock out, scarce one has to be procured and stored irrespective of its value, volume and frequency of movement.

(d) SOS (Seasonal and Off Season) Classification

Inventories can be classified as Seasonal or Off–Seasonal items affecting demand and supply.

(e) GOLF (Government, Open suppliers, local suppliers, Foreign suppliers)

Classification

In this system, the materials are classified according to the nature of suppliers like government, open market, local and foreign suppliers.

Use of control Ratios

Inventory turnover ratio is also one of the methods of exercising inventory control.. High ratio indicates fast moving stock whereas a low ratio is an indicator of slow moving stock.

$$\text{Inventory stock turnover ratio} = \frac{\text{Cost of material}}{\text{Cost of average stock}}$$

Where,

$$\text{Average stock} = \frac{\text{opening stock + closing stock}}{2}$$

Inventory turnover may also be indicated by the number of days the average inventory is consumed. If the length of the inventory turnover period is short, the material is said to be fast moving and vice versa.

$$\text{Stock turnover period} = \frac{\text{Days / months in a year}}{\text{Inventory turnover ratio}}$$

PROBLEMS OF OLD STOCK

Goods which are not sold during a normal period of time could be called old stock. This may happen due to the following reasons: (1) Seasonality of the commodity (2) Perishability of the commodity (3) Fashion sensitivity of the commodity (4) Changes in consumer habits (5) Wrong assortment policies (6) Wrong purchases (7) Wrong placement in shops (8) Wrong storages (9) Lack of sales promotion (10) Wrong prices (11) Poor quality.

Measures to Reduce old Stocks: The following measures may reduce the problems of old stock: (i)no more purchase (ii) negotiate with the supplier for return (iii) find out the market demand (iv) reduction sales (v) link sales (vi) auction sales.

14

Inventory Control Models for Co-operative Wholesale Stores

P. Sundara Pandian and V. Manohar

INTRODUCTION

Inventory management plays a vital role in managing finance, profit planning and the overall working of business enterprise. Organization unable to manage its inventory in an efficient manner cannot maintain its operations Successfully. Every enterprise should, therefore, manage its inventory at an optimum level in a quantity necessary for its trade and marketing cycle on an ongoing basis. Every organization has to keep/maintain inventories to carry on production/business cycle uninterrupted and also with a view to reducing its ordering costs.

A Co-operative organization should have at all times sufficient inventories to ensure a smooth flow of activity to meet market demands. If inventory holdings fall below the minimum level quantity (MLQ) the sales may be interrupted or spot purchases of materials at higher rate have to be made. If delivery schedules are interrupted customers may cancel orders. In addition to inventories to meet the normal production needs, a society may maintain stocks to the safety needs. These stocks provide the cushion or the safety margin in case of emergencies like traffic bottlenecks, supply breakdown, and so on.

INVENTORY CONTROL

Inventory control means regulating the availability of right materials of right quantities coordinated with lead time, thereby ensuring consistently with production and sale needs the maintenance of an adequate but not excessive bank of materials at all times to maintain an economical and uninterrupted flow of production and maintenance activities and to ensure minimum blocking up of capital.

ROLE OF INVENTORY CONTROL IN CO-OPERATIVE STORES

It is of common experience that the costs of all products are increasing every day. To keep the product competitive in the market, and at the same time make reasonable profit, the management of co-operative organization is left with a few options. Cost reduction is one of them. It can be shown that a mere 5% reduction in inventory cost can increase the profitability by 30%. By this ultimate members of the co-operative society will be benefited. This brings the opportunity to increase the standard of living of the members. Carrying cost is a part and parcel of inventory cost which is quite substantial. Scientific inventory control system can reduce the carrying cost.

In Co-operative Wholesale Stores, a large variety of products are kept. It holds more than 5,000 items. Some of them are used in bulk, others in small quantities. Some are seasonal, others are not. There are still a few items which are imported, others are indigenous. In addition, uncertainty of demand and supply, frequent price changes, obsolescence and substitution necessitate the use of systematic methods and scientific techniques to manage the inventory. The capital tied-up in inventory does not add value to the product but cost. Hence it should be reduced. Moreover, with the credit squeeze imposed by financial institutions, the industries are forced to release the working capital from the excess inventory through scientific inventory control system.

INVENTORY MODELS

Inventory models are representation of inventory problems in graphical or analogous form for solution. Such solutions refer to the determination of decision variables by considering the various aspects of the problem simultaneously. In inventory problems, the decision variables are economic ordering quantity, safety stock, re-order level. In Co-operative Wholesale Stores there will be a large number of items, most of which are different in nature and hence requiring individual treatment from inventory control point of view. But this is extremely costly and time consuming. On the other hand, use of single inventory model for all items is easier and less time consuming but does not satisfy the different nature of items. Hence, a compromise is to be struck. Three models have been used in this study.

MODEL - I

In practical situations, neither the lead time nor the consumption is deterministic. It is also recognized that it is much more economical to allow a limited number of short stock-outs with less stock holding than absolute protection against stock out with very high inventory.

When the lead times and consumption during the lead time is normally distributed the first model is proposed with a risk of stock out in 'n' years is a follows.

$$EOQ = \sqrt{\frac{2\ Cp\ D}{Ci\ I}} + m\ (km\text{-}ka)\ \frac{Dn}{24}$$

$$\text{no- 2}$$

$$SS = \frac{(km - ka}{48}$$

$$ROL = ka + SS$$

Where

EOQ = Economic ordering quantity,

SS = Safety stock

ROL = Re-order level

D = Expected annual demand (Units)

Cp = procurement cost (Rs. Per order)

Ci = units price of item (Rs.)

I = Annual inventory carrying cost (as per cent of item cost)

N = Permissible risk of run out, i.e., number of years in which one risk of run out is permitted.

O = number of Orders per year.

Km = Normal maximum consumption during normal maximum lead time.

Ka = Average consumption during average lead time.

In this model, it is assumed that the replenishment rate is infinite, i.e., bulk supply takes place.

MODEL - II

For sometimes, it is observed that the material is not supplied at a time. Whatever quantity is ordered or contracted, material is dispatched at a more or less regular rate. Assuming normal distribution for lead time and consumption during the lead times, model –I is modified as below.

$$EOQ = \sqrt{D(2Cp + \frac{\frac{Ci\,n}{24} km - ka)}{Ci\,I(1 - da/R)}}$$

$$SS = \frac{no - 2}{48} \text{ (km-ma)}$$

$$ROL = ka + SS$$

Where da = Daily average consumption

R = Replenishment rate.

Others have the same notations as given in model-I.

The two models belong to perpetual reviewing system where stocks are continuously reviewed. As soon as the total stock level reaches Re- order level, procurement action is taken for a fixed quantity equal to EOQ.

MODEL - III

For C – class of items, enough information are not generally recorded. Moreover, as they are numerous in number, it is much time consuming to analyse their demand or lead time distribution for inventory control purpose. Karl Pearson has developed a well known system to represent practical probability distribution provided the first four moments about the mean are known. The more moments we know, the more we know about the distribution. If we don't know at least the first two moments, means and variance of distribution, we can't do anything with our present state of knowledge.

It is well-known that there may be infinite number of probability distributions with the same average and variance. Hence, no optimal inventory policy can be made with any specific distribution of known average and variance only. Also owing to a large number of items in C- class having different possible distributions; it is required to have a probability statement which will be true for every specific probability distribution having the same average and variance. The answer is given by Techebyecheff. The Techebycheff's inequality states that for any probability distribution whatsoever, there is a simple relationship expressing the probability that the given variable will differ from its mean by some multiple of its standard deviation. Expressed mathematically:

$$P(Y - Z \geq KS) \leq 1 \backslash K^2$$

Where Y –Z = Absolute value of difference

S = standard deviation

Z = mean

K = A factor determined on the basis of acceptable risk of service level.

Safety stock may calculated as

$$SS = da\ Tm \text{ when } Tm \leq (Ta+KS) \text{ or}$$

$$SS = da\ Y \text{ when } Tm > (Ta + KS)$$

Where

Y = Ta+KS

Ta = average lead time

Tm = maximum lead time

Replenished inventory level (RIL) is defined as a level which is desired to be replenished every time an order is placed. This is calculated as

$$RIL = SS + EOQ$$

According to this model, stock is reviewed at the end of each cycle and procurement action is taken for the quantity determined by

$$EOQ = RIL - STOCK$$

Items having different number of orders per year will have different number warning period. The values of warning periods (W) for different number of order (n) are given below.

No. of orders per year (n)	*Warning period 'W" (in weeks)*
4	1.5
3	2
2	3
1	6

How to Reduce Inventory Carrying Cost?

In the process of reducing cost inventory control plays an important role. The following measures are to be taken to reduce inventory carrying cost.

- Rational and consistent stocking policies.
- Proper source Development
- Lead time Analysis and control
- Wastage control
- Standarisation
- Monitoring surplus early disposal action
- Good codification system (Avoid duplication)
- Reliable information system (Timely/Dependability)
- Better co-ordination among all departments.
- Above all, better consciousness among all the staff that inventory is idle money.

CONCLUSION

Inventory management is a part of the over all management system. Efficient management of an inventory will increase the efficiency of the Co-operative Wholesale Stores. It can be said that inventory control must be looked upon as integrated function. Close co-operation is required from all departments to make this function effective. Inventory management may produce wonderful results. Controlling pilferage and wastes may contribute greatly to alleviate the liquidity crunch. Most of the Co-operative stores are making losses due to the ineffective and poor inventory management system. Stock control procedures can be improved at the distribution centers so that stock levels are better balanced. Though the models have been successfully implemented, further refinements are also necessary.

15

Materials Management Practices in District Consumer Cooperative Wholesale Stores: A study

B. Baskar

INTRODUCTION

A Consumer Cooperative is an association of consumers having a common aim of buying pure, unadulterated, and better quality stuffs at reasonable prices to distribute among themselves. The origin of consumer's cooperatives was incidentally the origin of the successful cooperative movement in the world *i.e.*, the first successful cooperative organized by the Rochdale Pioneers of England in 1844. In India, the emergence of the cooperatives starts from 1904 wherein the enactment of law for the cooperatives took place. Even in that, the organization of different types of cooperatives started in consumer's cooperatives *i.e.*, starting of consumers' cooperative at Triplicane, the then Madras province. The spread of the consumers' cooperatives in India is energetic during the post-independence era. Now the consumers' cooperative stores cover 7.57 million individuals in 24,190 primary consumer cooperative stores with 627 district cooperative wholesale stores, 26 state level consumer cooperative federation and a national consumer's cooperative federation.

The main activities of these stores are purchase of required materials from the available sources at reasonable cost with right quality and distribute them to its members. Being the federation of the primary consumer cooperative stores, it facilitates the actives like purchase of commodities in bulk, supply them to the primaries. The Wholesale stores deals with almost all essential commodities needed by its member societies. Naturally it deals with a variety of commodities which warrants a systematic and scientific management of the materials.

MATERIAL MANAGEMENT: THE CONCEPT

The emergence and spread of material management as a specialized branch of management was only after II world war. The term material management denotes an integrated approach to purchasing, inventory control, store keeping and other allied functions concerned with materials.

It covers purchase of materials from outside source, keeping the materials in stock and maintaining optimum level of inventory of materials as and when required, transporting the materials to its place of destination and finally keeping an overall account of materials in the stores.

The proper management of materials is sine-qua-non to reduce the cost of sales, cost of administration, the overall cost of inventories and to facilitate better utilization of capital assets of an organization.

MATERIALS MANAGEMENT IN DISTRICT CONSUMER COOPERATIVE WHOLESALE STORES

The District Consumer's Cooperative Wholesale stores, being the federation of Primary consumers' cooperative stores, undertake a variety of activities so as to facilitate the smooth functioning of the primaries for the sake of the ultimate consumers. All the functions of the materials management viz., materials planning including demand forecasting, material purchase, storage and preservation, movement and transportation, surplus and scrap disposal are undertaken by the wholesale store. All the cooperative wholesale stores do not function in isolation. In fact, they practice the cooperation among cooperatives especially the horizontal integration can be seen practically. They form Joint Purchase Committee (JPC) among themselves and that committee invites cooperative marketing societies, the suppliers of the materials for the efficient performance of the functions of the store with special reference to purchase.

In Tamil Nadu, Cooperative Wholesale Stores also undertake distribution of controlled products along with non-controlled commodities through their branches, self service sections, fair price shops, and primaries to the needy people.

A study has been conducted to appraise the existing practice of the material management practices in the selected cooperative wholesale stores in Tamil Nadu. The Wholesale stores selected are Dindigul District Cooperative Wholesale Store and Salem District Cooperative Wholesale Store.

The details of the practice of materials management functions by the Wholesale stores are presented here under.

DEMAND FORECASTING

Indent Preparation

The indent preparation is done in two parts. In the first part, an indent is prepared for the non-controlled items which are to be marketed through the primary consumer cooperative stores and through self service section and branches of the wholesale store. In the second part, an indent is prepared for the controlled items.

Indent Preparation for the non-controlled Items

- Demand from the Primary Consumer Cooperative Societies will be given each month probably within the first week of every month. Their requirements are expressed both in quantity and quality with item-wise details.

- Like-wise the demand is also made from the branches of the wholesale store and self service section run by the wholesale store.
- The store keeper, after receipt of all the demands from all the primaries, branches and self service sections, consolidates the demand and prepares a consolidated indent. If stock is available, the indent is reduced to the tune of available stock.
- The consolidated indent is crosschecked by the Secretary and the Special Officer the store in terms of its arithmetical accuracy, list of items and its quality and quantity.
- The crosschecked indent, then sent to the Joint Purchase Committee for further processing.

Indent Preparation for the Controlled Items

- As far as the controlled items such as rice, sugar, kerosene, wheat are concerned, demand is prepared by the staff of the fair price shops run by the Wholesale store at different places in the district. This is based on the number of ration card holders under various categories. The demand is sent to the Wholesale store in the first week of every month.

PURCHASE

JPC stands for Joint Purchase Committee (JPC) which undertakes the systematic purchase of required items of the wholesale stores. The members of the JPC are the Special Officers of the District Wholesale Stores of nearby region which is ranging from 8 to 16 and special officers of Cooperative Marketing Societies in that region. The other members of the JPC are individuals or representatives or authorized dealers of the products.

It is required that the Cooperative Wholesale stores should submit its consolidated indent to the Cooperative Wholesale store wherein the meeting is scheduled. The indent should reach the office one week before the date of conduct of the JPC meeting to enable the JPC meeting function smoothly.

The suppliers are also required to send their sample items (ranging from 500 grams to 750 grams) to the wholesale store for their quality test in the lab. The quality testing laboratory checks the quality of the sample supplied by the suppliers. The test is based on the standard norms fixed by the Prevention of Food and Adulteration Act of 1954. Civil Supplies Corporation norms will be adhered for the controlled goods.

Upon satisfying the quality of the products, i.e., equal to or above the norms of the concerned act, the report of the quality is to be placed in the ensuing JPC.

JPC meeting is normally held on every second Saturday of a month. The venue to conduct the JPC meeting is decided by the JPC from time to time. Normally it is held in a common place wherein all the members of the JPC could meet. The venue is also, in certain cases, fixed on rotation basis.

The JPC meetings start on the forenoon and prolong upto late evening depending upon the proceedings of the meeting.

The suppliers have to register their company (even the authorized dealers) by depositing a sum of Rs. 5000 with their RC copy to the JPC. They have to come and attend the JPC meeting along with sample products with price details.

The Special officers of the concerned Wholesale store has to be empowered with information related to the availability of products, its current market price and product related aspects well before the JPC meeting.

The suppliers, those who fulfill the quality standards, are called in the JPC meeting and contacted individually to quote their prices. If the price quoted by a supplier is lower than the other supplier and lower than the current market price, he is given a chance to supply the goods for the whole indent for the month. Negotiation is also held with them with regard to price fixation.

The supply order is placed with the selected supplier, with a request to supply the required quantity to the concerned wholesale store itself.

Mostly the pulses are purchased from NCCF and cosmetics are purchased from private firms.

The JPC deals with only certain items. The remaining items are directly purchased from the producers or their authorized dealers directly.

STORE KEEPING

Upon receipt of materials by the suppliers, the items are once again undergone quality checking. If the quality of the product supplied is as per the quality of the sample already sent by them, they are accepted and bills are passed for settlement.

The settlement of the materials purchased from JPC are of one month (30 days) credit. For other items purchased from other sources, one week to 10 days credit is allowed. The tasks undertaken in store keeping are checking of the products as per the indent, sent for quality check, storing the goods in First In First Out method on item wise in the godown and entrusting the liability with the Store keeping.

DISTRIBUTION

Distribution of the materials is in accordance with the indent received from the concerned primaries, branches and self service sections and fair price shops.

The store keeper has to distribute the entire stock item with in the month.

The distribution of materials to the primaries and others is carried by the vehicle owned by the Wholesale store.

Price Fixation: The profit margin fixed on the items is ranged from 3% to 50% and for certain other items it is fixed at the MRP. A committee has been constituted for fixing the price fixation at the wholesale store level. The fixation of the price is as per the guidelines given by the Registrar of Cooperatives. Out of the profit earned in the controlled products 40 : 60 is for by wholesale store and Primaries.

DISPOSAL OF WASTE AND SCRAPS

While dealing with variety of materials, the movement of the goods is frequent, naturally the waste and craps are inadvertent parts in the inventory. They are having their own value. The Wholesale store disposes it off by adopting an appropriate measure.

CONCLUSION

Even though the Cooperative Wholesale Stores follow all the material management practices in their own way, they require adaptation of certain tools and techniques of materials management so as to serve the public at large efficiently. The essentials tools to be followed to minimize the cost of operation are inventory control techniques, Economic Order Quantity, Scientific codification, arrangement and safeguard of materials in the godown, application of the concept of Just In Procurement, quality circles, Computerization of the inventory management, efficient working capital management –maximizing the inventory turnover, maximizing the debtor turnover and the like.

16

Working Capital Management in Consumer Cooperatives

S. Jayakumar

INTRODUCTION

Management of working capital is playing an important role in consumer cooperatives. A consumer cooperative store is investing more than 70% of its working capital in inventories. Therefore, its management calls for a better working capital management.

Effective management of working capital ensures success of the business. It is having a close relationship with the current day-to-day operations of the business.

Working capital generally refers to the excess of current assets over current liabilities.

Therefore, the working capital management is concerned with the problems arising out of managing current assets and current liabilities.

Inadequacy or mismanagement of working capital leads to business failures. Excessive working capital also is bad for a business concern, as it implies idle funds.

The objectives of working capital are to produce maximum profitability and liquidity. Therefore working capital is regarded as a life blood of the business.

The working capital should be sourced (i) at the right time (ii) at reasonable cost (iii) at the best possible terms.

CONCEPTS AND COMPONENTS OF WORKING CAPITAL

There are two components of working capital:

Gross Working Capital

It represents investments in current assets. Current assets are those assets which in the ordinary course of business can be converted into cash within a short period of one accounting year. It deals with the problems of managing individual current assets in short term. It is a financial concept but not an accounting concept.

Net Working Capital

It represents the difference between current assets and current liabilities. When current assets exceed current liabilities, then net working capital is positive and when the current liabilities exceed the current assets, the net working capital is negative. It is an accounting concept.

Net Working Capital = Current Assets–Current Liabilities

Current assets and current liabilities are listed below:

Current Assets Include

(1) Cash and bank Balances (2) Investments (marketable securities) (3) Fixed Deposits with banks (maturing within one year) (4) Receivables arising out of sales (5) Stock in trade (6) Finished goods (7) Other consumable spares (8) Advance payment for tax (9) Prepaid expenses.

Current Liabilities are

(1) Short term borrowings (2) Unsecured Loans maturing within one year (3) Public deposits (4) Sundry creditors (5)

Interest and other charges due for payments (6) Advanced payments from customers (7) Deposits from selling agent (8) Payable/Other liabilities.

KINDS OF WORKING CAPITAL

The working capital is classified as under: (1) Permanent or Fixed working capital (2) Temporary or Variable working capital (3) Reserve working capital

Permanent or Fixed Working Capital

Minimum amount of current assets needed to conduct a business even in the dullest season of the year is called a permanent or fixed working capital. It is otherwise known as the funds required for the business to produce goods and services to satisfy the demand at a particular point of time. It is required on a continuous basis over the entire year.

The characteristics of permanent or fixed working capital are; (i) It is classified on the basis of time factor (ii) It constantly changes from one asset to another (iii) Its size increases with the growth of the business operations.

Temporary Working Capital

It is the additional current assets required for a short period to meet the seasonal needs of a business. It represents certain amount of fluctuations on current assets during a short period.

Reserve Working Capital

It is the excess amount over the requirement of regular working capital, provided for contingencies arising at the time of strikes, rise in prices, depression etc.

Sources of Working Capital

The following is a snapshot of various working capital available to a business organization:

Determinants of Working Capital

Working capital requirements are affected by a number of factors. These factors are related to monitory, general economy, business environment etc., The determinants of working capital are discussed below:

Long term sources	*Short term sources*	
	Internal	*External*
Ploughing back of profits	Depreciation fund	Trade credit
Loans	Taxation provision	Bank credit
Public deposits	Accrued expenses	Customers' credit
		Government assistances
		Security of employees

1. **General nature of business:** Trading business requires large amount in current assets but less amount in fixed assets investments. Manufacturing concerns require sizable amount for working capital along with fixed assets investments.
2. **Terms of sales and purchase:** Credit terms granted to customers as well as credit terms granted by suppliers affect the working capital. The ratio between the cash and credit sales/purchases also affect the level of working capital. When an organization buys and sells on cash basis, it requires less amount of working capital, as the funds are not tied up in debtors or bills receivables.
3. **Manufacturing cycle:** The quantum of working capital needed is influenced by the length of manufacturing cycle.
4. **Rapidity of turn-over:** If the inventory turn over is high, the working capital turn-over will be low. When an organization is carrying on a large amount of slow moving stocks, it needs a large amount of working capital.
5. **Business cycle:** Cyclical changes in the economy also influence the quantum of working capital. In a period of boom, there will be increase in sales, rise in price etc., Therefore, a large amount of working capital is needed.

During depression period a heavy amount of working capital is needed, as the inventories remain locked unsold and book debts remain uncollected.

6. **Changes in technology:** Changes in technology may lead to improvement in the processing of raw materials, reduction of wastages, greater productivity etc., These factors may lead to reduction in working capital requirements.
7. **Seasonal variations:** Working capital requirements depend on the conditions of supply of raw materials also. When the raw material is available seasonally and production operations are carried out throughout the year, large inventory is required. Even if the supply is unpredictable and scant, large inventory is required.
8. **Market condition:** When competition is keen, a large inventory of finished goods is required to promptly serve customers. Further generous credit terms may have to be offered to attract customers in a highly competitive market.
9. **Seasonality of operations:** Highly fluctuating working capital is required to an organization, which has seasonal markets like textile business. To have a fairly even sales throughout the year a stable working capital is needed.

Dangers of inadequate working capital

When working capital is inadequate, a business faces the following problems:

(i) It may not be able to take advantages of cash discount.

(ii) It cannot buy its requirements in bulk and unable to utilize the production facilities fully.

(iii) It may not be able to take advantage of profitable business opportunities.

(iv) It's low liquidity may lead to low profitability. In the same way, low profitability results in low liquidity.

(v) Short-term liabilities cannot be paid off because of inadequate working capital.

(vi) Credit-worthiness of the organisation may by damaged because of lack of liquidity. Thus, it will lose its reputation.

(vii) Low liquidity position may lead to liquidation of the business. When it is unable to meet its debts at maturity, there is an unsound position.

(viii) Fixed assets cannot efficiently and effectively be utilized on account of lack of sufficient working capital.

Danger of Excessive Working Capital

When there is excessive working capital, it is also dangerous. Excessive working capital raises the following problems:

(i) A business may be tempted to over trade and lose heavily.

(ii) The situation may lead to unnecessary purchases and accumulation of inventories.

(iii) There arises an imbalance between liquidity and profitability.

(iv) Excessive working capital means funds are idle. When funds are idle, no profit is earned. When it is so, the rate of return on its investment goes down.

(v) The situation leads to greater production which may not have matching demand.

(vi) The excess of working capital may lead to carelessness about cost of production.

RATIOS PERTAINING TO WORKING CAPITAL MANAGEMENT

Current ratio/working Capital Ratio

Current ratio is an indicator of the organization's commitment to meet its short term liabilities. It shows the relationship between current assets and current liabilities. It is also known as working capital ratio.

$$\text{Current ratio} = \frac{\text{Current assets}}{\text{Current liabilities}}$$

Generally 2:1 is considered ideal for a business. That is

value of current assets should be twice the value of current liabilities.

Quick ratio/Liquidity ratio/Acid test ratio

This ratio indicates the relation between liquid assets and liquid liabilities. The term quick assets refer to current assets which can be converted into cash immediately and it comprises all current assets minus stock and prepaid expenses. Liquid liabilities comprise all current liabilities minus bank overdraft.

$$\text{Liquidity ratio} = \frac{\text{Liquid assets}}{\text{Liquid liabilities}}$$

Super Quick Ratio

This ratio considers only the absolute liquid assets (cash in the marketable securities and liquid/quick liabilities).

$$\text{Super quick ratio} = \frac{\text{Cash and marketable sec urities}}{\text{Liquidity / quick liabilities}}$$

Working Capital turnover Ratio

This ratio indicates whether or not working capital has been effectively utilized in making sales. If higher volume of sales is achieved with relatively small amount of working capital, it is an indicator of efficiency of the business operations.

$$\text{Working capital turnover ratio} = \frac{\text{Net sales}}{\text{Net working capital}}$$

Stock turnover Ratio

This ratio indicates whether or not the investment in inventory is efficiently used. When ratio is higher, it shows that finished stock is rapidly turned over. A low stock turnover ratio reveals that there is accumulation of obsolete stock or too-much stock.

$$\text{Stock turnover ratio} = \frac{\text{Cost of goods sold}}{\text{Average stock}}$$

where,

$$\text{cost of goods sold} = \text{sales} - \text{gross profit}$$

$$\text{average stock} = \frac{\text{opening stock} + \text{closing stock}}{2}$$

Debtor turnover ratio

Debtors turnover ratio establishes the relationship between credit sales and average receivables of the year. It measures the number of times the receivables/debtors rotate in a year in terms of sales.

$$\text{Debtors turnover ratio} = \frac{\text{Credit sales}}{\text{Average debtors}}$$

where,

average debtors =

$$\frac{\text{opening sundry debtor} + \text{closing sundry debtor}}{2}$$

Debt Collection Period

The purpose of this ratio is to find the period over which receivables/debtors remain uncollected.

$$\text{Debt collection period} = \frac{\text{Month / Days in a year}}{\text{Debtors turnover}}$$

Creditors Turn over Ratio

Creditors turn over indicates the number of times the payable rotate in a year. Creditors turnover ratio shows the relationship between the net credit purchase for the whole year and the total payable. When the period of outstanding payable is longer the requirement of working capital is lesser. But when the business organization does not pay off its creditors within time it may adversely affect the business.

$$\text{Creditors turnover ratio} = \frac{\text{Net credit purchase}}{\text{Average sundry creditors}}$$

$$\text{Average payment period} = \frac{\text{Month / Days in a year}}{\text{Creditors turn over ratio}}$$

FORECASTING TECHNIQUES OF WORKING CAPITAL

There are many popular methods available for forecasting working capital requirements, which are as follows; (1) Cash forecasting method (2) Balance sheet method (3) Profit and Loss adjustment method (4) Percentage of sales method (5) The operational cycle method (6) Regression analysis method.

1. **Cash forecasting method:** In this method the position of cash in the end of the period is shown after considering the receipts and payments to be made during that period. This shows the deficiency or surplus of cash at the definite point of time.
2. **Balance sheet method:** In the Balance sheet method of forecasting a forecast is made from various assets and liabilities of the business. Afterwards the difference between the two is taken to indicate either cash surplus or cash deficiency.
3. **Profit and Loss adjustment method:** Under this method the forecast profits are adjusted after adding the cash inflows and deducting the cash outflows. The basic idea under this method is to adjust the estimated profit on the cash basis.
4. **Percentage of sales method:** In this method the working capital is determined as a percentage of forecast sales. It is decided on the basis of past observations. If over the year, relationship between sales and working capital is found to be stable, then this relationship may be taken as a standard for the determination of working capital in the future also.

This relationship between sales and working capital and its various components may be expressed in three ways:

(a) As number of days of sales

(b) as turnover

(c) as percentage of sales

5. **Operational cycle method:** This method of working capital forecast is based on the operational cycle and it refers to the period that a business enterprise takes in converting cash into cash.
6. **Regression analysis method:** In the sphere of working capital management, it helps in making projection after establishing the average relationship in the past years between sales and working capital. The analysis can be carried out through the graphic portrayals (scatter diagram or through mathematical formula).

Examples of Working Capital Forecasting through Operational Cycle method

Under this method the estimated requirements of working capital for a trading business and manufacturing industry are to be calculated on different basis.

(i) Trading Business–Its Working Capital Assessment

Data required to forecast the working capital requirement.

1.	Projected annual sales	= Rs. 65,00,000
2.	Percentage of net profit on cost of sale	= 25%
3.	Average credit period allowed to debtors	= 10 weeks
4.	Average credit period allowed to customers	= 4 weeks
5.	Average stock carrying (in terms of sales requirement)	= 8 weeks
6.	Contingencies	= 10% on working capital

Calculation of working capital requirement forecast

1. Per week sales = $\frac{65,00,000}{52}$ = 1,25,000

2. Cost value of sales (per week) = $\frac{1,25,000 \times 100}{125}$ = 1,00,000

3. Current assets

Stock (8 weeks on cost value)	1,00,000×8	=8,00,000
Debtors (10 weeks on sales value)	1,25,000×10	=12,50,000
		20,50,000
Less current liabilities		
Creditors (4 weeks on cost value)	1,00,000 × 4	= 4,00,000
		16,50,000
Add 10% for contingencies		1,65,000
Total requirements of working capital		18,15,000

(ii) Manufacturing Industries–Its Working Capital Assessment

Data required to forecast the working capital requirement.

1. Percentage of various elements of cost bears on the selling price:
   - (a) materials 50% on sales
   - (b) labor 20% on sales
   - (c) overhead 10% on sales
   - (d) profit 20% on sales
2. Production = 2,00,000 units
3. Selling price = Rs. 9 per unit
4. Expected raw material to remain in stores = 1 month
5. Expected finished goods to stay in warehouse = 2 months

6. Expected period of stock of materials in work-in-progress = 1 month
7. Credit allowed by suppliers to material = 1 month
8. Debtors allowed for credit sales = 2 months

Calculation of Working Capital Requirement Forecast

1. Total sales (2,00,000 × 9) = 18,00,000
2. Current assets

(a) stock of raw material
(18,00,000 × 50/100 × 1/12) 75,000

(b) stock of finished goods

(i) materials
(18,00,000 × 50/100 × 2/12) = 1,50,000

(ii) labor
(18,00,000 × 20/100 × 2/12) = 60,000

(iii) overhead
(18,00,000 × 10/100 × 2/12) = 30,000

2,40,000

(c) work-in-progress

(i) materials
(18,0 0,000 × 50/100 × 1/12) = 75,000

(ii) labor
(18,00,000 × 20/100 × 1/12) = 30,000

(iii) overhead
(18,00,000 × 10/100 × 1/12) = 15,000

1,20,000

(d) Debtors

(i) materials
(18,00,000 × 50/100 × 2/12) = 1,50,000

(ii) labor
(18,00,000 × 20/100 × 2/12) = 60,000

(iii) overhead

(18,00,000 × 10/100 × 2/12)	= 30,000
	2,40,000
Total current assets(a + b + c + d)	6,75,000

3. current liabilities
   (a) creditors (18,00,000 × 50/100 × 1/12) 75,000
4. working capital = current assets – current liabilities
   = 6,75,000 - 75,000
   = Rs. 6,00,000

CONCLUSION

The management expenses of consumer cooperatives are relatively higher than that of private traders. By controlling costs and supply line essential, consumer cooperatives endeavor to afford protection to their members. The cooperative sector can only service, if they are effectively able to adopt all types of costing methods and management accounting techniques in the management of inventory and working capital.

The efficiency of consumer cooperatives depends on how quickly it is in a position to convert the goods in to cash. Then the need for working capital would be less. To face the competitive consumer market, consumer cooperatives should equip themselves to meet the emerging challenges.

Another notable feature in cooperative stores is inadequate and inefficient stock control system. Stock deficit is inevitable in consumer cooperatives. In many cases, lack of proper follow up action and periodical stock verification have resulted in erosion of working capital. The average stock level maintained by the stores will result in neither piling up stocks nor leading to stock outs.

Effective inventory control methods will result in working capital efficiency.

17

Management of Working Capital in Cooperative Wholesale Stores

S. David Amirtha Rajan & P. Gnana Soundari

INTRODUCTION

Co-operative Movement in India is a century old. It was sponsored and developed with lot of hopes and expectations. In 1904 through enacting "Co-operative Credit Societies Act". Henry W. Wolff quoted it as "a turning point in economic and social history" and Sir Daniel Hamilton noted its significance as "the way from poverty to plenty". It is a system sponsored to help the poor. In this sense, it is a method to extend a helping hand for the growth of nation's economy.

Such an old system though well established is facing certain problems. This may be due to changing attitude of customers and government in general. In those cases when attitudes are changing, there is a need to analyse the reality of its marketing and accounting. In this paper an attempt is made to analyse its accounting reality. As a part of it, a study was conducted on "Management of Working Capital in the Co-operative Wholesale Stores in Madurai".

WORKING CAPITAL MANAGEMENT

The basic aim of financial management is to maximise the shareholders' wealth. This can be achieved only when there is a sufficient profit in any organization. The amount of such profit largely depends upon the magnitude of sales. It is a fact that sales do not convert into cash immediately. There is always a time gap between the sale of goods and receipt of cash. In this juncture, working capital becomes vital to sustain the sales activity. In case adequate working capital is not available for this period, the company will not be in a position to sustain the sales since it may not be in a position to purchase raw material, pay wages and other expenses required for any manufacturing or trading activities. According to Guthamann and Dougall "Working Capital is excess of current assets over current liabilities". The basic objective of working capital management is to manage the firm's current assets and current liabilities in such a way that the satisfactory level of working capital is maintained (that is neither inadequate nor excessive).

Therefore, working capital management is concerned with the problems that arise in attempting to manage the current assets, the current liabilities and interrelationship that exists between them. The management of working capital in Madurai District Co-operative Wholesale Stores is discussed here.

MANAGEMENT OF CURRENT ASSETS

The current assets consist of cash, debtor, bills receivable and stock. The management aspects of these are presented in the forth coming paragraphs.

MANAGEMENT OF DEBTORS

The Madurai District Co-operative Wholesale Stores provides credit facilities to its member societies. This facility is allowed for one month time. This means 30 days credit facility is given to its customers. However, it may be extended for more than 30 days in case of Government institutions.

CASH MANAGEMENT

Cash sales are allowed in general. In case of credit sales, one month credit facility is allowed. The mode of collection from these debtors is cheque. The cash as well as cheque collections are remitted to the Head office after a thorough check up. This is done by all branches of the main stores. The branches or main stores cannot hold any cash for a long period. It means, the collected amount should be deposited in the Head office and then it should be deposited in the District Central Cooperative Bank, Madurai.

It is a century old procedure followed in the stores. Further, as per its bye-laws it can keep only minimum cash in hand.

MANAGEMENT OF BILLS RECEIVABLES

Bills are not used and as such there is no such procedure existing in the trade activities of the wholesale stores.

INVENTORY MANAGEMENT

The usual purchase is made from leading companies which are mostly approved by the government. The stock may be maintained only on the basis of demand. No proper technique is adopted to assess minimum, maximum, re-order and danger levels and Economic ordering quantity. In case of pricing the stock, they adopt cost plus method strictly. There won't be flexibility in price fixing for any product. It is also noted that any scientific method is not followed in inventory management.

MANAGEMENT OF CURRENT LIABILITY

Current liabilities are creditors, bills payable and so on. The management of working capital also implies managing current liabilities. The details of these are discussed below:

MANAGEMENT OF CREDITORS

The purchase of goods is usually done from authorized leading-companies. Indeed, these companies provide one month credit facility to the stores. Against this, the payment is made by cheque. Here the centralized way of payment is carried out.

MANAGEMENT OF BILLS PAYABLE

There is no chance in using bills payable for credit at any cause.

SUGGESTIONS

Based on the above discussion, the following suggestions are made for better working capital management in the wholesale stores:

(a) Lock–Box system should be followed for quick collection of cash or cheque from debtors. The present system of collection is not at all an admirable one.

(b) In case of inventory system, the costing technique should be adopted. The levels of stocks being mentioned in cost accounting should be followed. The flexi-method of pricing should be adhered. Both trade and cash discount may be allowed. Steps should be taken to clear the old stock as early as possible.

(c) The collection period allowed to customer should be reduced.

(d) Scientific methods of accounts receivable and accounts payable may be considered and adopted.

SUMMARY

The present pattern of co-operative stores needs a change in all aspects in management of working capital. If it is done, there is a scope to compete with competitors. There is also a necessity to change its policy at its gross root itself.

18

Working Capital Management in Dindigul District Co-operative Wholesale Stores

R. Seerangarajan

Business enterprises, while making decisions should actively take into account the needs and desires of the members of the society. Howard R. Bowen suggested that businesses should consider the social implications of the enterprise's decisions and actions.

Thus, wholesale co-operative stores have been established with a view to serve the public in providing timely supply of essential goods and services such as rice, wheat, sugar, kerosene, etc., at reasonable prices. These are operating with a greater social responsibility of caring for the needs of weaker sections of the society through distribution of goods.

The degree of value creation by wholesale co-op stores is very high in the context of satisfying the social needs. As these stores do not involve in any manufacturing of goods, they essentially undertake distribution of goods and services. Thus, working capital occupies significant share in total assets. Sometimes the it exceeds 95% of the total assets.

Therefore, the management of working capital is a crucial factor in determining the profitability of the business and periodic evaluation is essential for assessing the health of the business. Working capital sustains a business by bridging the time lapse between incurring expenditure in supply of products and receipt of the revenues. Therefore, working capital should be as low as possible and it has direct bearing on the profitability of the stores.

The success of the business operations in a wholesale stores is dependent on the appropriate level of investment in current assets and it will be the first and foremost responsibility of the administrator. Working capital investment strategies are highly volatile and the management should always seek to fix appropriate level of investments in current assets.

In this direction, certain tools and techniques may help the management to spot out problem areas for necessary corrective action. Among such tools, ratio analysis is a simple but effective tool. In this context, the management can evaluate the working capital policies through estimating the average inventory holding period during a particular accounting year and compare the same with that of the previous years. A lower holding period reflects an efficient utilization of inventory. This indicates that inventory is held for shorter durations in the warehouse/go down and is fast converted into receivables/cash through sale. And too high inventory holding period is not considered good due to its impact on profitability and liquidity of the business. Longer durations mean that more funds would be locked up in inventory earning nothing. Such situations may need immediate attention for further investigation. And the management, sometimes might be interested to know the efficiency of the various components of inventory in managing current assets through estimation of operating cycle.

The components operating cycle comprises raw material cycle, conversion cycle, storage cycle and collection cycle. All the above components should be related to the total time to find out the proportion of each of them.

Thus, the present exercise is addressed to the evaluation of the component cycles over a period of ten years in the Dindigul Dist. Co-op. wholesale Stores. The exercise is also addressed to the impact of the components of the operating cycles on the gross profits of the study unit.

COMPONENT CYCLES

Raw Material Cycle

This cycle measures the efficiency of raw materials holding period in the go-down before it is sent for further processing. Shorter durations are preferable. This is computed by dividing the average stock of raw materials with that of consumption raw material per day. Such analogy will be helpful in comparing the performance in a particular accounting year with the predetermined standard set by the management or with the industry standards or with the past performance. In this regard a significant variation from the acceptable standard may invite corrective actions from management in respect of quantity of raw material to be ordered, timing and other related aspects that may have a bearing on this.

Conversion

If work-in-process inventory turnover ratio is divided into the number of days in a year it will give the conversion period which can be compared with some acceptable standard to evaluate the performance.

$$\text{Conversion period (In number of days)} = \frac{\text{Average W.I.P. inventory}}{\text{Cost of goods manufactured per day}}$$

This ratio establishes a relationship between the value of goods produced and the value of average work-in-process.
Thus

$$\text{Work-in-process inventory turnover ratio} = \frac{\text{Cost of goods manufactured}}{\text{Average W.I.P. inventory}}$$

A higher turnover ratio indicates lower inventory accumulation and lesser funds as tied-up working capital .A falling turnover means either management has become lax in controlling the productive processes or some external factors have retarded the production movement at its final turn-up.

Storage Cycle

Firms produce goods in order to sell them in the market. However, there may be a delay in their sale or in meeting seasonal demand for finished goods. There is, however a limit to the period for which finished goods should be in store. If the finished goods are turned over faster, the amount of locked-up funds would be less: otherwise, it will be more.

Storage cycle can be computed as below:

$$\text{Storage cycle} = \frac{\text{Average stock of finished goods}}{\text{Average value of sales per day}}$$

The same can be converted into finished goods storage period if the number of days in year is divided by the finished goods inventory turnover ratio. That is,

$$\underset{\text{(in number of days)}}{\text{Finished goods storage period}} = \frac{\text{Average stock of finished goods inventory}}{\text{Cost of goods sold per day}}$$

Generally, lower storage period is considered good. But too low a storage period is risky.

It is worthwhile to compute finished goods inventory turnover ratio for comparison purposes. Finished goods inventory turnover ratio attempts to capture the above aspect. It is calculated as:

$$\underset{\text{turnover ratio}}{\text{Finished} - \text{goods inventory}} = \frac{\text{Cost of goods sold}}{\text{Average finished goods inventory}}$$

Collection Cycle

For getting additional insight into the managerial aspects of receivables, the ratio can be divided into the total number of days in a year (say 365),to give average collection period.

$$\text{Average collection period} = \frac{365 * \text{Average balance of receivables}}{\text{Total sales}}$$

(or)

$$= \frac{\text{Average balance of receivables}}{\text{Sales per day}}$$

Average collection period calculated above indicates the number of days for which receivables remain uncollected. This can be compared with the credit period offered by the management to its customers. If actual collection period as calculated above is more than the one which is offered, it indicates slackness on the part of management. This calls for toning up of its systems and procedures of collection. If there is a wide and continuing variation, the whole approach towards recovery of dues needs to be streamlined, modified or changed as per the severity of the problems. Otherwise the concern may have to face severe liquidity crisis.

ANALYSIS OF COMPONENTS OF OPERATING CYCLE IN THE STUDY UNIT

Raw Material Cycle (Table I)

The Study Unit has recorded a gross raw material cycle ranging from four days to twelve days during the study period of 1994 -95 to 2003 -04 Lowest gross raw material cycle was recorded is 1999-2000 due to high volume and value of raw materials consumed coupled with lower stocks of raw materials maintained in the same period. In all the years, the business has recorded low duration of raw material cycles as it has dealt mainly with the essential commodities that are to be distributed to the public in time.

The credit durations for the purchases effected by the stores varied from one day to 6 days. Lower durations were attainted due to limited purchases that were made on credit basis and most of the purchases were made against payment as they sourced most of the goods from Civil Supplies

Table I
Operating Cycle
Net Raw Material Cycle

(Rs.in Crores)

Sl. No	Particulars	94-95	95-96	96-97	97-98	98-99	99-00	00-01	01-02	02-03	03-04
1.	Opening stock(Rs)	0.51	0.58	0.67	0.61	0.54	0.38	0.32	0.53	0.70	00.63
2.	Purchase(Rs)	17.53	18.86	25.10	25.88	22.85	27.52	25.76	27.65	26.06	25.03
3.	Total (1+2) (Rs)	18.04	19.43	25.78	26.49	23.38	27.90	26.08	28.26	26.76	25.66
4.	Closing stock(Rs)	0.58	0.67	0.61	0.54	0.38	0.32	0.53	0.70	0.63	0.47
5.	Consumed goods (3-4) (Rs)	17.46	18.76	25.17	25.95	23.00	27.58	25.55	27.56	26.13	25.19
6.	Avg.value of consumed (Rs) goods 5/365(Rs)	0.05	0.05	0.07	0.07	0.06	0.08	0.07	0.08	0.07	0.07
7.	Avg.value of stock (1+4/2) (Rs)	0.55	0.62	0.65	0.58	0.46	0.35	0.42	0.62	0.67	0.55
8.	Gross R.M.cycle (7/6) in days	11	12	9	8	8	4	6	8	10	8
9.	Total purchase(Rs)	17.53	18.86	25.10	25.88	22.85	27.52	25.76	27.65	26.06	25.03
10.	Avg.daily purchase in credit (9/365) (Rs)	0.04	0.05	0.07	0.07	0.06	0.07	0.07	0.08	0.07	0.06
11.	Avg.sundry creditors. (Rs)	0.07	0.09	0.10	0.09	0.10	0.12	0.20	0.21	0.29	0.35
12.	Credit cycle (11/10)	2	2	2	1	2	2	3	3	4	6
13.	Net Raw material cycle in days(8-12)	9	10	7	7	6	2	3	5	6	2

Corporation, Government of TN. The wholesale stores recorded net raw material cycle ranging from 2 days to 10 days with the lowest duration was recorded in 1999-2000 and 2003-04. Longer duration of net raw materials cycle was recorded in 1995 - 96 due to low volume of goods consumed for processing and moderately high stocks of goods maintained when compared to other periods.

No doubt that the stores has maintained lower duration of raw material cycle days contributing to more number of business cycles. The staff managing inventories have done commendable work in this regard.

Conversion cycle (Table II)

Conversion cycle in a district wholesale stores which is basically in distribution business will be mainly in standardizing the quantity, quality and repacking of the goods in 1 kg and ½ kg packs etc., And there will not be any value addition through conversion process except inspecting quality and packaging.

The Store has recorded conversion cycles ranging from four days to twelve days during the study period. Lowest conversion cycle of four days was recorded in 1999-2000.

As in the case of net raw material cycle, longest duration of twelve days was recorded in 1995-96. The longer durations of 12 days was recorded due to higher volume of average inventory of semi finished goods coupled with lower volume of cost of goods manufactured. Despite fluctuations in the duration of conversion cycles, the stores has done fairly well in managing the conversion process with very low durations. The management can think of bench marking the duration of conversion cycle to that of the average of ten years and efforts may be taken to contain the conversion cycle days well with in 9 days(average for ten years) through regulating the inventory levels of semi-finished goods.

Storage cycle (Table III)

Storage cycle reflects the unit's inventory policy and marketing policy in general. Storage cycle also tracks the efficiency of

Table II
Conversion Cycle

(Rs.in Crores)

Sl. No	Particulars	94-95	95-96	96-97	97-98	98-99	99-00	00-01	01-02	02-03	03-04
1.	Opening stock	0.54	0.58	0.61	0.61	0.54	0.38	0.32	0.53	0.70	0.63
2.	Cost of consumed goods	17.46	18.76	25.17	25.95	23.00	27.58	25.55	27.56	26.13	25.19
3.	Total(Rs.)	17.46	18.76	25.17	25.95	23.00	27.58	25.55	27.56	26.13	25.19
4.	Closing stock(Rs.)	0.58	0.61	0.61	0.54	0.38	0.32	0.53	0.70	0.63	0.47
5.	Total (Rs.)	16.88	18.09	24.56	25.41	22.62	27.26	25.02	26.86	25.50	24.72
6.	Trade charges	0.15	0.20	0.28	0.31	0.22	0.26	0.21	0.29	0.27	0.26
7.	Cost of goods producted	17.03	18.29	24.84	25.72	22.84	27.52	25.23	27.15	25.77	24.98
8.	Avg.value of transactions	0.05	0.05	0.07	0.07	0.06	0.08	0.07	0.08	0.07	0.07
9.	Avg.stock(Rs.)	0.56	0.62	0.65	0.58	0.46	0.35	0.42	0.66	0.67	0.55
10.	Con.cycle in days	11	12	9	8	8	4	6	8	10	8

Table III
Storage Cycle

(Rs.in crores)

Sl. No	Particulars	94-95	95-96	96-97	97-98	98-99	99-00	00-01	01-02	02-03	03-04
1.	Opening stock	0.51	0.57	0.68	0.61	0.53	0.38	0.32	0.61	0.70	0.63
2.	Cost of goods (19)	17.53	18.86	25.10	25.88	25.85	27.52	25.76	27.65	26.06	25.03
3.	Total (23+24)	18.04	19.43	25.78	26.49	23.38	27.90	26.08	28.26	26.76	25.66
4.	Less closing stock	0.58	0.67	0.61	0.54	0.58	0.32	0.53	0.70	0.63	0.47
5.	Sales	17.46	18.76	25.17	22.95	23.00	27.58	25.55	27.56	26.13	25.19
6.	Avg.value of sales per day (27/365)	0.05	0.05	0.07	0.07	0.06	0.08	0.07	0.08	0.07	0.07
7.	Average stock of finished goods	0.55	0.62	0.65	0.58	0.46	0.35	0.42	0.66	0.67	0.55
8.	Storage cycle in days	11	12	9	8	7	4	6	8	10	8

Simulation Table for a bench mark of 9 days

(Rs. in Crorès)

Sl. No.	1	2	3	4	5	6	7	8	9	10
Avg. Stock Finished Goods	0.10	0.20	0.30	0.40	0.50	0.60	0.70	0.80	0.90	1,00
Cost of goods Sold per day	0.0111	0.0222	0.0333	0.0444	0.0555	0.0666	0.0777	0.0888	0.0999	0.111
Expected sales (Rs. in crores)	4.05	8.11	12.15	16.20	20.25	24.05	28.38	32.412	36.50	40.50

distribution of goods and services once they completed the conversion process. As the stores deals with essential commodities for public distribution, the storage cycle ought to be as low as possible to ensure timely delivery of goods to the needy public.

In this regard, the store has recorded storage cycles ranging from four days to twelve days during the study period of ten years. Again the lowest duration of four days was recorded in 1999-2000 and the longest was recorded in 1995-96 as in the case of other component cycles. The average of storage cycle in all the ten years was at 8.3 days or 9 days. The management can think of making this 9 days duration as a benchmark for fixing the level of inventory in terms of finished goods that are ready for distribution. In such a condition of bench marking of 9 days, the stores may think of following options for inventory and cost of goods sold.

The simulation table will help the managers of the whole sale store to decide on the levels of average inventory to be maintained and the annual sales proposed to be made in crores of rupees. The manager should aim at reducing average inventory levels and enhancing the sales as explained above.

Hence, the management can think of reducing the storage cycle days through effective logistics and transportation system.

Collection Cycle (Table IV)

The wholesale stores has recorded collection cycles ranging from two days to four days during the study period of ten years. The duration of the collection cycles is quite stable in the range of two to four days and the duration is quite shorter than other components of operating cycle. Collection cycle deals with the velocity of collection of dues from sundry debtors for the sales made on credit. The total credit sales ranged from Rs. 18.00 crores to Rs. 28.48 crores. The average

Table IV
Collection Cycle

(Rs.in crores)

Sl. No	Particulars	94-95	95-96	96-97	97-98	98-99	99-00	00-01	01-02	02-03	03-04
1.	Total credit sales	18	19.46	26.0	26.8	23.75	28.48	26.94	28.07	26.62	26.06
2.	Avg. daily credit sales	0.05	0.05	0.07	0.07	0.06	0.08	0.07	0.08	0.07	0.07
3.	Avg. sundry debtors	0.1	0.1	.012	0.15	0.15	0.20	0.30	0.30	0.30	0.30
4.	Collection cycle in days	2	2	2	2	3	3	4	4	4	4

Table V
5. Total Operating cycle and Turnover of Working Capital

(Rs.in crores)

Sl. No	Particulars	94-95	95-96	96-97	97-98	98-99	99-00	00-01	01-02	02-03	03-04
1.	Net R.M. Cycle	9	10	7	7	6	2	3	5	6	2
2.	Conversion cycle	11	12	9	8	7	4	6	8	10	8
3.	Storage cycle	11	12	9	8	7	4	6	8	10	8
4.	Collection cycle	2	2	2	2	3	3	4	4	4	4
5.	Total cycle days	33	36	27	25	23	13	19	25	30	22
6.	T.O.W.C	11.06	10.13	13.52	14.60	15.86	28.08	19.21	14.60	12.16	16.60

sundry debtors was found to be lower in the range of Rs. 0.10 crores to Rs. 0.30 crores as the despatch of goods are made against payment or on short credit days. The average duration of collection cycle for the ten years period will be 3 days which is a commendable performance in containing collection cycle and management of working capital.

Turn Over of Working Capital (Table V)

The total operating cycles for Dindigul district wholesale co-op store ranged from 13 days to 36 days during the study period. The average of operating cycles in ten years is twenty five days. The store has performed well in containing the operating cycle within 30 days. Thus, one cycle is made once a month. This could be possible due to the nature of the goods dealt with by the unit and all the items are essential goods which require faster and efficient business cycles. Thus, the WCS has recorded a turn over of working capital (TOWC) ranging from 10.13 to 28.07 crores.

Lowest turnover was recorded in the year 1995-96 as it has done less volume of business or value of goods sold was lowest when compared to other years. Highest turnover of working capital was recorded in 1999-2000 which could be considered as the best performing year among the study periods considered. Looking at the overall performance, the store has managed the working capital successfully in terms of operating cycle concept.

Operating Cycle and Gross Profit (Table VI)

Table VI explains the Gross Profit and Turnover of working capital ratios during the study period of ten years. The turn over of working capital was found to be highest in 1999-2000 and Gross profit was also found to be Rs. 0.64 crores which is the highest. In other years these two variables have recorded partly concurrent and contrasting trends.

Table VI
Operating Cycle and Gross Profit

Sl. No	Year	Total Operating Cycle in Days	Turnover of working Capital	Gross Profit Rs. in Crores
1.	94-95	33	11.06	0.39
2.	95-96	36	10.13	0.50
3.	96-97	27	13.52	0.55
4.	97-98	25	14.60	0.54
5.	98-99	23	15.86	0.53
6.	99-2000	13	28.07	0.64
7.	2000-01	19	19.21	0.18
8.	01-02	25	14.60	0.22
9.	02-03	30	12.16	0.22
10.	03-04	22	16.60	0.55

SUGGESTIONS

Suggestive measures for improving the performance are that the management can think of involving bench mark for the components of the operating cycle and evolve suitable methodologies to control the inventory levels at each stage. From the performance of working capital management, the store is quite efficient in fast delivery of goods and services to its retail network which are mainly public distribution shops and retail stores. With the expertise, the store can think of entering distribution of other items that are not covered under essential goods. Such efforts will help to augment profitability and enhance the volumes in the business. In recent years SHGs are coming in a big way in production and marketing of household consumer non-durables. The district level wholesale co-operatives may help the SHGs and respective federations in marketing their products through networking and co-ordination. According to Hagel III & S. Brown, capacity building is the most powerful strategic advantage and it is the only sustainable edge. The catalyst for such capacity building will be 'off shoring'. This will not only facilitate the units to enhance its business capabilities but also push their performance to new levels faster by forming partnerships with SHGs and other participating business units.

REFERENCES

Anthony, Robert and J.C. Reece (1995), 'Management Accounting: Text and Cases, Richard Irwin, Illinois, p. 206.

M.A.Poecock and A.H. Taylor (1982), 'Handbook of Financial Planning', Gower Publishing Co. Ltd., Westmeeds, U.K., p. 186.

P.Gopalakrishnan (1996), 'Handbook of Materials Management', Prentice Hall of India Pvt. Ltd., New Delhi, p. 175.

Hingorani & Ramanathan (2003), 'Management Accounting-Text', Sulthan Chand & Co. New Delhi.

John Hagel III S. Brown (2006), 'The Only Sustainable Edge' Harvard Business School Press, U.S.

Kuchhal, S.C., 'Financial Management, Charange Publishing House; Allahabad 1998.

19

Status of Management Accounting System in Co-operative Wholesale Stores

S. Manivel

ACCOUNTING SYSTEM: ERSTWHILE PROCEDURE

Cooperative accounting system, otherwise known as Receipts and Payments System of Account Keeping, was followed in the cooperative wholesale stores. The duties and responsibilities of the personnel in the accounting sections are not clearly specified in many cases. The accounts personnel, besides maintaining accounts, have to look after the purchase, sales, business development and so on. Though it is desirable, from the administrative point of view it becomes an unbearable burden on the individuals and thus they fail to do justice to their work.

It is under these circumstances, the NCCF through its consultancy and promotional cell deviced an accounting system which would upgrade the quality of the existing accounting system besides assisting the management in the decision making process. The system so promoted was known popularly as management accounting system. The Wholesale store at Dindigul in Tamil Nadu is one of the 29 stores in the state which adopted the MAS in the year 184. It was believed at that time that it would bring revolutionary changes in the accounting and management planning and control practices of the stores. Almost two decades have passed since. Whether the stores, have gained anything out of MAS? Has the store in a position to adjust to the requirements of MAS? To find answer to these questions a detailed study was conducted and the results are presented in the subsequent paragraphs. The responsibility of writing the Day Book, the only book of original entry was entrusted entirely with an individual accountant, which is not an easy task given the volumes of business. This resulted in non-completion of account books in time, leading to inordinate delays in finalization of accounts and thereby of audit of the accounts. Thus, the Stores failed to organize itself properly and the way in which the system was practiced and made the accounting system least useful in matters of decision-making.

The accountant and accounting assistants by themselves, found it very difficult to prepare the financial statements. The final accounts and the balance sheet were, therefore, prepared by the department auditors. This resulted in delay of finalizing the accounts and completion of final audit. As a result, right information could not be passed on to the management and to other authorities at the appropriate time. Therefore, the decision-making authorities had to rely more on individuals and intuitive measures/judgments in taking business decisions.

In the absence of properly organized accounting system, the Stores on many occasions, lost opportunities of using an important source of information called internal accounting, which led to: (i) loss of control over cash and inventories in the godown and its branches; (ii) mounting time-bared stock and stock deficit; (iii) delay in finalisation of accounts and completion of audit; (iv) continuous loss; and (v) loss of image and goodwill among the members and the non-member customers.

ADVENT OF MANAGEMENT ACCOUNTING SYSTEM

Management Accounting System (MAS), as advised by the Consultancy and Promotional Cell (CPC) of the National Cooperative Consumers Federation (NCCF), was introduced in the year 1984 with the following objectives:

(i) overcoming the inadequacies in the existing accounting system;

(ii) providing necessary internal check and controls;

(iii) ensuring uniformity by standardizing books, forms and procedures;

(iv) setting out in clear terms the exact method of operation; and

(v) providing adequate management information for planning and control.

Thus the MAS introduced in Stores aimed at effecting task control as well as internal control, besides brining in uniformity in the accounting system.

THE CURRENT STATUS OF FINANCIAL ACCOUNTING

Management Accounting System (MAS) has been introduced in order to overcome the defects, drawbacks and inadequacies in the existing system and making the financial accounting simple, clear, easy to handle, refer and interpret. The major purpose of MAS is to equip the executive of the stores with the necessary information to perform the decision-making most effectively and to assess the performance of the stores.

The first step towards the adoption of a standard plan of accounts, is to decide the procedure under which accounts are grouped and codifield. Codification is based on three digits. The first digit stands for Main Group; the second one stands for Main Head; and the last one for practical Head. This would help the store to ensure systematic preparation and presentation of accounts. The consultancy and promotion cell of national consumer cooperation federation has given the plan of action taking into account the possibilities of computerization of accounting system in consumer cooperatives in future.

Secondly, the stores has developed and introduced an improved form of primary records like cash and credit sales summary which facilities classification of sales by commodity group and tax-category-wise. Salesmen's Daily Statement, which is a summary of daily cash transactions, and stock liability balance of sales staff have also been introduced as part of the MAS.

Salesmen's Daily Statement is prepared in duplicate. The original copy of the Daily Statement, along with sales summaries, bills and supporting documents for receipts and payments of cash, is furnished daily by salesmen. Based on this statement, the cashier accepts remittance and acknowledges receipts of cash. The cashier makes an endorsement of the amount received in the original copy of the Daily Statement, enters the amount in the scroll and then passes on the Daily Statements to the accounts section for making entry in the Day Book. In the accounts section, sales summaries are scrutinized and tabulated commodity groupwise before entering them in the Day Book. In the case of purchases, purchase invoices/bills received are entered in the Invoice Control Register. The Stores-in-charge who receives the invoice and the goods has to compare and verify the invoice with the copy of the purchase order with him, note the variations, if any, verify the stocks received and certify the correctness of stock in the Control Form. Stock Control Form is prepared in duplicate, one copy for the godown and the other for the accounts section. The Purchase Department fills up the Stock Control Form initially to enable the Godown Keeper to certify and enter the particulars of stock received with its sales price. The account section receives the Stock Control Form with the purchase invoice and a copy of the purchase order. These are checked before making entries in the Purchase Book.

It must be noted that sales summaries and Salesmen's Daily Statement are submitted every day. Hence, entries are made without delay. On the contrary, submission of Stock Control Form, with the purchase invoice and order by purchase department takes 10 to 15 days and, consequently entries cannot be made in the Purchase Book in time.

Thirdly, sub-day books for sales, bank, sundry creditors other than societies, societies' credit sales, employees' advance, stock shortage recoverable, income, operational expenses, non-operational expenses, suppliers etc. are maintained. Their totals are incorporated in the Day Book.

Fourthly, Columnar Day Book is introduced. Accounts which have frequent transactions have separate columns in the Day Book, such as sales, bank, customers, income, suppliers, trade charges, and expenditure. A common column is provided for other accounts which have frequent entries. The columnar division of the day book is to classify and group transactions and to summarize them at the end of the month for monthly posting in the General Ledger. Columns are also provided for noting account code number to facilitate summarizing and posting in the ledger accounts. Totals of the concerned column in the Day Book are posted monthly in the General Ledger. The sub day books carry detailed classification of accounts. Based on the Ledger totals, Receipts and Disbursement Statement is prepared every month.

Fifthly, the accounts section has been reorganized. Duties, functions and responsibilities are specified. This has been done on the instructions of the Registrar of Cooperative Societies. Citing want of organization in the accounts sections as the main cause for delay in finalization of accounts division of wholesale stores in Tamil Nadu (see Fig. C1.3). The Stores in Tamil Nadu were asked to choose any one of the three, depending on their volume of business. The Registrar also suggested that the tendency to depend upon the departmental personnel to write the accounts should be gradually reduced and the employees of the Stores should be motivated and encouraged to write the accounts with enthusiasm. Based on the suggestions the Stores has reorganized its accounting division.

Figure
Organization Structure of Accounting Division in Cooperative Stores as Suggested by the Registrar of Cooperatives

Option 1	*Option 2*	*Option 3*
Account Officer	Accounts Officer	Chief Accounts Officer
Accountant	Assistant Accounts Officer	Accounts Officer
Assistant Accountant	Accountant	Assistant Accounts Officer
Supporting Accounting Personnel	Assistant Accountants	Accountants
	Supporting Accounting Personnel	Supporting Accounting Personnel

Sixthly, the Stores follow an action programme for speedy and effective completion of accounts. The action programme fixed deadlines for completion of various accounts like purchase, sales, cash, imprest, stock liability control account, operational and non-operational expenses account, statement of receipts and disbursements, valuation of stock, final account, and the balance sheet. As per the action programme, accounts should be finalized by the end of April every year. Reorganisation of financial accounting system has brought in several advantages. They are:

- Integration of physical and financial accounting and thereby better control over the functions of the Stores.
- Complete control is established over cash receipts and payments.
- Final accounts can be completed on time.
- Dependence on departmental personnel to write the accounts is reduced to a certain extent.

- Information could be provided easily and quickly.
- Confusion in understanding the accounting information is avoided.
- Branch-wise accounts could be obtained.
- Classification of sales helps a great deal in inventory control and purchase planning. Credit sales are controlled. Receivables are easily collected. Bad debts are avoided.

In a nutshell, it could be stated that the induction of new books has brought clarity to the accounting system and that it has also facilitated optimum utilization of the available human resources.

However, there are still certain loopholes which need to be plugged. No doubt, the Stores has succeeded in controlling stock at its branches; but it is yet to ensure control of stock at the godown, from where the goods are lifted to the branches. In the godown, it is understood, stocks are controlled on unit basis and in the branches the stock is controlled on liability basis. In the godown, though it is insisted upon under the MAS, the stocks are not controlled on liability basis since the godown keeper's work load increases considerably in the event of maintaining both unit and liability system of stock control. Godown keepers are to be charged with all purchases at resale price in the purchase book. Monthly total of goods purchased at resale price is to be debited to the godown keeper's stock liability account. This has not been practiced for the reason that since the goods are unloaded at any time of day or night and, several godown keepers have to work in shifts, since a single godown-keeper cannot be present all the time to receive the goods, and in the circumstances liability cannot be fixed on one godown-keeper. Further, goods, especially the controlled goods, are directly sent to the retail outlets and only the invoices are sent to the godown-keeper. Under such circumstances the godown-keeper has to assume that goods have been unloaded at the godown and then delivered to the retail outlets. This system prevents the implementation of stock liability control account effectively.

Despite the measures taken by the Registrar and by the NCCF in designing the MAS, the Stores has been unable to introduce the system properly and has not produced the desired result because of the faulty approach followed in the implementation of the system. The system designed should have been introduced with reorganization of duties and responsibilities based on responsibility centre accounting. But the Stores found it very difficult to reorganize because of the existing arrangements relating to buying, selling, storage and decision-making practices. Decisions were made at the top level, based on the advice of the Registrar of Cooperatives. Information from accounting sources was hardly found useful by the staff for internal management. It was found useful only to the Special Officer and to the Registrar of Cooperatives.

Secondly, the system is comprehensible only to people with high intellectual caliber. The personnel in the accounting section do not have adequate exposure even to the simple principles of management accounting, and hence they lack interest in the system. Moreover, the system has been thrust upon the Stores all of a sudden without being accompanied by modern equipment like computers, adequate training and orientation to personnel and clear-cut demarcation of duties and responsibilities of the personnel in the Stores. Had it been introduced in a phased manner along with the above-said factors, the Stores would have put it in practice and made use of it in the day-to-day operations of the organization.

Figure 1
Organizational Structure of the Cooperative Wholesale Stores Limited

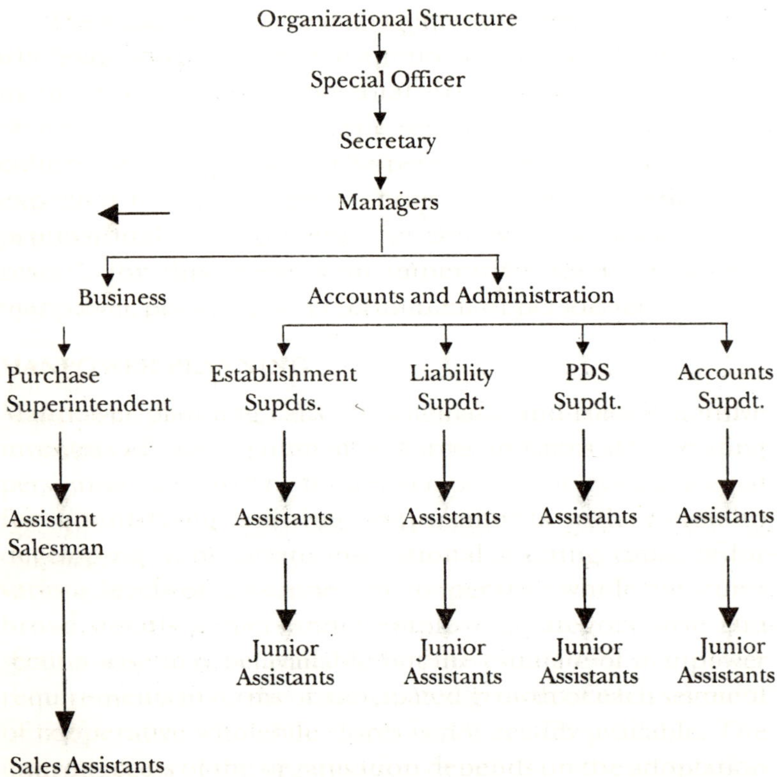

Figure 2
Organizational Structure of Accounts Department of the Wholesale Stores

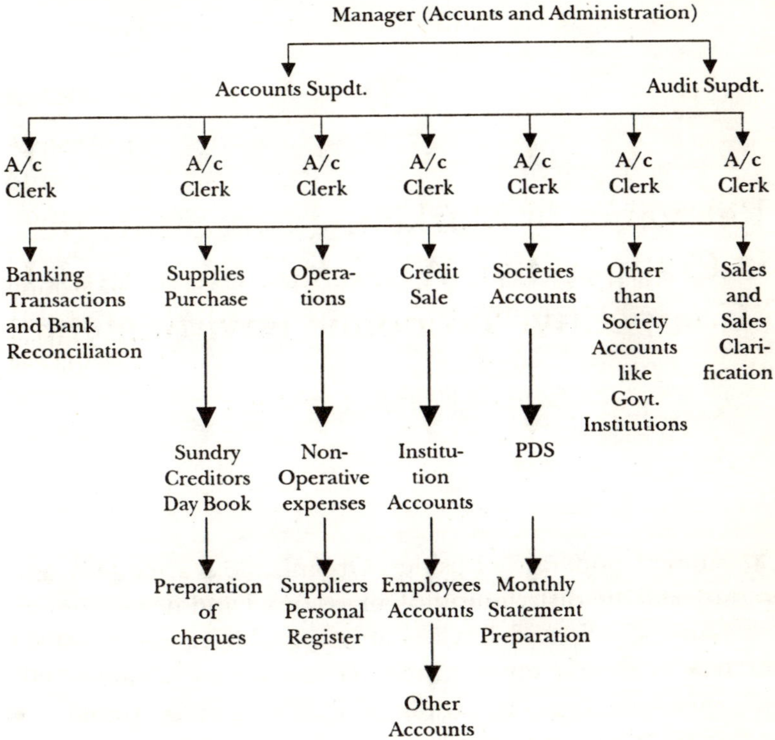

20

Relevance of Marketing Mix Strategies in Co-operative Wholesale Store under Competitive Economic Environment

Samuel Kakuko Lopoteum

Consumer Cooperative Business Organizations are significant in undertaking distribution of all essential and non-essential consumer goods and services at reasonable prices. Even in the new economic environment, consumer cooperatives are still ensuring regular supply of quality goods, supply of original, pure and unadulterated goods. They engage themselves in the purchase of bulk articles of domestic consumption and sell them in wholesale and retail, purchase or hire processing plants for the purpose of processing or manufacturing goods into a state fit for consumption or use, act as agent of government and/or cooperative societies to procure and stock food-grains and other commodities, sell processed or manufactured goods to affiliated primary stores at wholesale rates, to undertake retail distribution of goods purchased, processed or manufactured by it, to open branches and supermarket for retail distribution at suitable locations within the area of operation. The overall business performance of CWSs is more or less remained weak and stagnant. Infact, large numbers of factors have contributed-non-performance in their growth and development of consumer cooperatives. The four tier structure of consumer cooperatives in the country (primary consumer cooperatives, wholesale/central stores, State Federation and NCCF) are not making adequate profit. Infact, it is disheartening that, about 50 % of the consumer cooperative societies have been incurring losses.

They continuously sustain losses on account of: borrowing funds at high cost for their business operations which ultimately affect their economic viability, prevalence of competition with other cooperative outlets, high cost of distribution, outdated facilities and equipments, lack of training and motivation, weak distribution network, obsolete technology, the low level of margin available, low employee morale, high unit cost relative to competitors, entry of low cost foreign competition and products of low prices, entry of substitute products and management by non-professionals leading to mismanagement.

In the new competitive economic environment, consumer cooperatives have greater role and responsibility to ensure their survivability, profitability, productivity, economic viability and sustainability. It must cater to the changing needs of the consumers, buyers and economically weaker sections of the society. The changed economic environment has created enormous challenges and threats to the consumer cooperatives, therefore, there must be paradigm shift in the New Competitive Economic Environment.

Accordingly, what is needed right now is the adoption of better marketing mix strategies and other business diversification strategies to be implemented by the consumer cooperative organizations to face the New Competitive Economic Environment. The LPGs have greater impact in the sense that national and international private organizations have now entered and expanded into rural markets, full load of planes and ships of consumer products are coming from abroad (FMCGs), withdrawal of subsidies by government, poor sections of the society can not afford exorbitant prices, high pressure of advertisement, propaganda and publicity, changing preferences of consumers and the daily increase of cut-throat competition. The marketing mix strategies and other essential support strategies are completely discussed in this paper in terms of (i) price, (ii) product, (iii) promotion, (iv) Place (Distribution), (v) People (Power), (vi) Total quality management and (vii) Joint venture and collaboration, (viii) Promotion of inter-CWS's products and business (ix) use of cost-effective methods (packaging and labeling) (x) use of product diversification strategies (xi)inculcating the culture of professionalism and up-gradation of human resources (manpower) development management (xii) implementation of internal checks and controls (xiii) use of Information and Communication Technology and (xiv) setting up of quality testing laboratory.

It is highly essential to prevent ever mounting financial losses in cooperative Whole Sale Stores by adopting the best marketing mix strategies. In this research paper, the best strategy is simply defined as the best operational plan of action to achieve the specified objective under competitive circumstances (herein referred to as New Competitive Economic Environment, Economic Liberalization, Open Market Economy, Global Market, and Globalization of Trade and Business Process). Moreover, strategies are dynamic and subject to modification to suit the prevailing new economic environment. By adopting the best marketing strategies, the CWS's can insulate themselves from strong competitive pressures, gain superior image and reputation, avoid poor market image, remove outdated equipments and facilities and attain better strategic directions, etc. Some of the cooperative wholesale stores are undertaking diversified business activities such as provision of fruits and vegetables, liquor, drugs, petroleum products, textbooks and notebooks, grocery, cosmetics, rice, oil, crackers, spirit, controlled commodities, household goods. The self-service counters are air conditioned and computers are being used for preparation of cash bills. Eventually, there is imperative need for the overall revival and complete rehabilitation of Cooperative Wholesale Stores in the new competitive economic environment.

PRICING SYSTEM

Most of the CWSs are following the active price policy which means that they are charging a lower price in market only and in such a way that it can not permit resale of the same product/commodities. This concept must be understood by the management of the consumer wholesale stores so that they hold the price line.

It is essential that the interest of the potential buyers is maintained eventually, which would encourage impulse buying to the greatest extent possible in order to succeed in the open market economic system.

CWSs must also promote retail marketing system. And a formal contractual relationship would ensure discipline in the functing between federation, CWS, and members' cooperatives.

There are unfavourable costs, due to insufficient market demands for their products within the cooperative movements.

In order to serve in the open market economic system, CWSs can mingle with private wholesales as dictated by the prevailing market environment.

NEED FOR INTEGRATION WITH PRODUCER COOPERATIVES

Consumers must enter into contractual relations with the producer cooperatives. There is full potential and this has even remained unexploited. The CWSs can think in terms of adopting the joint venture and linking business relationship on contractual basis between consumer cooperative with the marketing cooperatives.

They can engage themselves on the basis of business Industrial cooperative which is mutually advantageous to both the cooperative business organizations.

Hence, cooperation among cooperatives on the basis of cost and efficiency shall be the main destiny for Joint-Business Operation. Even weavers cooperatives and industrial cooperative producing consumers products can be co-opted and this would lead to mutual growth and development of the cooperative sector. Also the cost, quality, and consumer preference must be considered while undertaking such type of collaboration and cooperation.

FACTORS CONTRIBUTING PURCHASING COSTS IN CWSS

It is essential and imperative to find out the areas of inefficiency and waste to enable the management to take corrective action in time, also, there is need to install the purchase management all of which is dynamic to face the new economic environment.

There is need to use value analysis of purchases and other cost reduction techniques to make savings in all the business transactions and operations.

This is even better than price analysis because it aims at minimizing cost and it takes into consideration alternative possibility such as the quality and quantity sources, while pursuing decisions. Similarly, it is essential to get maximum value of goods required at the point of purchase.

RIGHT QUALITY

The Managers of CWSs must understand and know that right quality means, the best quality for a purpose and having regard to suitability and cost consciousness while dealing with the products to be sold to the customers.

- It should be economical and customer-oriented and need not pay premium price for quality in excess of his needs or requirements.

- It must have reasonable lead time.
- It must have customer patronage.
- It deals with all assortment of goods.
- It must always meet the needs of different income groups

STRATEGY OF BUSINESS DIVERSIFICATION

- It must, side by side, diversify their business operations from time to time.
- India is a developing country experiencing shortages of many essential commodities, hence they must diversify their business operations.
- The danger of selling sub-standard, adulterated goods, must be completely avoided. Hence, the managers of CWSs must be careful in managing the cooperative affairs
- The CWCs managers must provide check of malpractices and shortages and adulteration of the goods/products on moral and ethical grounds.

TOTAL QUALITY POLICY AND GOVERNANCE

- To bring business unity within the CWCs
- Implementation of quality related programmes such as ISO, HACCP(Hazard Analysis on Critical Control Points), Integrated Agricultural Sanitary and Phyto-sanitary measures (IA PSM), are essential for the modern CWCs to facilitate competition in the new competitive economic environment.
- To meet the challenges of WTO, it is essential for the CWC's to adopt the total quality policy management and governance.

21

Marketing Strategy for Consumer Cooperatives

K. Selvarani and P. Pirakatheeswari

Consumer cooperatives are voluntary organizations formed and managed by consumers themselves. These cooperatives are organized for procuring the consumer goods in bulk from the production centers and then distributing equitably to the members at fair price. Members of the consumer cooperatives fulfill their requirements by themselves and enjoy the benefits of trading through collective action. The consumer cooperatives with their activities, in connection with the masses have got recognition for ensuring availability of consumer goods at affordable prices, developing fair trade practices, creating employment opportunities to the local people and educating the consumers of their rights and privileges under the Consumer Protection Act. To fulfill these objectives, the consumer cooperatives should frame strategies in such a way to satisfy both the groups i.e. producers and consumers.

As far as marketing is concerned, the consumer cooperative sector registers rather a slow progress vis-à-vis the private sector. There is no marketing strategy adopted in consumer cooperatives to increase the sale of their products, which in turn influences the production and marketing. Besides being a weaker organization, the cooperative institution do not adopt modern marketing techniques.

OBJECTIVES OF MARKETING STRATEGY

The consumer cooperatives' foremost objective is to render best possible services by buying consumer articles wholesale and distribute them to members, thus replacing, as far as possible, the middlemen and divert the profit to the consumer members. A consumer cooperative aims to satisfy the needs of its members more economically than is done by private individuals and institutions. It sells generally for cash and leaves the customer free to demand quality stocks, reasonable prices and correct weightment or measurement. On the other hand, private shopkeepers deliberately encourage credit/debt and ultimately enslave the consumer. Profit making is a secondary aspect. To ensure effective services, the consumer cooperatives should try hard and evolve a suitable strategy with regard to production and marketing. The consumer cooperative at once acts as producer and seller, so it has to take care of the marketing aspect in right sense.

PRODUCT STRATEGIES

For survival and growth, the consumer cooperatives should frame an effective product strategies in such a way to appeal the consumers to go after the cooperative products. Product strategy guidelines are needed for changing the existing products, adding new ones and decisions are also needed regarding branding, packaging, colour and other product features to satisfy the consumer. The consumer expects that the quality of the product he buys will not only be uniform and consistent but will also have an improvement in quality over time. Consumer cooperatives must have adequate capital to maintain stock.

Consumer cooperatives have to change their product mix to remain active in the market. Consumer cooperatives can include durable consumer goods like T.V, Mixie, Refrigerator, etc according to market requirement. All the consumer cooperatives should also enter the market of durable goods, where there is a vast scope for consumer cooperatives. The traditional products like Pickle, Pappad, soap, Masala Powder, Agar Patti, Herbal Powder, etc have good market in foreign countries. The consumer cooperatives should encourage such types of products that may attract foreign customers because of their taste and tradition.

PRICING STRATEGY

Pricing plays a dominant role in the market. The main aim of consumer cooperatives is to sell the products at a reasonable price to the consumers. Usually consumer cooperatives fix up the price of their products on cost plus margin basis. The consumer cooperatives should be very careful in calculating the cost and margin and try to fix the price lower than their counterparts.

Consumer cooperatives should ensure production of only saleable varieties. The market and the products should be identified, which suit the consumers and fix the price according to each segment of the market. The price of a particular consumer product (variety) should not vary from one society to other. All the societies in the state should fix a uniform price for all varieties.

PHYSICAL DISTRIBUTION

The consumer cooperatives, at present have dealers, retailers and their own retail show room. The primary societies are expected to supply around 50% of their total production to the apex body and the apex body sells it through their retail outlets. This system widens the gap between the producers and consumers and it encourages competition among the consumer cooperatives. This has to be changed to stop the competition.

There is a wide range of price spread between the producers and consumers due to the intervention of middlemen in the name of whole seller. The consumer cooperatives should try to sell their products directly to the consumers to eliminate the middleman in order to get better margins.

PROMOTION STRATEGY

Under the present market conditions, the consumer cooperatives should undertake sales promotional activities seriously for their survival. The following promotional strategies should be framed to increase the sales volume of the cooperatives.

- It has been found that lack of salesmanship is a prime factor for low sales volume of cooperatives. Hence, it is imperative that the sales staff are to be trained in latest sales techniques and business tactics. This will help in clearing all stocks in time.
- To get an idea about the taste and demands of the customers as well as the position of their competitors, the consumer cooperatives should conduct annual surveys.
- It has been experienced that the sales outlets of consumer cooperatives are not in good shape and customers are not easily attracted. So the consumer cooperatives should display the products in such a way to attract the customers. Proper display of products will certainly boost the sales of consumer cooperatives.
- Consumer cooperatives go for massive and nation wide publicity campaign for the consumer products and the government should also come forward to help the cooperatives in this regard. This will promote the sales of cooperatives.

It has been discussed in detail the need for marketing strategy in consumer cooperatives, but mere formulation of strategy will not produce a good result unless, it is implemented in a right manner. The result of strategy can be evaluated with the two aspects viz. increase in sales and production and the success of consumer cooperatives. This will indicate that the consumer cooperatives are going in right direction.

22

Supply Chain Management Applications to Cooperative Wholesale Stores

A. Abdul Rahman

COOPERATIVE WHOLESALE STORES

The Cooperative Wholesale Stores are engaged in the distribution and sale of controlled commodities and purchase and sale of non-controlled commodities. The cooperative wholesale stores are at the district level, which sell the commodities to the consumers. The structure of Consumer Cooperatives in Tamil Nadu continues to be a three tier one with the Tamil Nadu Consumer Cooperative Federation at the apex level, 35 Cooperative Wholesale Stores including 2955 Students' Cooperative Stores at the base level [CFCP Policy Note Page 2005]. As a policy, the Government of India has been encouraging the development of consumer Cooperatives so as to protect the interests of the common consumer in the country. Consumer Cooperatives have playing a significant role in the distribution of consumer goods, particularly supply of essential consumer items at fair prices to the rural community, especially in the remote, inaccessible and hilly areas. The objective of the consumer cooperatives has been to eliminate the middlemen and to protect the interest of the consumers. They have no profit motive as they buy goods in bulk from wholesalers and sell them at reasonable prices. Consumer cooperatives have received a good deal of support from the Government, as they help to check rise in prices of consumer goods (www.tn.gov.in/consumer).

PERFORMANCE OF CONSUMER COOPERATIVES

There are 709 wholesale stores with 430 department stores and 5124 other types of branches. The total membership of such stores is 21.21 lacks, comprising 18.38 lacks individuals, 39716 consumer cooperatives and 0.40 lacks other institutions and/or Government. The total sales turnover achieved was Rs. 21527.63 millions, which includes sales of controlled commodities amounting to Rs. 12295.87 millions during 2003-2004. The setting up of big Department Stores by consumer cooperatives have, however, not kept pace with the rapid urbanization and mex the growing needs of the urban population. There is a crying need for setting up of more such Department Stores.

In both the rural and urban areas, the primary consumer cooperative stores play a vital role in serving the consumers as well as their members. Some of the consumer cooperative stores organized by the employees of large undertakings/ business houses are well-managed institutions. As per the information furnished by the respective the Registrars of Cooperatives Societies of the States/Union territories, the total number of primary stores in the country is 23173. Of these 8318 primary stores were in profit, 7471 stores in loss, 2528 primary stores were either defunct or under liquidation while 1490 stores were working on no profits or no loss. Information regarding the remaining 3366 stores is not available. The sales and turnover of these primary stores was Rs18200.38 millions of which sales worth Rs. 11717.89 millions was of controlled items. Profit earning consumer cooperatives are proportionate only 35.98 per cent. Nearly eleven per cent consumer cooperatives are defunct, 6.42 per cent consumer cooperatives have incurred loss and 14.52 per cent consumer stores are not duing well. The sales turnover also is very poor among these consumer cooperatives. The poor sales performance may be due to the lack of professional management capability of the sales persons. Application of supply chain management may improve the sales performance since the supply chain process has the ways and means for making good sales.

APPLICATION OF SUPPLY CHAIN MANAGEMENT IN COOPERATIVE WHOLESALE STROES

A supply chain is the stream of processes of moving goods from the customer order through the raw materials stage, supply, production, and distribution of products to the customers. All organizations have supply chains of varying degrees, depending upon the size of the organization and the type of product manufactured. These networks obtain supplies and components, change these materials into finished products and then distribute them to the customers. Managing the chain of events in this process is what is known as supply chain management. Effective management must take into account coordinating all the different links of this chain as quickly as possible without losing any of the quality or customer satisfaction, while still keeping costs down.

APPLICATIONS

The first step is obtaining a customer order, followed by production, storage and distribution of products and supplies to the customer site. Customer satisfaction is paramount importance. Included in this supply chain process are customer orders, order processing, inventory, scheduling, transportation, storage, and customer service. A necessity in coordinating all these activities is the information service network.

In addition, key to the success of a supply chain is the speed in which these activities can be accomplished and the realization that customer needs and customer satisfaction are the very reasons for the network. Reduced inventories, lower operating costs, product availability and customer satisfaction are all benefits which grow out of the effective supply chain management.

The decisions associated with supply chain management cover both the long-term and short-term. Strategic decisions deal with corporate policies, and look at overall design and supply chain structure. Operational decisions are those dealing with every day activities and problems of an organization. These decisions must take into account the strategic decisions already in place. Therefore, an organization must structure the supply chain through long-term analysis and at the same time focus on the day-to-day activities.

Furthermore, market demands, customer service, transport considerations, and pricing constraints all must be understood in order to structure the supply chain effectively. These are all factors, which change constantly and sometimes unexpectedly, and an organization must realize this fact and be prepared to structure the supply chain accordingly.

Structuring the supply chain requires an understanding of the demand patterns, service level requirements, distance considerations, cost elements and other related factors. It is easy to see that these factors are highly variable in nature and this variability needs to be considered during the supply chain analysis process. Moreover, the interplay of these complex considerations could have a significant bearing on the outcome of the supply chain analysis process.

There are six key elements to a supply chain:

- Production
- Supply

- Inventory
- Location
- Transportation, and
- Information

The following describes each of the elements:

Production

Strategic decisions regarding production focus on what customers want and the market demands. This first stage in developing supply chain ability takes into consideration what and how many products to produce, and what, if any, parts or components should be produced at which plants or outsourced to capable suppliers. These strategic decisions regarding production must also focus on capacity, quality and volume of goods, keeping in mind that customer demand and satisfaction must be met. Operational decisions, on the other hand, focus on scheduling workloads, maintenance of equipment and meeting immediate client/ market demands. Quality control and workload balancing are issues which need to be considered when making these decisions.

Supply

Next, an organization must determine what their facility or facilities are able to produce, both economically and efficiently, while keeping the quality high. But most companies cannot provide excellent performance with the manufacture of all components. Outsourcing is an excellent alternative to be considered for those products and components that cannot be produced effectively by an organization's facilities. Companies must carefully select suppliers of raw materials. When choosing a supplier, focus should be on developing velocity, quality and flexibility while at the same time reducing costs or maintaining low cost levels. In short, strategic decisions should be made to determine the core capabilities of a facility and outsourcing partnerships should grow from these decisions.

Inventory

Further strategic decisions focus on inventory and how much product should be in-house. A delicate balance exists between too much inventory, which can cost anywhere between 20 and 40 per cent of their value, and not enough inventory to meet market demands. This is a critical issue in effective supply chain management. Operational inventory decisions revolve around optimal levels of stock at each location to ensure customer satisfaction as the market demands fluctuate. Control policies must be looked at to determine correct levels of supplies at order and reorder points. These levels are critical to the day to day operation of organizations and to keep customer satisfaction levels high.

Location

Location decisions depend on market demands and determination of customer satisfaction. Strategic decisions must focus on the placement of production plants, distribution and stocking facilities, and placing them in prime locations to the markets served. Once customer markets are determined, long-term commitment must be made to locate production and stocking facilities as close to the consumer as is practical. In industries where components are lightweight and market-driven, facilities should be located close to the end-user. In heavier industries, careful consideration must be made to determine where plants should be located so as to be close to the raw material source. Decisions concerning location should also take into consideration tax and tariff issues, especially in inter-state and worldwide distribution.

Transportation

Strategic transportation decisions are closely related to

inventory decisions as well as meeting customer demands. Using air transport obviously gets the product out quicker and to the customer expediently, but the costs are high as opposed to shipping by boat or rail. Yet using sea or rail often times means having higher levels of inventory in-house to meet quick demands by the customer. It is wise to keep in mind that since 30% of the cost of a product is encompassed by transportation, using the correct transport mode is a critical strategic decision. Above all, customer service levels must be met, and this often times determines the mode of transport used. Often times this may be an operational decision, but strategically, an organization must have transport modes in place to ensure a smooth distribution of goods.

Information

Effective supply chain management requires obtaining information from the point of end-use, and linking information resources throughout the chain for speedy exchange. Overwhelming paper flow and disparate computer systems are unacceptable in today's competitive world. Fostering innovation requires good organization of information. Linking computers through networks and the internet, and streamlining the information flow, consolidates knowledge and facilitates velocity of products. Account management software, product configurators, enterprise resource planning systems, and global communications are key components of effective supply chain management strategy.

THE ISSUES

The supply chain has also been called the value chain and the service chain, depending on the "fad of the moment", or sometimes, we think, the weather, or sun spot activity. Just like anything else, supply chain management is no panacea, nor should it be embraced as a religion. It is an operational strategy that, if implemented properly, will provide a new dimension to competing: quickly introducing new customerized high quality products and delivering them with unprecedented lead times, swift decisions, and manufacturing products with high velocity. The wholesale/consumer cooperatives will succeed and earn profit if their officials are trained in supply chain management.

23

Need for Strengthening the Managerial Excellence in Cooperative Wholesale Stores

A. Xavior Selvakumar and C.P. Jayaseelan

INTRODUCTION

The cooperative wholesale stores have been playing a vital role in the distribution of essential consumer goods at reasonable prices. Management of cooperative wholesale stores has to be based on certain guiding principles, ethos and values. If a cooperative wholesale stores runs successfully and achieves the optimum output from the services, the members, the managing committee and the employees are required to be brought under a discipline of cooperative culture and management excellence. They must cultivate basic ingredients of human qualities in themselves to imbibe and to develop a sense of honesty and selflessness. At present, there are 1156 cooperative wholesale stores functioning throughout our country.

The cooperative wholesale stores is more distinct in its management structure than other enterprises management structure. It is composed of two elements namely, it belongs to all its members individually and equally and the members pay for the entire costs of operation of the cooperative according to their patronage in the stores. Cooperative wholesale stores soley depends on the introduction of management techniques at all levels of its operations. Today management excellence holds an important place in the marketing network.

MANAGEMENT COMMITTEE

The management committee is the highest elected executive institution in the cooperative wholesale stores. Everything done in the cooperative must be approved by the management committee. Generally speaking, members of this committee are not paid for their services, and the time they devote to meetings is limited. This committee should nourish and nurture the following qualities of cooperative philosophy to bring management excellence and success to their mission.

- Confidence in approach
- Orderlines in activity
- Outspokenness against irregularities
- Potentiality in imparting authority or execution
- Expressiveness of ideas and views
- Resourcefulness in thinking and working
- Accommodative in nature under an environment of diversified attitudes and approaches
- Tactfulness in handling crisis
- Inquisitiveness for knowing problems
- Vigorousness in mind to accept challenges and competitiveness
- Effectiveness in planning and execution.

Members of the management committee are "blind" in the sense that they depend entirely on the manager for the submission and explanation of issues. The Management has a global responsibility for all acts of the cooperative though there may not always be an immediately discernable connection. It must decide on the executive acts of the manager and bears responsibility for the successes and failures of that official.

STRENGTHENING OF MANAGEMENT EXCELLENCE

Due to the socio-economic consequences of the implementation of economic reforms, the cooperative wholesale stores have to work out its strategy to develop competitive framework to compete nationally and globally in the liberal economic environment and to neutralise the social costs in terms of increase in poverty levels and reduction in employment opportunities. Keeping this view, it is necessary to examine the role of value-based management in the growth and development. The cooperative wholesale stores leaders and officials have to balance their profits motive with the promotion of welfare of their members. In this context, the question of value based professional management in wholesale stores comes to the forefront.

In Tamil Nadu, many cooperative wholesale stores have tended to implement the cooperative values paradigm through their own developmental efforts. They have demonstrated a remarkable capacity in terms of caring for the development of rural areas through the infrastructural facilities. In this process, the cooperative wholesale stores have reflected a great sense of social responsibility, a phenomenon which is rarely found in the functioning of private sector enterprises. The crucial issue before the cooperative wholesale stores in India specially in Tamil Nadu at present is the implementation of value-based system for guiding the consumer cooperative movement in their business policy and in the day-to-day functioning.

NCUI ACTION PLAN

The National Cooperative Union of India (NCUI) worked out an Action Plan for Actualisation of Cooperative Identity which was placed before the 13th Indian Cooperative Congress held in New Delhi in January 1997. This action plan envisages that each cooperative society should lay down responsibility norms for its members. The issue relating to professionalisation of management, members and workforce was also discussed at the 14th Indian Cooperative congress held in September 2001. It was recommended at this Congress that NCUI and National Council for Cooperative Training (NCCT) should take into account training needs of different sectors of cooperatives in the context of changing economic environment and lay special emphasis on promoting modern management practices and information technology at various levels of cooperative fold especially cooperative wholesale stores.

Efforts are being made by cooperative wholesale stores officials to promote professionalism in cooperative management for excellence among cooperative personnel. If the managerial personnel of the cooperative wholesale stores are efficient and are professionally competent, the goals of cooperative organisations would be achieved quickly with a minimum cost. The wholesale stores managers/officials, however have to be clear about their role, perception and freedom of operations. This scenario implies that various cooperative organisations have to formulate their personnel management policies keeping in view the overall objectives and long term perception. There has to be cooperation among cooperatives with emphasis on organisational discipline with the structure of cooperative movement. Management excellence should be strengthened to four important areas like MIS & IT, human resource development and cooperative leaders.

MANAGEMENT INFORMATION SYSTEM AND INFORMATION TECHNOLOGY

Efforts are being made to develop an effective management information system along with information technology for the use of the Board of Directors and members of the wholesale stores; also for opinion builders and policy makers. It is agreed that access to updated latest information about the functioning of the national economy and the various segments of the cooperative wholesale stores for the management and members would facilitate quick and well thought-out decisions which can stand in good stead for the growth, prosperity and management excellence in cooperative wholesale stores.

HUMAN RESOURCE DEVELOPMENT

It has been observed that in many segments of cooperative wholesale stores, human resource development policies and practices are oriented towards out-dated Government system. For bringing about management excellence in wholesale stores, there is an urgent need to review and strengthen the existing personnel management policies within the wholesale store and through this process evolve suitable parameters for bringing about management excellence. The selection of parameters would be in tune with the local conditions along with promotion of modern management practices and information technology. This is likely to create a conducive environment for the entry of professionals and experts into the cooperative wholesale stores. For brining about over-all management excellence in cooperative wholesale stores, promotion of leadership development programme is essential and should be strengthening an integral part of human resource development strategy within the overall plan of growth and development of cooperative wholesale stores.

The leadership training programme should aim at developing certain attributes needed for effective leadership. The following leadership development programmes must strengthen management excellence competencies.

1. Management of attention : ability of leaders to listen to others.
2. Management of meaning : ability of leaders to communicate meaningfully.

3. Management of thrust : getting wholesays acceptance of their role by the followers.
4. Management of employees/staff : effectively and efficiently
5. Always ready to look for challenges and having the capacity to face them.

COOPERATIVE LEADERS

Presently, the management excellence in cooperative wholesale stores while implementing the cooperative principles, values and ethos is at cross-roads. One of the objectives of wholesale stores is promotion of welfare of their members. While promoting the welfare of their members, the business may not maximise their profits and as such, they may not distribute sufficient amount as dividend to the member constituents. The cooperative leaders have to balance their profit motive with the promotion of welfare of their members. For ensuring management excellence in cooperative wholesale stores, the cooperative leaders have to ensure the following activities:

- Review of existing activities being undertaken in the organisation.
- Examination of the expansion potential of the activity concerned.
- Decisions regarding goals for each input or group of inputs going into the cooperative system.
- Working out norms for ensuring work effectiveness, efficiency and excellence.
- Evaluation of the process of various activities being undertaken in the organisation.
- Comparison of the management excellence achieved vis-a-vis the goals set up at the initial stage.

CONCLUSION

Cooperative wholesale stores have come to occupy a significant place in our distribution system. To compete with the private traders, the stores must enhance their quality of service by applying scientific management principles for the excellence of management. Management excellence in cooperative wholesale stores should aim at improving service quality and delivery and making serious efforts in adopting service quality initiatives, information technology initiatives and partnership initiatives. They should develop a vision to incorporate quality with cost reduction and consumer focus and launch quality initiatives.

If introducing new projects and programmes, the management of consumer cooperative wholesale stores should pay adequate attention to project planning, monitoring and budget allocations for proper implementation. Therefore, cooperative wholesale stores should strengthen the management excellence to obtain maximum functional efficiency backed by professional management and skilled workforce. This is the need of the hour.

24

Human Resource Management in the Cooperative Wholesale Stores

W. Raja Solomon and K. Kalidoss

INTRODUCTION

The establishment of cooperative movement in our country ensures valuable service to people. To safe-guard the consumers from the exploitation of the traders and merchants the consumer cooperatives were established. The main objective of the consumer cooperative wholesale stores is to hold the price line and ensure equitable distribution of essential consumer goods to the general public at reasonable price. Cooperative wholesale stores is a leading institution in the field of consumer services, professionalisation and management of human resources.

Human resource management is a segment of management science. It recognizes the human power as a vital resource contributing to the fulfillment of wholesale stores goal and objectives. It involves the planning and implementation of a variety of activities and functions for optimum utilization of human resources for the benefit of the individuals in cooperative wholesale stores. In the new economic environment, this is an important area which needs continuous attention. It is unpredictable and also dynamic.

MISSION

The mission of human resource management in cooperative wholesale stores is to assure a steady source of sound people that can contribute to the success of the stores. The cooperative wholesale stores have to effect operational efficiency, improvement in quality of products and services, developing managerial and technological excellence, enhancing strong financial and human resource base with full autonomy and adequate infrastructure facilities.

OBJECTIVES

The objectives of human resource management in cooperative wholesale stores must be evolved as an effective system to attain the highest efficiency standard.

- to secure and maintain a satisfactory and satisfied working group.
- to ensure the welfare of an employee as an individual in the stores, so that he may give his best to the enterprise.
- to enable each person to make his maximum contribution and thereby promote the productive efficiency of the stores; and
- to maintain good human relations within the stores.

SCOPE

Scope of human resource management in cooperative wholesale stores is a wide area and covers a broad spectrum of activities. These may be classified under three headings:

Employee Welfare	Personnel Administration	Individual Relation
(working conditions, health, safety welfare amenities such as ventilation, good environment, canteen)	(Recruitment & selection, placement, compensation, training, development & promotion)	(trade union, joint consultation, collective bargaining, settlement of disputes and redressel of grievances)

IMPORTANCE

"To keep an efficient manpower to run the consumer wholesale stores successfully" is the very important aim in human resource management.

- Cooperative wholesale stores is user's organisation and to satisfy the needs of members efficient service is necessary. This can be provided only by efficient personnel with great professionalisation.
- Wholesale stores are not monopolistic organisations. Many of the services undertaken by the wholesale stores are also provided by private and public sector concerns. To thrive in that competition, cooperative wholesale stores need to improve the quality of their personnel.
- Viability of cooperative wholesale stores has become a vital aspect of their survival. They have to expand their turnover and business. This is possible only by efficient professional management in general and personnel management in particular.
- Cooperative wholesale stores need to follow efficient personnel policies to absorb the best talent available in the market.
- Wholesale stores must become model employer. They need to change their recruitment, wage policies and incentive systems. This calls for a comprehensive personnel management system.

HUMAN RESOURCE MANAGEMENT

Human resource management in cooperative wholesale stores is the planning, organising, directing and controlling of the operative functions of procurement, development, compensation, integration and maintenance of human resources of a stores for the purpose of contributing towards the organisations' goals. It is thus concerned with the proper recruitment, management and development of human resources and their effective utilisation.

Factors that manage the human resources in cooperative wholesale stores, can be classified into three main categories, namely individuals and their growing expectations; groups and their inability to mesh as a team and the Trade nion with its collective bargaining power. The following table summarises the factors to be considered in each of these areas:

Efforts for	*Factors to be considered*
Individuals	• Initial efforts for good interaction
	• Constant communication
	• Recognition of talents and aspirations
Groups	• To contain negative effect of 'Groupism'
	• Mechanism for inter-group party
	• Sociological concerns
Trade Union	• 'Co-education' with managers
	• Regular system of election
	• Human resource development effort for workmen

In the face of the emerging present challenges, upgradation of the management system is now, more than ever before, the most vital need of the cooperative wholesale stores. The significance of professionalisation of management in wholesale stores, indeed, transcends mere management considerations. It influences their very identity and autonomy. It has been seen that cooperative wholesale stores which have developed good management culture of their own are interfered by the Government more than by those who have failed to develop a satisfactory managerial infrastructure. If they were only to function with a reasonable degree of efficiency they can get the better of any competition.

The human resource management system in cooperative wholesale stores is a set of institutions that has to be designed in the framework of the total organisational goals and objectives and thus has to represent an integrated functional culture of management. Cooperative wholesale stores are expected to attain higher norms of economic efficiency, professional management and achieve sound social-end results, for this there is an imperative need for proper manpower planning and recruitment of personnel.

MANPOWER PLANNING

Manpower planning calls for systematic and comprehensive inventory of existing human resources and aims at forecasting personnel needs for the future. Manpower surveys are needed for quantifying training requirements with a view to developing appropriate institutional training capacity for various levels of personnel. In cooperative wholesale stores broad details of personnel employed, category wise and section wise may be available but the estimate of manpower requirements in terms of anticipated growth of each segment of cooperative wholesale stores is not readily available. The entire success of the organisation depends on the adoptation of proper manpower planning and survey. Forecasting of manpower requirements could be made at both micro and macro levels in the wholesale stores, because manpower planning is intimately linked to the corporate vision that a cooperative seeks to set for itself. Therefore, manpower planning in cooperative wholesale stores will thus be integrated with a whole range of important issues such as:

- Policy of personnel development to enable systematic identification of existing personnel and building them up for suitable upward or lateral movement.

- Wage structure attractive enough to retain competent personnel, as also recruit new ones with merit.
- Availability of career development opportunities, so that the deserving ones can look forward to advancement within the organisation.

RECRUITMENT

As per the tentative manpower plan, recruitment of right type of people for specific jobs is an important one. But there is no uniform recruitment policy that is followed among the cooperatives. The cooperative wholesale stores prefer to choose local people even if they lack quality. Particularly, they resort to informal and non-institutional methods of recruitment. At present, there are three methods of recruitment in cooperative wholesale stores, namely:

(i) Direct recruitment

(ii) Deputation from Government or from sister cooperative institutions.

(iii) Promotion.

Deputation is widely used as a method of recruitment in cooperative wholesale stores particularly for key positions. During the recruitment they have to face the following problems:

- They have to yield to local pressures and influence.
- Relatives and friends of the Board of Directors find easy entry into the cooperatives.
- Very often the recruitment producers adopted are informal methods.

To overcome these constraints, it is necessary to streamline the recruitment policies and system, so that right type of people are recruited and retained.

CONCLUSION

Human Resource Management in cooperative wholesale stores determines the combination of factors of production.

Money, materials and machines are easy to manage but management of human resource is very difficult because each of them have their own attitudes, emotions, aptitudes and feelings. Hence the management of human resources is the most difficult task of management, and it has to overcome the professionalisation of management.

Cooperative wholesale stores are playing an important role in economic development besides providing maximum welfare to the masses. The crucial areas of human resource management viz., professionalisation, manpower planning, recruitment are largely concentrated by the cooperative wholesale stores. Thousands and above employees working in wholesale stores, the managers and the officials are the key persons. If the key persons properly handle the human resources, the cooperative wholesale stores is sure to grow in future.

REFERENCES

Jyothi, S.S. (1985), "Human Resource Management in Cooperative Sector", Inter-India Publications, New Delhi.

Krishnaswami, O.R. (1987), "Human Resource Management & Industrial Relations", Rainbow Publications, Coimbatore.

Gandhiraj, V. (2004), "Human Resource Management in Cooperatives", Tamil Nadu Journal of Cooperation, May 2004 (p. 3 & 4).

Recommendations of the National Workshop on Human Resource Development in Cooperatives", held on 5, 1990 at New Delhi.

25

Bringing About the Managerial Effectiveness in the Officials of Cooperative Wholesale Stores through Behavioural Approach

D. Joel Edwinraj and S. Adaikala Charles

INTRODUCTION

The history of consumer cooperative movement in India is as old as cooperative movement of the world. They are established with the objectives of acting as market leader, protect consumers against exploitation by private traders, supply of quality consumer goods with affordable price, develop fair trade and improve consumer awareness. The first registered consumer cooperative stores was established in Madras in 1904. *i.e.*, Triplicane Urban Cooperative Society. The consumer cooperatives in Tamil Nadu try to meet the present challenges that are build up daily from the competitors. The proper professional management of consumer cooperatives is perhaps the greatest need in modernizing the management.

The officials of the cooperative wholesale stores depend on their knowledge, skill and attitude. Most of the officials are satisfied with their daily routine managerial activities, they are not willing to take risk and add innovative managerial activities to their work. They possess very good behavioural approaches in their minds, but they and not put into practice to their work.

This paper is an attempt to bring about the managerial effectiveness in the officials of the cooperative wholesale stores through some behavioural approaches.

AN OVER VIEW

What makes a cooperative wholesale stores manager effective? There are no definite answers to this question. But some research and experience indicate that few behavioural dimensions help managers to become effective in the wholesale stores.

The first duty of being a cooperatives wholesale stores official is to get effective results, not activity. Officials spend too much time working on problems rather than letting their people solve the problems. The officials of cooperative wholesale stores work should lend itself to impact, significant achievement and results. The effective officials eliminate the non-essentials. It is possible for the officials to be very busy and still not be very effective. They may be busy doing things that do not count very much.

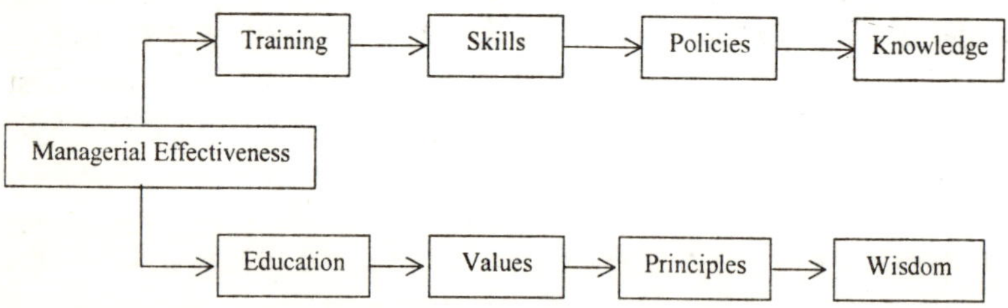

Managerial effectiveness besides knowledge, needs wisdom. Indeed, wisdom subsumes and transcends knowledge.

A wise worker and an integrated personality may be taken as synonymous. The true effectiveness of officials for the managerial development efforts, they seem to equally concentrate on the upper and lower limb of the below mentioned wisdom working model of managerial effectiveness.

BEHAVIOURAL APPROACH

Managerial effectiveness is not an aspect of personality. It is not something that the official has. Effectiveness is best seen as something that an official of cooperative wholesale stores produces from a situation by managing it appropriately. It represents output, not input. The officials must think in terms of performance not personality. It is not so much what an official does, but what he achieves. Once an official has decided he wants to become effective, he should initially focus on how he can contribute more or more effectively than he is now doing.

The cooperative wholesale stores officials possess very good behaviour approaches in their mind. It should brought to practice brought to be more effective in their managerial role. Some of the behavioural approaches are explained as under.

Have High concern for Community and Productivity

The officials of cooperative wholesale stores are able to communicate by the things they do, not by the slogans they repeat. That they are equally concerned about the community and productivity and expect others to be similarly concerned.

Spend more Time in Managing

Official should spend most of their time in managing. *i.e.*, identifying opportunities for improvement, locating problems, training subordinates, developing contacts with others in the organization, working through inter-unit difference and the like.

Use a General Style

Cooperative wholesales stores' officials engage themselves in discussions with their subordinates. But due to their busy work schedule they cannot do it. They must engage in discussions with their subordinates about the overall scope and purpose of a work assignment, so that the employees are able to proceed on their own to accomplish the business.

Build Group Pride

The effective officials work with their employees in group or sub-groups on a regular basis. But the officials rarely work with their group. They allow the people to talk with each other and establish some common perspectives.

Keep People Informed

Achievement-ordented people, have found that it makes a real difference in their performance if people are given regular feedback and kept informed about what is happening in the organization.

Allow Employees to Influence them

Effective officials are aware of their own limitations and therefore, seek information and advice from others. They are open to good information, whatever be the source.

Take Pressure off in a Crisis

Crises are inevitable in the managerial work. Effective officials respond to such situations by taking some of the pressures off others and encouraging them to do their best.

Have Influence Upward

The ability to influence their own bosses' decisions is an essential characteristic of effective officials. They must be skilled as subordinates as well as proficient as supervisors.

Minimize Status Difference

Status symbols are an ubiquitous part of the managerial work. If wholesale stores officials emphasise status distinctions, they will be less likely to get the information they need and the cooperation they value.

MEASUREMENT OF MANAGERIAL EFFECTIVENESS

Managerial effectiveness in the officials of cooperative wholesale stores has been measured through ten behavioural approaches as to how he perceives his role in the organization. The are as follows:

1. Integration

When a cooperative wholesale stores official perceives that the role he occupies and the skills and capabilities he possesses are combined, such perception is referred as integration of self with the role. The integration of self and role increases the effectiveness of an official.

2. Proactivity

The officials take initiative and do something on their own, This is his proactive behaviour. The proactive behaviour increases effectiveness of an official.

3. Creativity

When an official perceives that he does something new or unique in his role, this is his creative behaviour. It increases his effectiveness.

4. Confrontation

Problems often arise in the business. The officials like to confront the problem in order to seek solution. It will increase his effectiveness.

5. Centrality

If the official perceives his role as our important one, then his effectives enhances.

6. Influence

The feeling that he is able to exercise influence in his role increases his effectiveness. The influence may be in terms of decision-making, implementation of policies, advice or problem solving.

7. Growth

When the official perceives that the role provides him opportunities for his personal growth/professional development, his effectiveness will be high.

8. Linkage

If the official perceives interdependency of his role with other roles, his effectiveness will be high.

9. Helping Attitude

The perception of the officials that helping should be attitude extended and received as and when required, increases effectiveness.

10. Superordination

The official's perception that he is contributing to something beyond his own, that he is serving the society, and is contributing to knowledge building etc., enhances his effectiveness.

CONCLUSION

The destiny, the success and the failure of cooperative wholesale stores in Tamil Nadu depend on the capability of officials to manage their operations effectively. The cooperative wholesale stores officials are highly effective in their role and operation. But in terms of behavioural approaches, they are not interested due to various reasons. If the officials of cooperative wholesale stores apply their behavioural approaches to the maximum levels to the managerial activities, their effectiveness will be at high level. Therefore, it is the right time the officials should bring out the managerial effectiveness for the success of the cooperative movement.

26

Control System in the Cooperative Wholesale Stores

M. Nagavel and M. Maruthamuthu

In this paper control system in cooperative wholesale stores with special reference to costing, auditing and budgeting are being discussed and presented.

Even though cooperation is an independent and democratic movement, when a cooperative engages itself in business, it should adopt the best system for improvement of its business. An effective control system is well required for the successful functioning of any business organization. As such cooperatives also have been suggested to adopt effective control system so as to achieve the goals of cooperation and also to achieve better business objectives.

Registrar of Cooperative Societies, Chennai, has issued many suggestions to adopt the best system of control over the purchase policy, stock control, costing, budgeting and management of cooperative wholesale stores. Apart form this, Director of Cooperative Audit, Chennai has also evolved the best system for the audit of the consumer cooperative wholesale stores

PURCHASE POLICY

Registrar of Cooperative Societies has issued elaborate instructions regarding the purchase policy for wholesale stores. Purchases are determined on the actual estimation and projection of market. As a whole, marketable goods have been listed in four divisions, and certain commodities have to be purchased only by the federation. The district wholesale stores can place their orders for requirement only to the state federations. Agriculture commodities can be purchased in two ways. One through Joint purchase committees (Appointed by the Government) and the other from Regulated Market Committees or Marketing Cooperatives through the State Federation. Manufactured goods can be purchased only from the appointed manufactures. Approved manufactures lists are periodically reviewed by a committee appointed specially for this purpose. Further, in an emergency situation purchases can be made without recoursing to the above formalities after getting a clearance from the state federation or from the Joint Purchase Committees.

SYSTEM OF MAINTENANCE OF STOCK

In all the wholesale stores "Double Compartmental System" is being followed for maintenance of stocks. Stocks are received at godown point and the value is arrived. After fixation of retail price, stocks are issued to retail points. But the godown stock and retail stock are valued at retail value. Foolproof system of issue of stocks at godown level, and at retail level is being followed to avoid any deficit.

Stock position is being monitored periodically both at the godown and retail points. Stocks are being monitored in such a way that the inventory turnover is being maintained as per best standard so that maximum benefit is derived by engaging the available capital in inventory. In general, 12 to 15 times of the capital employed is aimed and suggested. Further, physical verification of stocks both at the godown and retail level is undertaken every month and the results are monitored.

Deficits are arrived then and there and reasons are being probed, loopholes removed, and action is taken to recover from the persons responsible.

COST MANAGEMENT

Cost sheets are to be prepared for each and every purchase, on the basis of purchase bills and actual direct overhead charges incurred. This work is being monitored at the General Manager Level. Selling price is fixed normally with a margin ranging from 6% to 10%. Further, it is important to control the expenses as tightly as possible. The efficiency norms on various items in wholesale stores have been suggested (eg) Establishment charges 2% on sales, other expenses 1% on sales. Further, the wholesale stores have been advised to prepare a trading account separately for every class of goods at the end of every month, so that any loopholes in fixation of selling price and for regulating direct, overhead charges and for fixation of cost price. The major disappointing factor at this moment is mounting indirect overhead charges compared to the sales turnover.

BUDGETING

In these days of Golobalisation, budgeting plays an important role in designing the success of any business and it is also the most essential functions of the management. Forecasting of the business, the area of concentrating and sales projection are being undertaken by the wholesale stores on the basis of market survey and branch strength. On the forecast of local market, and all these factors, target is envisaged and fixed by the government. It is monitored periodically by the cooperative department. While fixing the sales target, available area of selling units, availability of sale personnel are considered. Normally to have a fair performance, Rs. 5/- to 10/- per sq. feet of selling unit per day is very essential. Further, sales to per sales personnel should be between Rs. 1000/- to Rs. 1500/- per day so as to achieve a minimum efficiency.

Further, while projecting, the sales target, stocks outturn ratio is also to be taken into consideration. Considering all these factors, sales target is being envisaged and the budget forecast is completed.

ACCOUNTING PROCEDURE, INTERNAL CHECK AND INTERNAL AUDITS

The district wholesale stores are following Management Accounting System (MAS) formulated on the basis of the recommendation of the National Consumer Cooperative Federation. In the system, separate day books are maintained for purchases, sales, bank accounts, investments, borrowings, debtors, creditors, operational and non operational expenses allotting separate codes for each accounts. This facilitates easy accounting procedures and effective review. Further, it facilitates easy preparation of article-wise, trading accounts and finding out the trading results of each commodity and point out the loopholes in the business.

Effective internal check system has been suggested by the Registrar of cooperative societies for the wholesales stores. Cent per cent checking of sales, stock and liability of salesman are to be carried out by the internal checkers. The internal check system is to be monitored by the General Manager or some other executive at every stage, loopholes to be found out and cleared.

Further, the Registrar of Cooperative societies has already suggested that the wholesale stores should devise an internal audit system with the consultation of the Director of Cooperative Audit and implement the same. Even though all the wholesale stores have appointed internal auditors, the system is not effectively implemented.

AUDIT

Under section 80 of Tamilnadu Cooperative Societies Act 1983, the audit of cooperative wholesales stores is entrusted to the director of cooperative audit and as such cooperative audit department is conducting the statutory audit. At present , the audit is upto date and back log has been cleared. Apart from the usual financial audit of verification and valuation of assets and liabilities, examination of overdue debts, projection of profit or loss of the business. Audit departments is also concentrating on the purchase policy, Stock control, cost management, sales projection, sales effectiveness, sales promotion, stock turn over. All these aspects are scrutinized and stores are classified in accordance with the performance of the stores in the above aspects.

CONCLUSION

Even though cooperative wholesale stores are the pioneers of introducing self service centres, departmental stores, super markets and other modern developments in marketing in the state, their present situation is not so satisfactory. The financial position of the stores are not sound due to heavy, accumulated losses. Its high cost factor, acute competition, ineffective marketing staff and coordination, have barrier in the ability to function on the best performance lines. If effective modernization is carried out on these lines, the consumer cooperative wholesale stores shall come up to the expectation and be a boon both to the general public and to the movement.

27

Techniques of Control Mechanism in the Co-operative Wholesale Stores

S. David Amirtha Rajan and
P. Gnana Soundari

INTRODUCTION

A co-operative society is a voluntary association of persons and not of capital. In this system any person, irrespective of caste and creed, can join of one's free will and can leave at any time after serving due notice. The capital of a co-operative society is raised from members by way of share capital. Since it is started by weaker sections of the society, the share capital is very low. However, it is, by legislation eligible to raise loan from the state and central co-operative banks. In this system, democracy is an important feature. Further, it is organized with the motto of rendering service to its members. In case of surplus, the profit is distributed among the members. If any co-operative system is expected to survive, it will be a must to follow various modern control techniques and mechanism. In this context an attempt is made to study the "Control Techniques and mechanisms adopted by the co-operative whole sale stores in Madurai". This paper is mainly based on the interview held with the authorities of the Madurai District Co-operative wholesale Stores, Madurai.

CONTROLLING TECHNIQUES

The usual control techniques are budgeting, standard costing, Break-Point analysis, auditing and so on. In this study all these concepts are considered and analysed.

BUDGETING

Budgeting is a technique being used to forecast future financial position of the co-operative system. The Budget is a financial statement prepared on the basis of past records in order to predict the future. This helps to control finance.

In the wholesale stores, it is noted that budget is prepared once in a year. The main forecast is done on cash, purchase and sales. In case of deviation of actual values from budgeted figures, the matter is brought to the general meeting for further action or rectification. Slight increase over and above the previous year record is taken as the forecast figure in the formulation of budget. The account officer and purchase manager take the responsibility to finalise the budget.

But the consolidated statement is prepared by the General Manager for all the Madurai District co-operative whole sale stores. Whatever changes necessary in the middle of the financial year, changes are carried out and the same is ratified in the general body meeting. The traditional method of budgeting is adopted in this stores.

STANDARD COSTING TECHNIQUES

Standard costing is a control technique in which standard performance is compared with actual performance. This is used to find out variance on several performance indicators including purchase, production and sales. A detailed analysis of variance enables to have better control over business. But it is unfortunate to note that this technique is not followed.

AUDITING

The term audit is derived from the latin word known as "audire" which means 'investigating the truth' Auditing is a method to check the financial statement to assess the reality behind it. It is fortunate to understand that the work of audit is carried out. It is observed that the stores have both internal and statutory audits. In addition to these, interim audit is also performed. In all these cases, the co-operative audit department is involved . It is also noted that the audit work should be done only by the audit department.

The audit report is carefully studied and the comments stated are noted. In case of any adverse comments, these comments which are to be ratified can be modified immediately. Any suggestion being stated is considered for further action and the same in audited statement is ratified.

Misappropriation of cash or goods if detected and reported in the audited statement being found, the mater is viewed very seriously. A domestic enquiry will be conducted if the misappropriation is not huge and in serious cases, criminal action is initiated against the employee(s) found guilty. In most cases, the action is taken according to the enquiry report.

BREAK EVEN POINT ANALYSIS

Break-even point is a point where there is no profit or loss. This analysis is adopted to take vital decisions. In this study it is observed that the break even point analysis is followed. In general, marginal costing principle is considered for making decisions in crucial situations.

WASTAGE, SCRAP, SPOILAGE AND THEFT

In course of any trade, wastage, scrap, spoilage and theft are possible. But these may lead to a great loss to the organization. Therefore, the organization should take steps to minimise the risk. Accordingly, it is found that wastage, scrap or spoilage are permissible to a certain extent. The allowable wastage is 2 per cent in the stores. When this limit exceeds, it is viewed as abnormal loss.

In the cases of theft or abnormal losses, Insurance is taken as base for shifting risk.

On the basis of the above discussion it is found that the co-operative stores have a proper system for control of wastage, scrap and spoilage. In each case, the loss is attached with the insurance company.

SUMMARY

Madurai District wholesale Co-operative Stores follows proper techniques to control unnecessary losses. These techniques are budgeting, auditing, break even point analysis and avoiding wastage, scrap, spoilage and theft. Insurance is an important base to shift risk due to wastage, scrap, and theft.

28

Accounting-based Control System in a District Cooperative Wholesale Store: A Case Study

S. Manivel

INTRODUCTION

The Dindigul District Cooperative Wholesale Stores (Stores) a distributive society, established in the year 1964, is one of the 29 wholesales stores working in Tamil Nadu. The Wholesale Stores has been performing twofold functions viz., (i) Purchasing articles of domestic consumption in bulk and selling them to the public at a reasonable price; and, (ii) acting as an agent of the State Government to procure, stock and supply essential commodities through the Fair Price Shops and other retail outlets. The jurisdiction of the Stores extends over the whole of the district. With a membership of around 20,000 it serves the nook and corner of the district through its 21 branches, three self-service centers, one super market and 50 Fair Price Shops located in rural and urban centers. The Board of Management was superseded in 1976 under the Special Officer Appointment Act of the State Government, and since then, the affairs of the Stores have been managed by a special officer deputed by the State Government. The special officer so appointed by the Government has all the powers that the Board enjoys under the democratic set-up. Given the nature of business and the volume of business, these stores, have to follow scientific methods and systems in its management for better accomplishment of its objects. The wholesale stores is managed by a management team consisting of officers and officials in a democratic manner. The decisions pertaining to the operation of the stores are taken at various levels right from the society level to the state level. The stores have been expected to follow management accounting system(MAS) as designed and promoted by the consultancy and promotional cell(CPC) of the NCCF, Once this system is in place, it is believed that the store would be in a better place to take informed decisions. The stores has adopted the system and accordingly brought changes in the books of account and in several other accounting related practices. In this background, this paper attempts to examine and describe the practices pertaining to the major accounting-based control tools such as budgeting, costing, internal audit, and management reporting in the selected stores.

BUDGETING

Budgeting is in vogue in the Stores. But the system presents a unique feature. Two budgets-sales budget and administrative budget-are prepared and used. Sales budget which specifies the target that the Stores aims to achieve, by and large, is framed on the basis of the directives of the State Government and the Registrar of Cooperatives. The procedures followed in building the sales budget suggests the distinct character of the budgeting process in the Stores. The Registrar of Cooperative Societies based on the sales volume and the performance of the Cooperative Wholesale Stores in the previous year, fixes the target for the budget year. For this purpose the Wholesale Stores in the State are classified into three categories viz., (i) Stores which performed well; (ii)

Stores which recorded poor performance; and, (iii) Stores with moderate performance. Stores with better performance are assigned a higher sales target of 20 to 30 per cent more than the previous year's sales. Stores with poor performance are assigned a lesser target than the previous year's turnover and the last category of Stores are given a target of 10 per cent increment over the previous year.

The target of sales thus fixed is for the whole year. It is normally assumed that 60 per cent of the sales is from the sale of controlled commodities (which the Stores have to undertake as part of the agency service to the state government). The Stores upon receiving the target fixed by the state government prepares a major commodity-wise sales budget, especially for the forty per cent of the total targeted sale which the Stores have to cover from the sale of non-controlled commodities.

The Administrative Budget is primarily income and expenditure budget. Here again an incremental approach is followed. The estimates are made by applying the rule plus 10 or minus 10 per cent.

The Master Budget prepared by the Stores is reviewed by the Additional Registrar (Consumer Activities) who reports to the Registrar of Cooperatives. The Additional Registrar after receiving the budget from the Stores makes a through review of the various items included in the budget with reference to the instructions given to the stores and the particular wholesale store's past performance, before approving and passing it for implementation, by the society.

With regard to review of performance, the performance is reviewed at two levels. The Special Officer of the Stores convenes a meeting of the heads of different sections like purchase, sales, accounts and administration and sales personnel to review the performance of branch-wise sales every month. Branchwise actual sales are compared against the target. The deviations are noted. Causes for variance are analysed. Control measures are suggested based on the reasons and causes for variance. Sales performance alone is reviewed in such monthly meetings.

Figure 1
Budgeting Process in the Wholesale Stores

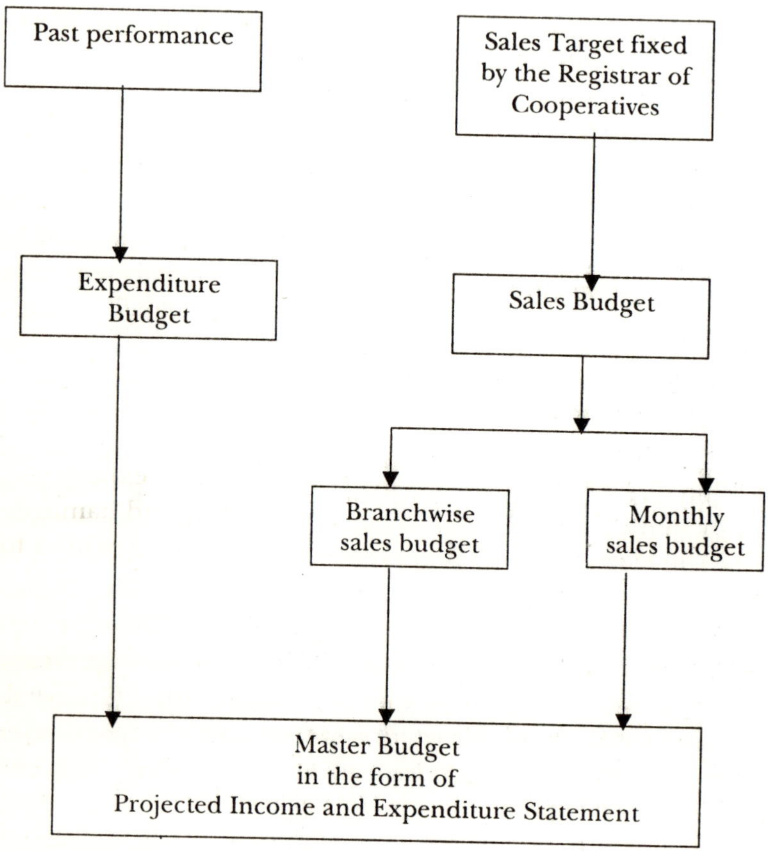

The second review is at a state-level meeting convened by the Registrar of Cooperative Societies every month for all the Cooperative Wholesale Stores in Tamil Nadu. This meeting is attended by the Registrar of Cooperative Societies, Additional Registrar (Consumer Activities), Special Officers of the Tamil Nadu Cooperative Consumers Federation and of the Tamil Nadu Cooperative Union and Special Officers of all District Cooperative Wholesale Stores in Tamil Nadu. Review or evaluation of the performance of the Stores against the targets fixed is mainly based on the data furnished by the wholesale Stores.

- Commodity-wise credit and cash sales are evaluated against the previous month's actual sales and the targeted sales for the month under review. So are the purchases.
- Commodity-wise and year-wise stock position, and time-barred and damaged stock are examined.
- Details of sundry debtors like bills pending for more than ten years, over five years but below ten years, below five years but above one year, and below one year are reviewed.
- Stock deficits are classified as dead and heirless, under arbitration, under execution petition, conditional attachment etc., and are analysed.
- Efficiency ratios like Gross Profit to sales, Net profit to sales. Establishment expenses to sales, Other expenses to sales, Sundry debtors to sales, time-barred and damaged stock to sales, Stock deficit to sales, sundry creditors to average purchase per month are also analysed in the review meeting.

Thus all the important variables which play a significant role in the business growth of the organization are reviewed, examined and analysed. However, a close look at the minutes of the review meeting reveals that the budgets of all the 29 Cooperative Wholesale Stores are reviewed in a day. As a result it could only be done in a superficial manner and not on an in-depth fashion.

To sum up, the following are the major characteristic features of the budgetary control process in the Stores:

- Budgets are targets fixed by the Registrar of Cooperatives. They are prepared on the instructions of the Registrar based on the past performance of the Stores.
- There are only two budgets viz., sales and administrative budgets.

- Personnel working in the different sections of the Stores are not involved in the preparation of the budget.
- The budget review and budgetary control are not effective in the Stores.

COSTING

Costing is not given much importance in the stores. One of the important areas where costing could be used is pricing. As the Stores has adopted the active price policy under which a fixed percentage of margin is added to the cost price, coasting has not been given much importance even in the fixation of price of commodities. However, in determining the administrative and establishment expenses, costing and cost control measures are adhered to. This is practised because of the provision (or standard fixed) that the administrative cost should not exceed two per cent of the total sales. No such norm is fixed for other costs. Of course, the administrative budget, to a certain extent, helps control cost. In the absence of established cost control methods the Stores used the budgets for cost control.

The monthly review meeting indirectly help in controlling costs because, in such meetings, the position of debtors, receivables, stock deficit, time-barred stock and inventory are analysed. Such review, sometimes, may possibly help in reducing the cost of excessive inventory, debtors etc.

INTERNAL AUDIT

The Stores has internal audit. Earlier, the internal audit section of the Stores was headed by a Cooperative Sub-Registrar, a departmental official. Now a Superintendent of the Stores heads the wing. He is assisted by two clerks. The internal audit section performs two tasks: (i) checking bills, and, (ii) checking liabilities. The audit is efficient to the extent of detecting omission in calculation of sales price. It also helps completion of external audit in time.

The external audit is statutory. There is a separate external audit wing in the Stores headed by a Cooperative Sub-Registrar assisted by two Senior Inspectors of Cooperatives. They audit the accounts of the Stores almost as a daily routine. The external audit, done by the department personnel, is largely confined to the examination of financial accounts and the purpose is to ascertain the accuracy of recorded financial facts. A review of the audit reports for the years 1992 to 1994 indicates that the auditors examine the performance of the Stores against certain commonly accepted efficiency standards of evaluation. To quote a few remarks of the external auditors:

> "The staff cost worked out 1.40 per cent of sales. This is less than the standard norm of 2 per cent. The stores may examine the possibilities of curtailing the operating and non-operating expenses or it may concentrate on increasing the sales".
>
> "The percentage of Gross Profit to sales works out to 3.45 per cent only. The sale of controlled goods and grocery contribute a major share. The profit margin on these sales are less. Further, there is an abnormal increase in the trade charges. All these are responsible for low percentage of Gross Profit. The Stores may take effective steps to promote the sale of non-controlled goods and to reduce the trade charges to earn a higher gross margins".

This is a good beginning. However, such observations are made only in the final audit report, and it could only be used in the planning process, not in the control process. Further, such observations are repeated year after year. No new observations are found and this shows the routine, mechanical and ritualistic nature of the audit and its reports. It also reveals that such reports are not given proper attention by the authorities.

REPORTING

Reporting forms, as developed by the Consultancy and Promotional Cell (CPC) of the National Cooperative Consumers Federation (NCCF), New Delhi, are circulated among the wholesale Stores. The report that are to be prepared by the Stores are:

- Sales Report (daily and monthly);
- Commodity group-wise Performance Report (monthly);
- Branch-wise Operation Reports (monthly);
- Stock Turnover Report;
- Report on sales per man-day/per sq.feet;
- Report on price variation;
- Report on damaged, slow-moving and obsolete stocks;
- Financial Reports.

These reports are prepared and sent to the Registrar of Cooperative Societies and to the CPC of NCCF, New Delhi. That is, they are mainly used for external reporting. They are neither for operational planning nor for day-to-day operational control.

Apart from the reports cited above, the Stores has to prepare a report on performance of the self-service centers. It is prepared regularly and sent to the CPC of the NCCF for it has extended financial help to start the self-service centers. Here again, the report largely serves an external purpose.

Thus, by and large the reporting is poor and seems to be done only to complete an official desk and shelf formality. The main reason for this is that, except one accountant, who is in charge of management accounting, many of the personnel do not understand the importance of reports in decision-making. Yet another reason is that the board or administration or whoever is incharge of management, has not been given the power to take decisions. As a result, they do not realize the need for proper reporting in the Stores.

CERTAIN HURDLES

Almost fifteen years have elapsed since the introduction of Management Accounting System in the Stores. MAS is still at the nascent stage. No doubt, it has greatly helped in brining some order to financial accounts which were once at sixes and sevens. Accounts are now planned and codified. Time schedule is fixed for finalization of accounts. However, MAS is yet to take firm roots in the area of budgeting and budgetary control, costing, internal audit and reporting. This is corroborated by the observations of the Cooperative Sub-Registrar who has been reviewing the functioning of MAS in all the Cooperative Wholesale Stores. To quote a few of his observations on the functioning of MAS in the selected Stores:

- The Stores has not prepared and submitted budget.
- Monthly operational reports are not prepared.
- Internal audit is not effective in the area of purchase, sales and personal accounts.
- Periodical review may be conducted to monitor arrears and to maintain the accounts up-to-date, which will facilitate effective control and efficient management of the business affairs.

All these clearly indicate that MAS is yet to take off in the Stores. The reasons for tardy, imperfect and incomplete adoption of MAS are many prominent among them are given below:

- Many a member of the staff at higher level in the Stores still feels that restructuring of financial Accounting is MAS. Many of them are yet to understand the scope of MAS.
- Only three staff members are trained in MAS. Of the three only one seems serious about MAS.
- MAS is not considered part of the total system. Many staff members still believe that the system is to serve external purpose and that it is largely concerned with the Accounts Department. Staff are not to be blamed because the system came from above without the ground being prepared.
- Inadequate staff strength.
- Poor salary and inadequate incentive are cited as the factors tending to make initiative a still-born proposition. Staff morale is low. Hence they do not want to take any extra effort.

- Frequent transfers of Special Officers. The interest of the Special Officers too varies. Some are interested in improving the business; some are keen to tone up the administration; some attach importance to financial accounting; some just meddle with the day-to-day affairs and some are satisfied with maintaining the status-quo. No Special Officer seems to have given serious thought to integrating account, business and administration.
- Special Officers do no not have orientation in the MAS. They don't understand the objective and purpose of the system.
- The staff of the Stores largely go by what the Special officers say. The Special Offices obey the orders of the Registrar of Cooperative Societies. In this chain what is ultimately done comes to bear little relevance to immediate realities.
- In the final analysis members get totally isolated as they do not know what is happening in the Stores. A complete apathy seems to have permeated the scene.

29

Laws as Applied to the Co-operative Wholesale Stores

G. Madhurai

Consumer Co-operatives in India face new problems and challenges under liberalized economy. However, private concerns and multinationals are coming up in a big way in setting up of supermarkets and departmental stores all over India. To overcome these problems, it is imperative to increase the membership base, streamlining their workforce, professionalisation of their cadres and service and have a sound financial management.

With the diversified expansion of the Co-operative Movement, the trend in co-operative legislation is fast changing. More and more provisions are being added or changed to meet the growing need of the movement. Besides, the consumer expectations are increasing in all respects of price, quality and service. Now the consumers know their rights and the outcome of so many Acts and Rules further boosted their capacity to buy commodities more diligently.

As Pluto said, "Human beings do not even make laws; it is accidents and catastrophes of all kinds happening in every conceivable way that makes the laws for us". Consumers needed an adequate protection against not only a private manufacturer or supplier of goods and services but also against undertakings run under the auspices of department of the state.

The enactments connected to consumer co-operatives may be broadly divided into two headings (1) Business and (2) Administration.

LAWS RELATING TO BUSINESS

The Indian Contract Act, 1872

All transactions in business are based on contract obligations. Any deviation from the Act will amount to an invalid or void contract. The Act sets out rules as to communication, acceptance and revocation proposals. The communication of proposal is complete, when it comes to the knowledge of the person to whom it is made. The contracts or agreements, if not entered by free consent or if caused by coercion, fraud or misrepresentation, then it becomes avoidable contract. When the contract has been broken, the party to the contract suffered by such breach may claim compensation for any loss or damage caused to him. Such compensation is not to be given for any remote and indirect loss or damage sustained by the reason of the breach.

The existing contract need not be performed, in case of:

(a) Novation - A fresh contract to substitute the original one

(b) Alteration - A change in one or more terms of a contract

(c) Rescission - Cancellation of contract with mutual consent and consideration

If any party fails to perform his obligation, it may be actual breach or anticipatory breach. The remedies for breach of contract are as follows:

1. Cancellation - A person rightfully cancels a contract can claim damages.

2. Restitution	-	Return of the benefit received.
3. Specific performance	-	Relief under Specific Relief Act, 1877.
4. Injunction	-	An order of court restraining the wrong doer from doing.
5. Quantum Meruit	-	Payment in proportion to the amount of work done.
6. Damages	-	To make good the loss, as he would have been, if performed.

A contract to perform the promise or to discharge the liability of a third party in case of his default is called Contract of guarantee. It involves three parties, creditor, principal debtor and surety. There must be separate contracts between principal debtor and creditor, guarantor and creditor and a third contract between principal debtor and surety.

The Act also deals with agency contracts. The duties of agent to principal are provided in the Act as follows:

1. Duty to act according to principal's directions
2. Duty to act with reasonable skill and diligence.
3. Duty to render accounts.
4. Duty to communicate.
5. Duty not to deal on his own account.
6. Duty to pay over all moneys.
7. Duty not to use information against a principal.
8. Duty not to set up adverse title.
9. Duty not to delegate.
10. Duty to protect the interest of the principal in case of death or insolvency.

The Rights of an Agent are provided as follows: (i) Right to remuneration (ii) Right to retainer (iii) Right of lien (iv) Right to be indemnified against consequences of lawful acts (v) Right to be indemnified against consequences of acts done in good faith (vi) Right to compensation.

Sale of Goods Act, 1930

This Act contains several provisions which show the spirit of doing business and consumerism. It deals with contract of movable property between seller and buyer, duties of seller and buyer, rights of unpaid sellers against the goods and suits for the breach of the contract.

Conditions and warranties are vital and go to the root of the whole contract. The condition is a stipulation essential to main contract and a warranty is a stipulation collateral to the main contract. Its breach gives rise to a right to treat the contract as cancelled. The breach of warranty does not defeat the purpose of the contract. It gives rise to a claim for damages.

The implied conditions are (1) as to title (2) sale by description (3) sale by sample (4) condition as to quality or fitness and (5) condition as to merchantability.

The implied warranties are (1) warranty of quite possession (2) warranty of freedom from encumbrances and (3) warranty annexed by usage of trade.

It is not a part of the seller's duty in a contract of sale to give to the buyer an article suitable for a particular purpose unless such purpose is made known to the seller (Sale of knife) exception is mail order purchases. The maxim Caveat Emptor means "let the buyer beware" and this is the fundamental principle of sale of goods.

If the seller has no title to the goods, the buyer does not acquire anything, even he may have acted honestly and may have paid value for the goods. This is the transfer of title by non-owner: The other types of sale are:

- **Sale by Mercantile Agent:** The buyer gets a good title to the goods as he buys them in good faith for value, though the mercantile agent is not the owner of the goods.
- **Sale by a joint owner:** Where one of several joint owners has the sole possession, with the consent of others, the ownership is transferred.

- **Sale by the seller in possession of goods after sale:** If the buyer has purchased the goods already sold with no knowledge of the seller's want of title, the first buyer can obtain only damagers from the seller but cannot recover the goods from the second buyer. The Act also deals with unpaid seller, who can, under certain circumstances, resell the goods.

Unpaid seller's rights are: (a) Right of lien (the right to retain possession of goods until payment in respect of them is paid) (b) Right of Stoppage in transit (c) Right of re-sale (d) Right of withholding (e) Suit for price (f) Suit for damages for non-acceptance and (g) Suit for interest.

The Consumer Protection Act, 1986

The Act is intended to protect the consumers from exploitation by the unscrupulous manufacturers and traders of consumer goods The Act empowers consumers and consumer associations to file public interest litigation in the consumer disputes redressal forums in district, state and national levels for protecting the following rights:

- **Right to safety** – to protect against marketing of goods which are hazardous of life and properties.
- **Right to be informed** – about the quality, quantity, potency, purity, standard and price.
- **Right to choose** – a variety of goods at competitive prices.
- **Right to be heard** – that consumer's interests will receive due consideration at appropriate forum.
- **Right to redressal** – against unfair trade practices and unscrupulous exploitation of consumers.
- **Right to consumer education** – to get awareness.

The Act provides to arrest unfair trade practices. For the purpose of promoting the sale, use or supply of any goods or for the provision of any service, a trader should not adopt any unfair methods or unfair deceptive practices.

As per the Act the unfair trade practices are:

- false representation of good/services as to standards, quality, quantity etc.,
- selling reconditioned good as new one;
- misleading representations connected to its usefulness;
- gives warranty without testing the length of the product's life.

The act also provides for *Restrictive Trade Practice* which means a consumer cannot be compelled to buy, hire or avail of any goods or, as the case may be, services as a condition precedent for buying, hiring or availing of other goods or services.

Who must be sued by a Consumer either Manufacturers or Seller is important question, which is clarified in the Act. Generally when a consumer finds the goods to be defective, he sues the person from whom he bought the goods. If the defect is a manufacturing defect, the customer may sue the manufacturer also along with the seller. This is an option available to the consumer. Thus the manufacturer is a proper person, but not a necessary person.

A complaint may be made against a trader who has charged a price in excess of the price in the following cases: (a) Fixed by or under any laws in force (b) Displayed on the goods (c) Displayed on any package containing the goods.

There are penalties for non-compliance of provisions. Every order made by the District Forum or State Commission or the National Commission may be enforced in the same manner as if it were a decree of the court. When any such person fails to comply may be punished with imprisonment up to three years and fine up to Rs. 10,000/ - or with both.

Essential Commodities Act, 1955

The object of this Act is to secure equitable distribution and availability of essential commodities at fair prices. The Act allows consumer associations to file written complaints with the special court set up for the purpose. The courts act as a criminal court and prosecute the offenders as under Criminal Procedure Code. The courts can receive complaint from consumer associations regarding offences of adulterations, hoarding or illegal movement of essential commodities.

Essential commodities are those that the Central Government may notify and declare to be an essential commodity for the purpose of this Act. This includes commodities like sugar, food crops, raw jute, edible oils, oil seeds, coal, cattle fodder etc.

Since Public Distribution System requires maintaining and supplying of essential commodities, this Act provides for regulating, supply and distribution of essential commodities.

Prevention of Food Adulteration Act, 1954

The provisions of this Act are designed for the prevention of adulteration in food articles to ensure safety and health to the consuming public at large in the country. The Act provides broadly to protect the interest of the consumers, a Central Committee for Food Standards, Central Food Laboratory, prohibition of import of certain articles of food, law on sea customs, powers of custom officers, prohibition and manufacture and sale of articles of food. The Act also deals with provisions of machinery of analysis of food to protect the interests of the consumers to ensure safety and purity of the food stuff.

Bureau of Indian Standards

Bureau of Indian Standards has laid down standards for most of the foods and processed foods. These standards are referred to ISI standards and cover raw materials and their quality parameters, hygienic conditions under which products are manufactured and packing and labeling requirements, specifications limits etc.

The food products sent for quality certification are analyzed as per BIS standards in their own network of testing laboratories or in some Government or Private Laboratories recognized by them. Manufacturers complying with standards laid down by the BIS can obtain the ISI mark which can be exhibited on the product packages.

AGMARK Standards

These standards are set by the Directorate of Marketing and Inspection (DMI) of the Government of India. The DMI enforces the Agricultural products (Grading and Marketing) Act and under this Act, grade standards are prescribed for agricultural and allied commodities. Manufacturers who comply with the standards laid down by DMI for the particular commodity are allowed to use "AGMARK" labels on their products. The provision of this Act is voluntary.The ultimate aim of all these acts and orders is to protect the consumer from health hazards arising from the consumption of unsafe/ adulterated foods.

The Indian Standard Institution (Certification Marks) Act 1952

The Act provides for the standardization and marking of goods which is a prerequisite to the establishment of a healthy trade. It performs to promote standardization, quality, control and simplification in industry. It also provides registration of marks applicable to products and arranging facilities to test the products.

The Standards of Weights and Measures Act, 1976

This Act provides for the establishment of standard of weights and measures on metric system, regulation of inter-state trade or commerce in weights, measures of goods which are sold or distributed, penalties for use of non-standard weights and measures and the establishment of an Indian Institute of Metrology for training inspectors and other persons.

The Prevention of Black Marketeering and Maintenance of Supplies of Essential Commodities, Act, 1980

This Act provides for effectively dealing with malpractices such as black-marketeering, hoarding, profiteering and unjustified rise in prices of essential commodities by providing for the preventive detention of person likely to indulge in such practices. It protects the interests of the vast consuming public in the country.

The Drugs and Cosmetics Act, 1940

The Drugs and Cosmetics Act regulates the import, manufacture, sale and distribution of drugs and cosmetics. Its main aim is to protect the consumers from sub-standard drugs and cosmetics.

In respect of patent or proprietary medicines there must be a list of ingredients or formula displayed in the prescribed manner on the label or container. Vaccines, etc must comply with W.H.O. (World Health Organisation) standards.

The Drugs and Cosmetics (Amendment) Act is an Act further to amend the Drugs and Cosmetics Act, 1940. Ayurvedic, Siddha and Unani drugs were brought within the purview of the Drugs and Cosmetics Act, 1940.

The Drugs and Cosmetics Rules are made under the Drugs and Cosmetics Act, 1940. The Act includes provisions for licensing of the import, sale, distribution, packaging, stocking, labeling etc of drugs and cosmetics. Many consumer groups are concerned about the inadequacy of the labeling requirements under Rule 96. There is no requirement to give directions as to how to use a drug, how often and in what manner to take it, whether it is suitable for adults or children, contra-indications and side effects or storage conditions. Since many drugs are sold over the counter, this is unsatisfactory and cases of, for example, aspirin poisoning are very common as a result. However, the failure to warn consumers on the label that a drug should not be used by children was held to be an unfair trade practice.

The Drugs (Control) Act, 1950

The Drugs (Control) Act has been enacted to provide for the control of the sale, supply and distribution of drugs. The Central Government can declare any drug to be essential for the purposes of the Act by notification in the Official Gazette and the maximum price is fixed by the Chief Commissioner. The quantity of the drug which the seller can have in his possession or can sell at any one time may be limited.

The Drugs (Prices Control) order gives the Government, power to fix the sale price of indigenously manufactured bulk drugs with a view to regulating their equitable distribution and supply.

LAWS RELATING TO ADMINISTRATION

The Employees Provident Funds and Miscellaneous Provisions Act 1952

The object of this Act is to make some provisions for the future of the workers after they retire or for their dependents in case of thier early death. Taking into account the various difficulties, financial and administrative, the most appropriate course appears to be the institution compulsorily of contributory provident funds in which both the worker and the employer would contribute.

Punishment for failure to pay contributions etc shall be, with imprisonment for a period upto one year with fine upto Rs. 4,000/- or with both.

The Act is applicable to every establishment in which twenty or more persons are employed. The contribution which shall be paid by the employer to the Fund shall be 12% per cent of the basic wages and dearness allowances. The employee's contribution shall be equal to the contribution payable by the employer in respect of him. The eligibility for employees to cover under this Act is for those who draw less than Rs. 6500 p.m as basic and dearness allownaces.

An employer who contravenes, or makes default in complying with shall be punishable with imprisonment for a period upto 3 years and not less than one year and fine upto Rs. 10,000/-.

This Act is not to apply to any establishment registered under the Co-operative Societies Act employing less than fifty persons and working without the aid of electric.

The Employees State Insurance Act, 1948

The object of this Act is to provide certain benefits to employees in case of sickness, maternity, and employment injury and to make provisions for certain other matters in relation thereto.

The insurance fund will be mainly derived from contributions from employers and workmen. The contributions payable in respect of each workman will be based on his average wages and will be payable in the first instance by the employer. The employer will be entitled to recover the workman's share from the wages of the workmen concerned. The eligibility for employees to cover under this Act is for those who draw less than Rs. 7500 p.m. as basic and dearness allownaces The Act would apply to an establishment only when the number of employees is 10 or more. Punishment for false statement shall be punishable with imprisonment for period upto six months or with fine not exceeding Rs. 2,000/- or with both.

Industrial Disputes Act, 1947

The object of this Act is to ensure social justice to both the employers and employees and advance the progress of industry by bringing about the existence of harmony and cordial relationship between the parties. It is a piece of legislation providing and regulating the service conditions of the workers and to provide them ordinary amenities of life.

The labour disputes are settled under this Act through conciliation proceedings, labour court etc.

The Payment of Bonus Act, 1965

The object of the Act is to maintain peace and harmony between labour and capital by allowing the employees to share the prosperity of the establishment reflected by the profits earned by the contributions made by the capital, management and labour. An employee working in the establishment for not less than thirty working days in that year is eligible for bonus. A minimum bonus shall be 8.33 per cent of the salary or wages earned by the employee during the accounting year or ten hundred rupees, whichever is higher, whether or not the employer has any allocable surplus in the accounting year.

The Payment of Gratuity Act, 1972

The object of this Act is to provide for a scheme for the payment of gratuity to employees engaged in factories, mines, oil fields, plantations, ports, railways, ships or other establishments and for matters connected therewith or incidental thereto.

Gratuity shall be payable to an employee on the termination of his employment on his super annuation, retirement or resignation or his death or disablement due to accident or disease after he has rendered continuous service for not less than five years.

Tamil Nadu Shops and Establishment Act, 1947:

Sec. 6: Tamil Nadu Government exempts permanently all societies registered or deemed to be registered under Tamil Nadu Co-operative Societies Act, except Section 31, 41, 43,50 and 51 of the said Act subject to the condition that the said societies shall exhibit their name boards in Tamil and wherever other languages are used the versions in those languages shall be below the Tamil version.

Sec. 31: Wages for overtime work–Twice the ordinary rate of wages.

Sec. 41: Notice of dismissal – Person employed for a period of not less than six months, except for a reasonable cause.

Sec. 43: Powers and duties of Inspection – Power to Inspectors to enter the premises for the examination of the place and registers.

Sec. 50: Rights and privileges under other laws, etc not affected.

Sec. 51: Commissioner of Labour to decide certain questions.

30

Laws Applicable to the Cooperative Wholesale Stores

R. Pothi Reddy

INTRODUCTION

The objective of the Cooperative Wholesale Stores (CWS) is to serve the consumers with the provisions of *Right Product*, of *Right Quality*, in *Right Quantity*, at *Right Price* (4 Rs). When the objective is deeply concentrated, they will achieve *Viability, Visibility, Values* and *Volume* (4 Vs). The business ethics is the core anchor which will lead to sustainability of the business.

The CWS have to deal with various kinds of provisions (commodities) to be supplied to consumers under one roof.

In the existing scenario, the officials of the CWS are accountable for the organizational *Safety, Surplus, Success* and *Sustainability* (4 Ss). The officials of the CWS need to have legal and awareness to aspects pertaining to business activities, managerial aspects in order to effectively run their stores.

The laws applicable to CWS are many in number. The present paper tries to identify a few among them. Ignorance of law is no excuse. It is therefore essential for the officials of the CWS to keep them in touch with all the relevant laws. Laws not only fix RESPONSIBILITY, but also enhances RESPONSIBILITY.

LAWS APPLICABLE TO CWS

The laws identified here may be grouped under Management, Labour and Business Laws Relating to Management:

- **Tamilnadu Cooperative Societies Act 1983:** All the CWS are registered under this Act–all the provisions are applicable.
- **Indian Contract Act 1985:** This Act is quite relevant for all the CWS.
- **Limitations Act 1963:** For taking action within the legal time limit.
- **Contract Labour Act 1970:** Works such as processing and packaging, cleaning etc are under this Act.
- **Child labour Act 1986: This Act Prevents the Employment of** Child labour which is not only illegal but also against the fair trade standards formulated by the International Federation for Alternative Trade (IFAT).
- **Tamilnadu Industrial Establishments (Conferment of Permanent Status to Workmen) Act 1981:** CWS running Fair price shops at times urgently need temporary men on daily wage basis for distribution of Kerosene, wheat and wheat products, sugar, rice, palmoil etc. This law, in that way is applicable.
- **Tamilnadu Shop & Establishment Act 1947:** Concerned with working hours, salary, over time, congenial working climate etc.
- **The Employees's Provident Fund and Miscellaneous Provisions Act 1952:** To provide for Provident Funds, family pension and deposit linked insurance plans and schemes for employees.

- **The Employees State Insurance Act 1948:** To introduce social insurance by providing for certain benefits in case of sickness, maternity and the like.
- **The Tamilnadu Industrial Establishments (National and Festival Holidays) Act 1958:** to facilitate the employees to go for national holidays compulsorily.
- **Provincial Insolvency Act 1920:** To be aware of and cautious in safeguarding the capital of the organization.
- **Criminal Procedure Code: 1908 (1973):** Is required where misappropriation, breach of trust, falsification of accounts, foregery, thefts, misuse of funds etc occur.
- **Indian Penal Code 1860:** For frauds, tampering of records and other aspects.
- **Code of Civil Procedure 1908:** For institution of suit and follow up.
- **Indian Evidence Act 1872:** To prove the cases effectively and to pin down the evidences.
- **The Tamilnadu Right to Information Act 1997:** To ensure transparency to the consumers and customers in the matter of working.
- **Constitution of India 1950:** To safeguard the rights of consumers and the general public.

LAWS RELATING TO LABOUR

The labour laws are a group of laws enacted. They cover various aspects relating to labour and employment. It includes the provisions for checking the exploitation and oppression of the employers, maintaining harmonious and good industrial relations, employee welfare and ensuring social security to the working class. The labour legislation can be classified as follows: (i) Industrial Relations (ii)payment of wages and social security (iii) employee welfare.

- **Payment of Wages Act 1936:** This Act is designed to secure payment of wages to the employees on due dates at regular intervals and expeditious disposal of claims relatively to wages.

- **Minimum Wages Act 1948:** The ILO way back in 1928 emphasized the need for a minimum wages fixing machinery. The Minimum Wages Act came in 1948. The objective is to prevent exploitation of unorganized labour.
- **Tamilnadu Payment of Subsistence Allowance Act 1981:** To make it obligatory on the part of management to make payment of subsistence allowance to the employees who are kept under suspension. 50% upto 90 days, 75% from 91 to 180 days and above 181 days 100%. Beyond 90 days, if the delay is due to the employee it is 50% only.
- **Payment of Bonus Act 1965:** The Act aims at providing payment of Bonus linked with profit or productivity.
- **Payment of Gratuity Act 1972:** Act envisages to provide a Retirement benefits to the workmen who have rendered long and unblemished service to the employer and thus have contributed to the prosperity of the organization (CWS). It is a reward for long and meritorious service.
- **Industrial Disputes Act 1947:** To provide conciliation machinery to bring about peaceful settlement of industrial disputes.
- **Factories Act 1948:** Applicable to CWS run processing units, mixing units, ginning factories and the like.
- **Workmen Compensation Act 1923:** Ensures social security for workmen in the shape of compensation etc.

LAWS RELATING BUSINESS

- **Income Tax Act:** The officials of the CWS should be conversant with the provisions of taxable income, exemptions available to cooperatives under the Income Tax Act etc.
- **Tamilnadu Sales Tax Act 1959:** Sales tax is directly affecting the sales turn over and profitability.

- **Sale of Goods Act 1872:** This Act is almost a part of Indian Contract Act streesed on "Buyer Beware".
- **Essential Commodities Act 1955:** CWS are the lead societies under public distribution system and dealing with essential commodities in retail and wholesale.
- The latest developments in Indian economic decisions indicate that India will soon have no essential commodities and an item will be declared as essential only in crisis.
- Public Distribution System also will come under core sector/priority sector leading to concessional finance.
- **Consumer Protection Act 1986 (2003):** To protect the consumers from unfair trade practices. Consumer Protection Councils and Consumer Redressal Forums are available to help the consumers.
- **Paddy pledged**–stock missing–society agrees for value of stock on the date of pledge. Member wants either the pledged stock or the value on date (market rate). Supreme Court: Cooperative Act can prevail. Consumer Protection Act also can prevail for additional relief. (Thirumurugan Cooperative Agricultural Credit Society vs. M. Lalitha (AIR 2004/SC 448/2004/2/LW/41)
- **Preservation of Food Adulteration Act 1956:** Till 1995, it was a State Act. The Government of India thought the subject as very important and they brought this subject under Central Act.
- **Weight and Measures Act 1976 and Standard of Weights and Measures Packed Commodities Act 1977:** The consumers have got a right to correct quantity and the full information on packed items and this Act ensures that.

Rights of the Consumers and values of Cooperative identity.

Consumer Protection Councils are now working for safeguarding the rights of the consumers. A few of their rights are catalogued hereunder: (i) Right to safety (ii)Right to be informed (iii) Right to choose (iv) Right to be heard (v) Right to redressal of grievances (NCRDC) (vi) Right to consumer education (vii) Right to healthy environment (viii) Right to basic needs.

COOPERATIVE VALUES

CWS as cooperative identifies with the basic values in them will be the right type of organizations to honour the consumer rights. The basic values with cooperatives (Lars Marcus cited in Dwivedi 1998) are:

1. Self help values (activity, creativity, responsibility, independence and do it yourself).
2. Mutual help values (cooperation, unity, collective action, solidarity and peace)
3. Non Profit interest values (resource conservation, elimination of profits as a driving force, social responsibility, utilitarian goal, not profiteering from others' work)
4. Democratic values (equality, participation, equity).
5. Educational & training values (Humanism, independence, constructiveness).
6. Voluntary effort values (commitment, creating power, independence, pluralism).
7. Universality values and values of cooperation (global perspectives; openness).
8. Purposeful values (Economic benefit to members).

The officials of the cooperative wholesale stores (CWS) are duty bound to see that the CWSs they manage, fully honour the values.

ETHICAL STANDARDS

The CWSs are to strictly adhere to ethical standards for continued existence in business. 'Ethics' are the fundamental rules. The various laws which we have discussed are only based on the ethical guidelines and moral values.

Businessmen perform a social function. Business is important to the public welfare. Today the whole society is a business environment. The ethical standards have been developed and advocated by The Rotary international; The Johnson Institute of Ethics; Gandhi Ashram, Thiruchengodu; and Gene Lacgniak.

(a) **The Rotary international** have developed a list of ethical principles that a business should follow.

(b) **The Johnson Institute of Ethics** have developed ethical values called "Six Pillars of Character".

(c) **Gandhi Ashram Thiruchengodu** have developed a code of ethical values as early as 1925 and they are following.

(d) **Gene Lacgniak** a social scientist has developed a set of five golden rules and propagated it.

(e) **IFAT**–International Federation for Alternate Trade has come out with a set of Fair Trade Standards (1997/2001) consolidating almost all the ethical standards. They are: (i) Creating opportunities for economically disadvantaged producers (ii) Transparency and accountability (iii) Capacity-building (iv) Promoting Fair Trade (v) Payment of fair price (vi) Gender Equity (vii) Working conditions (viii) Rights of the Children (ix) Environment.

CONCLUSION

Laws alone cannot make the CWSs a great success. It could be achieved with people's participation, ethical ingredients and the officials deportment.

31

Erode District Cooperative Wholesale Stores: A Success Story

B. Tamilmani and
S. Dhanasekaran

PRELUDE

The Erode Cooperative Wholesale Stores started functioning on 8.3.1964, with the objective of supplying consumer articles and necessary provisions to the members, societies and the general public. The membership of the store consists of 53 individual members, and 282 cooperative organizations with the state government. Providing quality goods at reasonable price with a correct measurement is the fundamental objective of the stores. This store has been one among a few, which has earned net profit continuously, in many of the years. What makes it different from other stores is analyzed below. The analysis is divided into two parts. The first part focuses on the business analysis which includes financial and functional analysis and the second part analyses their reasons underlining the success.

OBJECTIVES

The objectives of the study are:

1. To anlayse the business performance of the store over the period of 11 years and
2. To find out the underlying features of the success of the stores.

METHODOLOGY

Case study was adopted. The CWS was selected purposively, as it is one of few CWSs performing successfully over a period of time and being adjudicated as the best among CWSs in Tamil Nadu in the year 2004-2005. The study covered a period of eleven years starting from 1994-95 to 2004-2005. The Study depends on the secondary data which were collected from the Audit reports, annual reports, financial statements and ledgers. For collecting data from the CWS, a schedule was prepared. The data collected was tabulated under proper heads and they were analyzed in a meaningful way.

ANALYSIS AND DISCUSSION

This is the crucial part of the study. An attempt is made here to analyse the financial and functional areas of the study unit. The two areas are sub divided into: (i) Capital structure, (ii) Investment, (iii) Business activities, (iv) Business results and (v) Management and staff pattern. In course of analysis of the data, simple statistical tools namely average, percentage compound growth rates were used to arrive at meaningful statistical information.

(i) Capital Structure

The capital structure in CWSs is composed of equity capital and borrowed capital. Unlike the joint-stock companies, cooperatives are restricted to mobilize shares from the public but confined to members living within the jurisdiction. Reserve fund (created out of net profit) together with share capital constitutes owned funds. Owned funds strengthen the financial base as it facilitates for higher borrowing. The maximum borrowing power (MBP) is determined on the basis of five times of owned capital. The study average share capital was Rs. 11.82 Lakhs (see table1). The first seven years had greater share capital than the study average. Borrowed capital consists of deposits mobilized and loans borrowed from financing banks. Deposits pertaining to CWS are staff-security, trade and fixed. These deposits not to be treated on par with the ones the banking institutions tap from the public.

The staff security deposit is collected from the sales personnel as they are accountable to a sizeable amount of goods under their control (Salesman liability System). Trade Deposits are mobilized from the supplier of goods, as the CWS procure groceries and consumer provision from the panel of registered suppliers, who need to maintain trade deposits with the CWS.

Borrowings are made from District Central Cooperative Bank. The total borrowings consist of government loans, cash credit accommodations and short-term loans. Cash Credit accommodations are running accounts wherein the CWS is sanctioned to certain level of financial assistance for meeting the working capital requirements. Short term loans also do the same purpose, whereas Government loans are of long term nature.

(ii) Investment

In practice, CWSs make investments in shares of other cooperatives, shares of higher level organizations and in other firms of investments. The study unit has made similar investments. The investment picture shows (see table 2) a standstill whereas investment in other forms' shows a picture of variation.

(iii) Business Analysis

Business Activities of CWS refer to the purchase of goods in the most economic ways and sell them at a competitive price.

Table 1
Capital Structure

(Rs.in Lakhs)

S. No.	Year	Owned funds		Total (A)	Borrowed funds		Total (B)	Grand Total (A+B)
		Share Capital	Statutory funds		Deposits	Borrowing		
1.	1994-95	17.15 (20.23)	25.98 (30.64)	43.13 (50.87)	1.40 (1.65)	40.26 (47.48)	41.66 (49.13)	84.79 (100.0)
2.	1995-96	16.01 (21.52)	26.00 (34.95)	42.01 (56.49)	1.77 (2.37)	30.60 (41.14)	32.37 (43.51)	74.38 (100.0)
3.	1996-97	15.05 (12.37)	40.22 (33.06)	55.27 (45.45)	28.73 (23.62)	37.65 (30.95)	66.38 (54.57)	121.65 (100.0)
4.	1997-98	13.98 (12.07)	40.23 (34.73)	54.21 (46.81)	28.75 (24.82)	32.86 (28.37)	61.61 (53.19)	115.82 (100.0)
5.	1998-99	12.81 (14.92)	40.24 (44.58)	53.05 (58.78)	1.79 (1.98)	35.42 (39.24)	37.21 (41.22)	90.26 (100.0)
6.	1999-00	12.84 (9.28)	40.24 (29.10)	53.08 (38.38)	1.81 (1.31)	83.41 (60.31)	85.22 (61.62)	138.30 (100.0)
7.	2000-01	11.91 (10.45)	52.65 (46.20)	64.56 (56.66)	2.05 (1.80)	47.34 (41.54)	49.39 (43.34)	113.95 (100.0)
8.	2001-02	10.86 (11.25)	52.69 (54.57)	63.55 (65.82)	1.99 (2.06)	31.01 (32.12)	33.00 (34.18)	96.55 (100.0)
9.	2002-03	10.86 (8.20)	58.19 (43.94)	69.05 (52.14)	1.77 (1.33)	61.61 (46.52)	63.38 (47.86)	132.43 (100.0)
10.	2003-04	9.82 (12.63)	58.24 (74.91)	68.06 (87.54)	1.76 (2.26)	7.93 (10.20)	9.69 (12.46)	77.75 (100.0)
11.	2004-05	9.57 (9.25)	85.22 (82.36)	94.79 (91.61)	1.70 (1.64)	6.98 (6.75)	8.68 (8.39)	103.47 (100.0)
	Total	130.00	483.90	660.76	73.52	415.07	488.59	
	Avg	11.82	44.00	60.07	6.68	37.73	44.42	

(Figures in parenthesis indicate percentage to grand total)

Purchase of groceries and consumer goods constitutes the prime function where the other activities move around it. There must be a fool-proof system of purchase which would facilitate the CWS to perform better. An ill- advised or un-analyzed purchase decision would bring negative impacts upon the functioning and financial position.

Table 2
Business Activities

(Rs.in Lakhs)

Sl. No.	*Year*	*Sales (A)*	*GR*	*Purchases (B)*	*GR*	*Difference (A-B)*
1.	1994-95	3101.51	-	2947.52	-	153.99
2.	1995-96	3350.10	8	3131.01	6.22	219.09
3.	1996-97	3749.89	11.85	3552.07	13.44	197.82
4.	1997-98	4025.23	7.37	3730.40	5.02	294.83
5.	1998-99	3375.26	-16.12	3153.28	-15.47	221.98
6.	1999-00	3556.84	5.77	3361.07	6.58	195.77
7.	2000-01	3467.94	-2.87	3234.50	-3.76	233.44
8.	2001-02	3414.64	-1.53	3150.82	-2.58	263.82
9.	2002-03	3834.93	12.25	3547.03	12.57	287.9
10.	2003-04	3569.90	-6.84	3283.49	-7.42	286.41
	Total	35446.24		33091.19	-	2355.71
	Avg	3544.62		3309.11		235.51

CGR = 1.08

The purchase system as vogue in CWS clearly indicates the centralized purchase pattern. All the purchase decisions are taken by the Joint-purchase committee (JPC), which is the authorized nodal body to decide the matters on purchase of groceries for wholesale stores. In Tamil Nadu, the CWS are grouped under four JPCs, for regions of Chennai, Coimbatore, Madurai and Salem. One advantage of centralized purchase could be 'economy purchase' as the indents of CWSs of particular region are pooled together before a purchase decision is arrived at. But this does not workout well at all times, because when small quantity of goods is purchased the cost of breakeven would be higher. And in some instances, some regions are familiar with certain goods but which cannot

Table-3
Business Analysis – Major Classification

(Rs. in Lakhs)

S. No.	Year	Sales		Total	Purchase		Total	Difference
		Controlled	Non controlled		Controlled	Non controlled		
1.	1994-95	1341.67	1761.98	3103.65	1296.94	1297.17	2954.11	149.54
2.	1995-96	1424.79	1927.10	3351.89	1360.49	1786.74	3147.23	204.66
3.	1996-97	1401.21	2349.58	3750.79	1347.26	2224.03	3571.29	179.50
4.	1997-98	1184.01	2843.84	4027.86	1146.67	2619.65	3766.32	261.54
5.	1998-99	1250.10	2516.30	3766.40	1231.45	2283.58	3515.03	251.37
6.	1999-00	1447.05	2114.47	3561.52	1388.03	2464.44	3852.47	-290.95
7.	2000-01	1337.00	3335.46	4672.47	1273.17	3025.27	4298.44	374.03
8.	2001-02	1200.04	3073.15	4273.19	1143.72	2729.29	3873.01	400.18
9.	2002-03	1262.24	3082.88	4345.12	1195.81	2793.55	3989.36	355.76
10.	2003-04	993.84	3047.02	4040.86	960.95	2730.84	3691.79	349.07
11.	2004-05	1524.75	3050.24	4574.99	1467.95	2838.28	4305.91	269.08
	Total	14366.70	29102.02	43468.74	13812.44	26792.84	40964.96	2503.78
	Avg	1306.06	2645.63	3951.70	1255.67	2435.71	3724.08	227.61

be purchased by CWSs as they are not permitted. The JPC is convened once in a month. For purchase of goods in urgency to meet consumer demands, the CWSs have to wait for many days or compelled to buy the goods at a price for which suppliers are not ready. Another serious drawback is that the personnel involved in sales are not included in JPC, as a consequence, whatever the JPC purchases the sales personnel are compelled to take up the sales. All these shortcomings can be avoided by making the purchase system more effective and democratic. An ideal purchase system is need of the hour which features decentralized purchase and which gives no room for malpractices.

Table 4
Investment

(Rs. in Lakhs)

Sl. No.	*Year*	*Other investments*	*Share in coop. Investment*	*Total*	*GR*
1.	1994-95	36.16 (89.77)	4.12 (10.23)	40.28 (100.0)	-
2.	1995-96	6.64 (61.65)	4.13 (38.35)	10.77 (100.0)	-73.26
3	1996-97	5.86 (58.65)	4.13 (41.35)	9.99 (100.0)	-7.24
4	1997-98	6.20 (60.01)	4.13 (39.99)	10.33 (100.0)	3.40
5	1998-99	6.42 (60.85)	4.13 (39.15)	10.55 (100.0)	2.12
6	1999-00	5.74 (58.15)	4.13 (41.85)	9.87 (100.0)	-6.44
7	2000-01	4.49 (52.08)	4.13 (47.92)	8.62 (100.0)	-12.66
8	01-02	4.72 (53.33)	4.13 (46.67)	8.85 (100.0)	2.66
9	02-03	18.01 (81.34)	4.13 (18.66)	22.14 (100.0)	1.50
10	03-04	18.20 (81.51)	4.13 (18.49)	22.33 (100.0)	0.30
11.	04-05	21.45	4.19	25.64	0.148
	Total	139.89	45.48	179.37	
	Avg	12.17	4.13	16.30	

CGR = - 5.72

'Sales' is another crucial activity which determines profitability. Greater the sales higher the profitability and vice-versa. The CWSs effect sales in the following form: sale of controlled items (PDS), sale of goods to primary consumer cooperatives, (on wholesale basis), sale of petroleum products and sale of non-controlled goods to the public (Retailing). Of the four, retailing of non-controlled items assumes greater importance, and it is to be taken for efficiency test of sales performance. The reason is that the real competitive strength is witnessed through non-controlled retailing. Sale of goods to member cooperatives and public distribution system are effected on mandatory basis, which do not indicate competitive spirit. Sale of petroleum products is like non-competitive trading.

An analysis off business activities reveals fluctuation over the study period. High performance was witnessed on purchase and sales activities in 1997-98 as there was a boom in the market. There is a correlation of high performance between the two activities in 96-97, in 97-98 and 2002-03. It is also noticed that the sales performance was greater than purchase in all the years of study. The higher difference was found in 97-98, 2002-03 and 2003-04. The study average net difference was Rs. 235-51 lakhs, which was by passed by four years namely 97-98, 2001-02, 2002-03, and 2003- 04. This shows that the CWSs business performance had been maintained positively.

BUSINESS RESULT

Although Cooperatives are not for profit, the complexities of competitive world make CWS to earn profit. Otherwise, they cannot survive. Here, one should understand that profit earning is not our sole goals. Catering to the requirements of member-consumers, member-societies by supplying consumer goods and provisions at price advantage is the main goal. While undertaking business at cost plus price policy, CWSs happen to earn profit. In true sense, cooperatives are found working with two extreme objectives-values and profit. They neither should forgo their values for which they have been established nor should they go after profit. But, in the modern business world the performance of CWSs is scaled up with profit-making. Profit-making is an acid test which signifies the efficiency of business. The higher the profit the greater the efficiency the organization.

The study unit has earned gross profit in all the years of the study period. Gross profit is the positive result of trading activities. It was found to be varying from Rs. 113.16 to Rs. 206.90. The study average of the store was Rs. 178.22 lakhs which was surpassed by the gross profit for five years. Net profit is the result of income under expenditure. Net profit of the CWS is the net positive result. It is found that the store has earned profit in eight out of the ten years. The years 1996-97 and 98-99 found to be bad as the net loss crept in these years. The CWS was in a position to earn profit by minimizing cost, maximizing sales, and by avoiding over stock and other related reasons.

Table 5
Profits and Audit Classification

(Rs.in Lakhs)

Sl. No	*Year*	*Gross profit*	*GR*	*Net Result*
1.	1994-95	153.33	-	26.29
2.	1995-96	162.69	6.10	20.00
3	1996-97	181.43	11.51	-29.41
4	1997-98	234.85	29.44	15.16
5	1998-99	124.96	-46.79	-42.54
6	1999-00	207.44	66.00	1.46
7	2000-01	278.86	34.42	25.50
8	2001-02	248.64	1.00	41.61
9	2002-03	234.27	-5.77	62.81
10	2003-04	252.08	7.60	29.59
11.	2004-05	228.29	-9.43	16.40
	Total	2306.84	-	166.87
	Avg	209.71	-	15.17

MANAGEMENT AND STAFF PATTERN OF THE STORE

One added advantage of the CWSs is team work which is composed of decision-makers and implementing personnel. The Democratic Board of Management was done away with in the cooperative sector since 1976. The personnel at decision making are found to be wellversed with regard to business analysis, tax systems, auditing, budgeting and control. The staff strength has been maintained well below the level of approved strength. The actual staff strength was 154, which was lower than the approved strength of 251. The CWS could be in a position to save salary of the 97 personnel, if they had been appointed. Though it cannot be appreciated on labour point of view, but when it comes to question of efficiency, this would hold good.

The management of the stores is vested with the Special Officer appointed in the cadre of Deputy Registrar of Cooperative Societies. There is a General Manager who is working under the special officer. There are two managers, (purchases and sales) helping and coordinating the functions of the general manager. There are 153 employees at different cadres looking after the sales and administration of the stores.

Staff Strength

Sl. No.	*Category*	*Approved Strength*	*No. of Staff on Roll*
1.	Special officer	1	1
2.	General manager	1	1
3.	Mangers	5	2
4.	Superintendents	11	7
5.	Assistants (UDC)	23	17
6.	Junior Assistants (LDC)	36	17
7.	Salesmen	79	34
8.	Assistant salesmen	95	74
9.	Contract (Assistant on contract)	-	3
		251	154

REASONS ATTRIBUTED FOR SUCCESS

This part of the study attempts to bring out the important findings from the analysis which happened to be the causative factors for the success of the store. It can also be stated that all these factors together contributed to the success and made the CWS quite distinct from other CWSs in Tamilnadu.

1. **High Non-controlled Retailing:** The level of non-controlled retailing is considered to be the efficiency parameter in measuring the sale performance. Higher the level would be the greater the efficiency of the organization. In the competitive environment, pushing up the non-controlled retailing to a higher scale would be really a cumbersome task. The study unit had excelled by making greater sales to the tune of Rs.2645.63 lakhs (study average) which was hundred per cent greater than the controlled sales. The purchases under non-controlled also witnessed a similar trend.
2. **Computerization in Management:** Application of computers in administrative affairs would ease the functions. This would be highly useful to present the matters on time to enable the managers to make business analysis and take decisions. Now-a-days, it is rare to find private trading organizations functioning without computers. But for the CWS, it is still a distant dream, though they have voluminous business. The study unit is the only CWS in Tamil Nadu that has applied computers in its business operations and administrative affairs. Timely decision based on managerial information system was possible through computers.
3. **Location and Ambience:** Location of the business undertaking is a point of importance for its growth, that too if it is in the case of wholesale store, it becomes imperative. CWS could excel when they are located in the heart of the cities, dwelling centers, bus-stand and other busy places. The study unit has its retailing centers at Erode main bus stand. The retailing center happens to be the important center, as it puts up good sales performance. Equal importance is given to the ambience which would attract more number of consumers. The retail point at the bus stand no way inferior to the private shops, naturally it had won the hearts of the people.

4. **Realistic Management Control System:** Management control systems include budgeting, budgeting control, auditing control on purchasing, sales, financial matters. Budgeting puts forth the objectives in numerical terms. The study unit has the practice of budgeting every year for its key result areas and reviewing them at the end of the year. There was not much difference between the budgets and actuals when it was reviewed. Auditing is another area which helps to find out the exact financial position. As there is an internal auditor the business and financial matters were examined regularly and the final audit reports were brought out in time.
5. **Optimum Number of Personnel:** As of now, the study unit had been working with 157 employees for carrying out the business as well as administrative work. The actual strength of the employees was short of 94 of the sanctioned strength. It could be one way of minimizing the establishment expenses otherwise to that extent the amount would have to be spent as salary. This has resulted in the profit.
6. **Quality Assurance through Lab:** The unit owns a laboratory wherein all types of edible oils and food items are thoroughly tested for quality assurance. The lab was established with one time grant sanctioned by the Tamil Nadu Government. One has to understand that quality in performance will always speak louder among the consumers.
7. **Financial Soundness:** The study unit was in a position to develop its financial soundness over the years by way of enhancing business turnover. The financial gain largely obtained from its counterpart, on bifurcation of its assets. The sizeable amount it got from various sources was being used meticulously for widening the business horizons. The financial soundness had facilitated for the running of petrol bunks which normally requires huge funds.

CONCLUSION

It is concluded that the study unit is found to be stable, both in financial and functional areas. It has earned profit in eight out of the eleven years. The employees found to have understood the role and place of CWS in the competitive world. The management took decisions after careful analysis and performed activities seriously. On the effective performance carried over the years, the CWS had been adjudged the best CWS in Tamil Nadu. It deserves it.

32

Education and Training: Essential Ingredients for the Development of Consumer Cooperatives

X. Lourdes Xavier Wilson and N. Baluswami

In India, the consumer cooperatives have four tier structure comprising a National Consumer Cooperative Federation, State level Federations of Consumer Cooperatives, Wholesale/ Central Stores at the District level and the Primary Stores at the grossroot level. The consumer the cooperatives satisfy the consumers by supplying quality goods while at the same time, they have to improve their performance in the globalised era. The human resources in the consumer cooperatives should be encouraged. The investment in training and education should not be regarded as a wasteful expenditure, it must be considered as an investment in creation of professional and well informed employees and enlightened members. So, it is obvious that cooperatives will have to invest their resources in proper training and development of their own managers and employees with a new approach. According to Peter Drucker, the greatest benefit of training is not in learning new. It is to do better what we already do well.

INSTITUTIONS FOR TRAINING

National Council for Cooperative Training (NCCT), a wing of National Cooperative Union of India (NCUI) provides training and consultancy services for the cooperatives. Training programmes are organized at Vaikunth Metha National Institutes of Cooperative Management (VAMINICOM) at Pune, 5 Regional Institute of Cooperative Management and 14 Institutes of Cooperative Management located in different parts of the country, besides, junior cooperative training centers at districts.

With the revolution in the modern technology, professional management emphasises specialized knowledge, information and skills. Also commitment, character, competence culture, creativity, and credibility among the officials in cooperatives are essential to develop the consumer cooperatives.

IMPORTANCE OF VALUE EDUCATION

We are now in the Globalised World. Competition has intensified in most areas of business activities, including the sectors that were previously the domain of cooperatives, especially, consumer cooperatives. At this juncture, the employees of cooperatives should realize that the cooperatives are essential for their wellbeing. The efficiency of cooperatives is mainly based upon the employees. The success of the cooperatives depends on the integrity, loyalty, oneness, adjustability and other qualities of the employees. To inculcate these qualities, the employees should undergo value based education and training.

MANAGERIAL VALUES

The managers are influenced by the professional values of the cooperative organization. The policy makers at the top level must be able to differentiate personal values form

VALUE EDCUATION-CHART

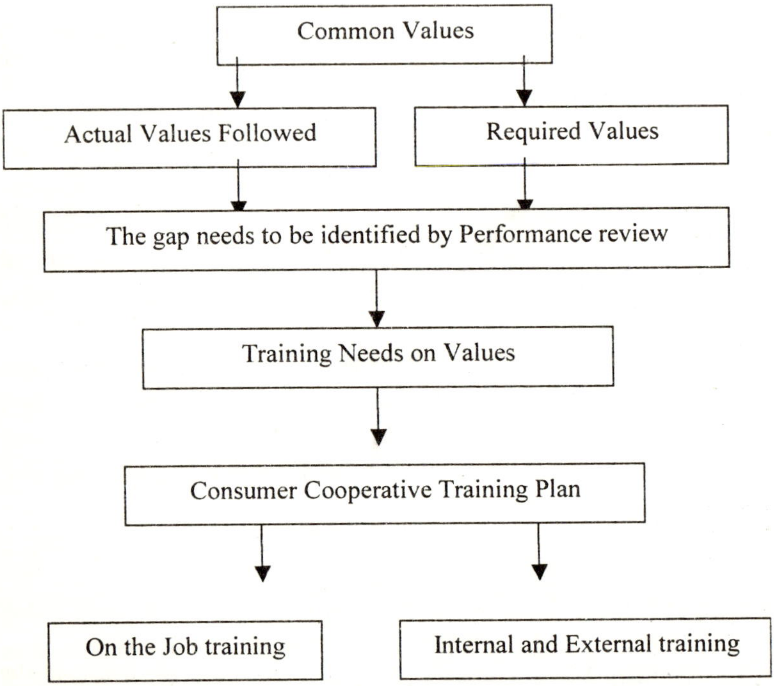

cooperative values. The participants sent for training programmes should be classified in such a way that they belong to clearly one of four categories such as:

- He who fully supports the cooperative view.
- He who accepts the cooperative view.
- He who lives with the cooperative view; though he has differences between his own view and those of his organization.
- He who completely disagrees with the cooperative views and this is the most difficult situation.

Based upon these views the tailor-made training is essential.□

'Values' Based Cooperative Education and Training

Training Areas	*Related Values*
Sales	Selling is an important activity to be performed with out adulteration. Products must be sold for the 'Public Welfare'. It must be informed.
Purchase	The consumer co-operative's success is based upon the proper purchase. The Functional welfare of co-operatives must be based upon purchase.
Accounting	Proper accounting helps to strengthen the activities of co-operatives. So 'Honesty' in account maintenance should be inculcated. Ethical use of accounting techniques
Receiving Consumers	Approaching customers is a vital function in co-operatives. So, the "Respect to Person" can be insisted upon in value education
Correct Weighment	'Justice' can be maintained through correct weighment. So it must be done properly.
Proper Billing	Proper billing to the society and also to the customer develops the' Loyalty'.
Packaging	The 'Promise –Keeping' is based upon the proper packaging.
Management	Value based management 'Ethical and Social' responsibilities of business.
Finance	'Ethical' use of money and the Social role of the official.
Auditing	Moral' duties of an auditor. Auditor's responsibility towards the society.
Customer Relations Management(CRM)	'Cordial Relations' with the member customers Benefits both the parties.' Hospitality' satisfies the customer
Conflict Management	'Cooperation' among cooperatives and in-between individuals will increase the sales volume of the consumer cooperatives.
Management Information System (MIS)	Communication should be sent in time to take the decisions easily.

CONCLUSION

The Consumer co-operative organizations should regularly ask for some of the important questions from time to time in order to get closer to the members and to serve them better. It is a process of introspection. The feedback provides valuable indicators and guidelines for further development. The training feedback should be measured. Certainly these will strengthen the skills of the employees.

33

Consumers' Perception: A Study with Reference to Consumer Cooperative Wholesale Stores in Dindigul

B.Tamilmani, V. Murugan and K. Gunaseela Prabhu

Cooperative wholesale stores play a crucial role in the structure of consumer cooperatives especially in delivering goods both in wholesaling and retiling. These wholesale stores aim at protecting the interests of the consumers, supplying essential goods with superior quality at reasonable prices, maintaining price stabilization, developing fair business practices and liasion with National and State Cooperative Federations and cooperative institutions. The Consumer Cooperative Wholesale-stores in order to render effective services to the customers, must run self-service sections, super markets, and retail outlets.

The Dindigul District Consumer Cooperative Wholesale Stores was registered on 19.03.1964 and commenced its functioning on 03.04.1964. The store has been functioning under the Tamil Nadu Cooperative Societies Act 1983. The area of operation of the stores is confined to the entire

Dindigul District. The main functions of the stores are procurement of articles in bulk and selling them in wholesale and retail trade. It acts as an agent not only to the government but also to cooperatives for procuring and storing of food grains and other commodities. It sells the goods to its affiliated primary consumer cooperative stores, members and the public at large.

STATEMENT OF THE PROBLEM

Initially the Dindigul cooperative wholesale store was running on healthy manner but in course of time the performance of store was not up to the expectation. The negative growth was witnessed on many of the key result areas. Losing of customer's patronage, volume of sales and its popularity were the phenomena. The researchers were interested to know the pulse of the consumers on the performance of the stores. What is the level of consumers' participation in the business? What is their share of purchase from the cooperative store? What is the level of satisfaction of the consumers? What are the expectations of the consumers? These are but a few questions to be answered, hence this study.

OBJECTIVES OF THE STUDY

(i) To understand the purchase behavior of the consumer

(ii) To measure the perception of the consumers with regard to price, quality, measurement and other essential parameters.

(iii) To know the place of cooperative wholesale stores in the minds of the consumers.

SCOPE OF THE STUDY

The study examined mainly the satisfaction level of the consumers on the services through some determined parameters like price, quality, measurement, behavior of sales personnel, location and ambience, working hours, customer relations after–sales service, packaging and location of the stores.

METHODOLOGY

It is an empirical study. Field survey method was adopted for the study. The data used in this study were collected through using structured interview schedule. Thirty consumer-respondents were selected randomly while they were purchasing the goods from the supermarket of the cooperative store.

ANALYSIS AND DISCUSSION

An attempt is made here to analyze the respondents' behavior especially on the share of purchase, which was correlated with their family size, occupation and expenditure. The purpose of analyzing these variables was to indicate the influence over purchasing.

Table 1
Family size and Share of purchase

Family size	*Families*			*Total*
Share of Purchase	*Small*	*Medium*	*Big*	
Below 25%	1 (3)	1 (4)	1 (3)	3 (10)
26 – 50%	7 (23)	8 (27)	-	15 (50)
51 – 75%	3 (10)	4 (13)	-	7 (23)
76 to 100%	2 (7)	2 (7)	1 (3)	5 (17)
Total	13 (43)	15 (53)	2 (4)	30 (100)

The respondents from medium-size families have greater share of purchase from the store, followed by the respondents from small-size families. Of the total household requirements, 50 per cent of the respondents had a share of purchase from 26 per cent to 50 per cent. The table implies that the big families have low-level participation in the business of the stores. It also reveals that 17 per cent of the respondents had the practice of buying three fourth of their family requirements from the store.

Of the different occupational status of the respondents, the participation of government employees found to be higher (37 per cent) followed by private employees (27 per cent). It was found that 50 per cent of the respondents procured the required goods of their family, from 26 per cent to 50 per cent. It is a good sign that 17 per cent of respondents procured goods from 76 Per cent to 100 per cent.

Table 2
Respondents' Occupation and their Share of Purchase

Occupation *Share of Purchase*	*Agri*	*Self Business*	*Govern-ment*	*Private employment*	*Total*
Below 25%	-	1	1	1	3 (10)
26 – 50%	1	7	4	3	15 (50)
51 – 75%	1	1	3	2	7 (23)
76 to 100%	-	-	3	2	5 (17)
Total	2 (6)	9 (30)	11 (37)	8 (27)	30 (100)

Table 3
Income and Share of Purchase

Income Group	*Amount in Rupees*				*Total*
Share of Purchase	*Below 3000*	*3001 to 5000*	*5001 to 7000*	*7000 and above*	
Below 25%	1	2	-	-	3 (10)
26 – 50%	5	5	3	2	15 (50)
51 – 75%	2	3	2	1	7 (23)
76 %and above	1	1	1	1	5 (17)
Total	9 (30)	11 (37)	6 (20)	4 (13)	30 (100)

The table shows that the people of low income and middle-income categories purchased frequently from the store. It is found that 50 per cent of the respondents had purchased up to 26 per cent to 50 per cent of their family requirements.

PERCEPTION OF CONSUMERS

In order to assess the perception of the consumers, nine variables were used as parameters, which reflected the performance of the store from the consumers' point of view. Four-point scale was used to measure the efficiency of the services of the store. The below table describes the variables along with scaling points:

Table 4
Key Variables and the level of Satisfaction

Sl. No.	*Factors variables*	*Highly satisfied*	*Satisfied*	*Dissatis-fied*	*Highly dissatis-fied*	*Total*
1.	Price	13 (43)	15 (50)	2 (7)	-	30 (100)
2.	Quality	13 (43)	16 (54)	1 (3)	-	30 (100)
3.	Weight or measurement	21 (70)	9 (30)	-	-	30 (100)
4.	Working hours	17 (57)	8 (27)	5 (16)	-	30 (100)
5.	Customer relationship	21 (70)	8 (27)	1 (3)	-	30 (100)
6.	After-sales service	13 (43)	16 (54)	1 (3)	-	30 (100)
7.	Availability of stock	3 (10)	7 (23)	20 (67)	-	30 (100)
8.	Packaging	18 (60)	10 (33)	2 (7)	-	30 (100)
9.	Location of stores	14 (47)	11 (37)	5 (16)	-	30 (100)

(Figures in parenthesis are percentage to the total.)

With regard to the price of the goods charged by the cooperative stores, 50 per cent of the respondents were satisfied followed by 43 per cent who were highly satisfied. The price policy followed by the store was cost plus price policy. Regarding the quality of the goods, 54 per cent of the respondents were satisfied followed by 43 per cent of respondents who got high level of satisfaction. The quality of goods is ensured as the purchase is made from the production centers or from manufacturers. The goods are purchased through joint purchase committee. The percentage of highly satisfied must be enhanced further. In case of weighment and measurement, 70 per cent of the respondents were highly satisfied and 30 per cent of the respondents were satisfied and no one reported dissatisfaction. This is because the goods dealt by them are already packed and served. Therefore, the chance for lower wieghment is avoided. On working hours, 57 per cent of respondents were highly satisfied; only 16 per cent of the respondents were not satisfied for it was not convenient for them to travel to the stores. On customer relationship, three- fourth of the respondents were highly satisfied and the rest were satisfied. The dissatisfied respondents portion was negligible. Now a-days there is much thrust on the customer relationship management. This helps the organization for further development.

After-sales service is considered an essential parameter of satisfying consumers. It was found that 54 per cent of respondents were satisfied, and 43 per cent of respondents were highly satisfied. Availability of sufficient stock would keep retaining the customer. Majority of 67 per cent of respondents were dissatisfied, as they did not get the required items they wished to buy. One fourth of the respondents reported to be satisfied.

Packaging helps the consumers to carry goods home conveniently. Consumers would prefer goods packed safely and easy to carry home. It was found that 60 per cent of respondents were highly satisfied, while 33 per cent reported to have satisfied with regard to packaging. Regarding the location of stores 47 per cent of the respondents were highly satisfied, while 37 per cent were satisfied. But 16 per cent of the respondents reported to have not satisfied at all.

FINDINGS

The following findings were arrived:

- Majority of the respondents found procuring their household articles from 26 per cent to 75 per cent of goods from the consumer cooperative stores.
- There was a high degree of relationship between occupation and the quantum of purchase and also income and share of purchase.

- It was found that 70 per cent of respondents were highly satisfied on the measurement and customer relations, 60 per cent on packaging and working hours. 54 per cent of respondents were satisfied, on price quality and after sales service. A two third of 67 per cent of respondents the were dissatisfied with level of stock of the goods maintained by the stores. No one was found to be highly dissatisfied.

CONCLUSION

It is concluded that consumers' perception on the service of the study unit was positive. The store maintained smooth customer relations and supplied articles at correct measurement. However, the prime areas like price and quality, a good number of consumers were only satisfied rather than highly satisfied. The wave of dissatisfaction was found only on non-availability of stock of goods. It is therefore, concluded that consumers' perception on the performance of the study unit was encouraging and positive.

34

Managerial Effectiveness in Consumer Cooperative Wholesale Stores: Proceedings of the State Level Workshop

B. Tamilmani

PRELUDE

Consumer Cooperatives have been functioning with the prime objective of supplying consumer articles and provisions at reasonable price. Their role is essentially witnessed in the fast growing materialistic world, as they combine business features with essential social ethos. They are not for earning profit but for protecting the consumers from the onslaught of unfair trade practices of some private traders. Organized in a small way in 1904 *(Triplicane Urban Cooperative Society)*, the movement has grown into a massive movement of 24,700 cooperatives with a membership of 9.7 million.

Cooperative Wholesale Stores (CWSs) are the District level Consumer Cooperatives performing both wholesale and retail businesses. They purchase goods in bulk, mostly, from the production centres and supply them to the consumers at a price advantage. Normally, these cooperatives adopt 'cost plus' price policy, which makes them function 'market checker' especially on price, quality and availability of goods.

In the globalized era, the CWSs have to pass through the challenges unleashed from all corners. When private wholesale/Department stores are growing at an accelerated pace, CWSs are now in a very critical situation more than ever before due to the globalisation of trade. They are hard pressed and are at crossroads. When 'survival of the fittest' is the mantra of the modern day, they are losing ground to the competitors. CWSs must strive for winning the race. Relying on the state, for assistance of all types, is to be done away with. Without any doubt, they need to redefine their policies, methods and management pattern to cope with the changing situation and circumstances. Application of modern management techniques, coupled with goal-oriented motivation of the employees, is the need of the hour. At this juncture, CWSs need to be adaptive in every respect and they must be capable of harnessing the opportunities and resources. Decisive strategies are to be evolved to strengthen CWSs to make them structurally strong and financially viable. Equipping the officials with necessary skill for enhancing the performance of CWSs is one way of getting close to make them functionally effective.

OBJECTIVES

The objectives of the workshop were:

(i) To provide a forum for analyzing the current status and performance of CWSs in Tamil Nadu, especially, in terms of growth and performance, market share and functional effectiveness.

(ii) To identify the training needs and managerial skills for better performance of the personnel.

(iii) To prepare operational and business guidelines for enabling the CWSs to be more competitive in the era of globalization.

With this background, a two-day state level workshop was organised on 19th and 20th January 2006, by the Department of Cooperation, Gandhigram Rural University (GR) with financial assistance from the unassigned grants of University Grants Commission, New Delhi.

METHODOLOGY

The methodology adopted in the workshop consisted of six technical sessions, four group discussions (parallel) followed by a plenary session. In total 45 papers were presented in the technical sessions under the identified sub themes of the workshop. There were four group discussion sessions, considered to be the main business element of the workshop. They were held parallel to synthesise the thoughts of academicians and practitioners on the theme of the workshop. In the plenary session, the findings of each group, were presented. The inaugural function preceded the technical sessions and valedictory function followed them.

The workshop had participants drawn from different backgrounds. The participants included personnel from managerial cadres of the cooperative wholesale stores of different districts of Tamil Nadu, faculty members from different Colleges and Universities, research scholars, faculty members from Gandhigram Rural University, and the students of II year M.A. Cooperative Management. The proceedings of the two day workshop are as under.

THEMATIC ISSUES

The major activity of the workshop was group discussions. The entire participants and delegates were grouped into four groups for discussing the identified topics of workshop in a detailed way. The group members after deliberations, came out with the conclusions.

Business Aspects

- The purchase policy must be reformulated and it must be decentralized. Purchase committees must be set up at

CWSs levels. In such committees representations shall be given to the purchase and sales personnel.

- For purchase of goods from manufacturers, the most advantageous sources must be selected.
- Purchase must be made from dealers on credit basis on terms mutually favourable.
- With regard to price fixation, active price policy which is followed at present should be continued.
- Concrete Credit policy for credit sales must be framed and put in practice.
- Advertisements through electronic and other media must be made frequently in an appealing manner.
- Sales incentives must be given to employees to enhance their sale performance.
- The margin available to cooperatives for distribution of commodities under Public Distribution System must be increased for all the items.
- Organic link must be strengthened between the CWSs and primary consumer cooperative stores.
- Democratic governance must be reinstated for better functioning and for ensuring accountability.
- CWSs must seriously think of enhansing the infrastructural facilities.

Inventory and Working Capital Management

The wholesale stores have to develop the managerial skills among the employees in making use of techniques such as Fast Slow non moving, Break Even Point, Vital Essential and Desirable, Economic Order Quantity. These techniques are essential in the present context, Product Port folio Analysis is to be made for making procurement and sales decisions.

- Consignment system of trading could be encouraged among the cooperative stores.

- All the techniques of inventory management and control must be adopted in all cases.
- All the Government assistance to be returned within a given time frame.
- Fixed deposits from the associated members and employees to be raised up to the necessity. The interest on deposit must be higher than the banks.
- Share capital of the members should be increased from Rs. 10 to Rs. 100/-.
- Interest on cash credit should be reduced by the District Central Cooperative Banks to ease the financial burden of the stores.
- Exempting cooperatives from paying tax would improve the working capital position of the stores.

Human Resource Management

- It is essential to estimate the demand and supply of necessary man power requirements. Manpower forecasting is a must for CWSs for competing with the private sectors.
- In the case of seasonal jobs, contract workers may be appointed.
- Recruitment should be based on merit. Cooperative Recruitment Board should be established, as it has been setup in Kerela.
- While selecting the candidates priority must be given to persons with degrees of M.B.A or M.A. Cooperation/ Cooperative Managements/B.Com(Cooperation) B.A.(Cooperation).

Cost Control and Cost Reduction

- For minimizing cost in their business and management transactions, the CWSs need to create and develop data base on cost, purchase, inventory and quality of the goods they deal in.

- The CWSs should establish norms for standardization of cost, quality, and price by availing professional help of experts in the locality.
- The existing arrangements for auditing the accounts of the cooperatives should be changed to annual auditing by assigning the responsibility to the management of the society.
- Cost minimization can also be achieved by increasing the business turnover with low margin for high sales.

RECOMMENDATIONS OF THE WORKSHOP

After having two day discussions and deliberations, the workshop came out with the following recommendations. The administrators and policy makers of the consumer cooperatives concerned could consider and take initiatives in line with the recommendations, for the better functioning of cooperative wholesale stores.

- Democratic system of governance should be reinstated in CWSs for better functioning and for ensuring accountability among the managerial cadres.
- The present system of purchases by joint purchase committee was found to have serious flaws. Therefore, purchase policy must be reformulated. Decentralization of purchase must be thought of. 'Purchase Committees' can be constituted at CWSs level, wherein the officials involved in the purchase and sales functions must be allowed to take part.
- To enhance the sale performance and to compete with private traders, attractive sales incentives must be provided to sales persons. Sales incentives in the form of bonuses, premium bonuses, rewards and other appropriate motivating measures should be considered for implementation.
- Organic link among the consumer cooperatives as well as with other cooperatives must be created, in order to

compete with the giant private departmental stores. Such link or effective network must result in cost effectiveness in operations for the benefit of the consumers. Consignment purchases, inter-cooperative exchange of goods are some of the measures that need to be taken.

- Measures for moving the CWSs from the financial crunch to financial soundness must be mooted. Increasing the share capital, tapping local resources in the form of deposits, debentures, etc., are a few note worthy measures mentioned. Financial adequacy would widen the business operations.
- 'Merit' should be the basis in the recruitment of personnel for filling posts with CWSs. Cooperative Recruitment Board should be established as it is in the case of Kerala. Priority must be given to those who are qualified in M.A. Cooperation/Cooperative Management or M.B.A. Cooperative Management/M.Com Cooperation) B.Com (cooperation)/B.A.(Cooperation).
- Management Development Programmes should be conducted periodically with the financial support of the Tamil Nadu Cooperative Union/Government in order to get the personnel oriented towards the managerial skills required for them in the normal course of business. These include; inventory techniques, Break Even Point, Economic Order Quantity, Sales promotion, effective management of working capital and other relevant skills.
- Member education programme should be conducted periodically to create member loyalty and to sustain their interest in their own cooperative organisations.
- CWSs must seriously think of enhancing the infrastructural facilities so as to attract the consumers in large numbers. The expenditure required for such renovation would be mobilized from banks guaranteed by the government.
- Advertisement campaigns through electronic and other media about the high standard of goods supplied by CWSs

must be made. Positive image of CWSs must be created in the minds of public through proper advertisements.

- Interest on cash credit extended by the District Central Cooperative Banks should be reduced and be given at a concessional rate.
- A data base system must be created and developed by CWSs on cost, purchase, inventory level, sales and incentives.

CONCLUSION

The two-day workshop was successful in all respects, as envisaged. The delegates, participants and paper presenters were very keen on their respective roles and involved themselves enthusiastically at every stage of the workshop. It must be appreciated that the workshop had a good mixture of participants drawn from personnel from practical / field as well as from academic institutions. Time allotted for paper presentation and discussion in the technical sessions facilitated the participants to learn concepts and take part in the discussion process. Theoretical aspects, ground realities, practical and functional problems confronted, the rough climate posed by Multinational Companies, and speedy measures to be taken in the midst of changing environment were elaborately discussed. In the group discussion, group members came out with some pragmatic measures for the better functioning of CWSs.